Submitted to the [Secretary]
of War & Genl. in c[hief]
A Lincoln
March 2, 1864

Executive Office
Washington City
May 5, 1865.

Respectfully referred to
the Surgeon General U.S.
Army. It is my
desire that Mrs. Doug-
las should be gratified
in the very reasonable request expressed within,
and I therefore respect-
fully ask that the Surgeon
General direct the reten-
tion of the Douglas
Hospital so long
as it can be con=

distinctly held and
used for hospital
purposes.

Andrew Johnson
President U.S.

Inform Mrs.
Douglas of the
President's
Decision.

Executive Mansion,
Washington, March 19, 1864.

[ ] B. Thomas.
My dear Sir

Below is an ans.
for the Sanitary Fair
request.

Yours truly
A. Lincoln

Buffalo March 9. 1864.

My Dear Sir,

I have your favor of
the 7th soliciting the manuscript
of my recent address at the opening of the ladies Christian commission
Fair in Buffalo, on the 22° day of
February last, and I cheerfully comply with your request by sending
you the original address in my
own hand writing as I wrote and
delivered it. It is somewhat soiled
because it has been in the hands of
the printers. Though it has been
attacked by the abolitionists, I adhere
to it as it is without changing a
word. Respectfully yours
H. P. McIntosh Esq. Millard Fillmore
Cleveland,

ch 16. 1864

[...] fever
rec'd.
[...] were
[...] was
cons-
note
[...] you

[...] field

Executive Mansion,
Washington, 21 May, 1864.

My Dear Sir
I have the honor
to acknowledge the receipt of
a photographic copy of
your allegorical sketch,
together with your letter
asking me to accept it
at the close of the Fair
to be held in Philadelphia.

I thank you
very sincerely for your

kindness but respectfully
request that instead of
being sent to me as
suggested, the picture
be sold for the benefit
of the Fair.

I am very truly
Your Obt. Servant
A. Lincoln

Chas. H. Richardson Esq.
Care Jacob Dunton
9[ ] Market St.

SANITARY FAIRS

A Philatelic and Historical Study
of Civil War Benevolences

BY
Alvin Robert Kantor
AND
Marjorie Sered Kantor

Book design by Michael Glass Design,
Inc., Chicago

Photography by Kenneth Cain,
The Newberry Library, Chicago

Indexing by Charles J. Peterson

Published by SF Publishing, Glencoe,
Illinois

Printed by Rohner Printing Company,
Chicago

Typeset by Paul Baker Typography,
Inc., Evanston, Illinois

Distribution by A-Three Services
Agency, Ltd., Northbrook, Illinois

ISBN: 0-9632603-0-8
Library of Congress Catalog Card
Number: 92-61024

"Sanitary Fairs, A Philatelic and Historical
Study of Civil War Benevolences" is
printed on Mohawk Innovation 80# text.
Cover insert is printed on 100# Mohawk
Superfine text. Endsheets are 80# Curtis
Tweedweave. The typeface is Sabon,
designed by Jan Tschichold in 1967.
It is a redraw of Garamond.

Much of the reference material from the
collection is now located in the Special
Collections Department of the Ablah
Library at The Wichita State University,
Wichita, Kansas.

For all Grandchildren...North and South...
but especially for

Lisa, Amy, Marc, Lori, Michael, Wendy and Katie

ERRATA

Page 31 captions should read:

Plate 25: Union Volunteer Refreshment Saloon and Hospital in Philadelphia
Plate 26: Citizens' Volunteer Hospital in Philadelphia

ACKNOWLEDGMENTS

We wish to acknowledge helpful Joe Eisendrath who was always ready to fill us in on a Civil War detail when we found our own knowledge inadequate or lacking. Also, Jim Milgram, who prodded us into this undertaking. The writing started on November 11, 1977, a day after he admonished us in his autograph in our copy of his *The Express Mail of 1836–1839* book to write on Sanitary Fairs. Were it not for the help of William W. Steele, our early education would have been doubly difficult. His lengthy and informative letters were not only a source of basic study but were a link to collectors of the 1930s and 1940s. We also wish to acknowledge the help of the late Len Persson whose information was ready and boundless. Also, thanks to Phil Bansner and Jim Czyl for their help and to Rich Hartzog for his advice on medals and tokens.

And a very special acknowledgment and thanks to Barbara R. Mueller, editor of the *American Philatelic Congress Book* and *The Essay-Proof Journal*, who not only guided us through the pitfalls of bringing this book to publication but also gave us her unstinted and ready help when we ran into anything that was beyond us.

And lastly, we wish to thank the members of the Collectors Club of Chicago and its Committee on Publications. The club's enthusiasm and dedication to the highest standards adds character to our hobby and to Chicago as a center for stamp collectors. The club under the able leadership of Bud Hennig, Charless Hahn, and now of Lester Winick is an inspiration to all who have the honor to be a member.

VALUATIONS

The valuations herein are based on what an informed collector would pay for an item, auction prices realized, and the quantities known to exist. The SF (Sanitary Fair) ratings by the authors comprise a rarity scale with SF1 as the most common and SF5 as the rarest for the Sanitary Fair and other related Civil War material.

SF Rarity Scale	Valuations (1992)
SF1	$25.00–$75.00
SF2	$75.00–$150.00
SF3	$150.00–$750.00
SF4	$750.00–$1,500.00
SF5	$1,500.00 and over

TABLE OF CONTENTS

But in silence, in dreams' projections,
While the world of gain and appearance and mirth goes on,
So soon what is over forgotten, and waves wash the imprints off the sand,
With hinged knee returning I enter the doors, (while for you up there,
Whoever you are, follow without noise and be of strong heart.)

I onward go, I stop,
With hinged knees and steady hand to dress wounds,
I am firm with each, the pangs are sharp yet unavoidable,
One turns to me his appealing eyes—poor boy! I never knew you,
Yet I think I could not refuse this moment to die for you, if that would save you.

I am faithful, I do not give out,
The fractur'd thigh, the knee, the wound in the abdomen,
These and more I dress with impassive hand, (yet deep in my breast a fire,
    a burning flame.)
Thus in silence, in dreams' projections,
Returning, resuming, I thread my way through the hospitals,
The hurt and wounded I pacify with soothing hand,
I sit by the restless all the dark night, some are so young,
Some suffer so much, I recall the experience sweet and sad,
(Many a soldier's loving arms about this neck have cross'd and rested,
Many a soldier's kiss dwells on these bearded lips.)

The Wound Dresser

Excerpts from "The Wound Dresser"—A Series of Letters Written from the
Hospitals in Washington During the War of the Rebellion by Walt Whitman.
Whitman served as a nurse and a member of the Christian Commission.

The Collectors Behind this Work
A Rationale for this Book

It was at a meeting of the Chicago Philatelic Society in 1961 that Bob first heard about Sanitary Fairs. Prior to that, he remembered seeing one of the stamps in the stock of an old-time dealer who could tell little about it except that it was of Civil War vintage. At that meeting Jim Hamilton displayed some of the more common stamps, probably the Philadelphia stamps, but no covers with stamps. It was only later on that we were able to secure stamps on cover.

The Sanitary Commission and the activities associated with it, such as the fairs and other benevolences of the Civil War period, represent one of the finest episodes of human endeavor in a period wrought with hardship, lack of medical knowledge, and a scarcity of effort in allaying the suffering of the wounded. The soldier was considered an expendable, endless resource to be tapped as more troops were needed in the field.

We have dealt briefly with the history of the United States Sanitary Commission, especially where it was a help in explaining a cover or postal usage. There are many fine books on the subject and an extensive bibliography follows the text for additional reading for both the philatelist and the history student. No near-complete bibliography has previously existed of this phase of American benevolent activity.

The material described is almost entirely from the authors' collection, and where it is from another source this is noted. Some of the material came to us unsolicited from other collectors, some was sought after, and some was found in unexpected repositories. As the collection grew in size and stature and was displayed from time to time, we were offered holdings intact to add to what we already had. Duplicates of fair stamps were kept as were covers even if they varied only slightly from others.

It was almost two years after hearing Jim Hamilton's presentation that one of the Boston dealers, Jack Molesworth, ran a small display advertisement in *Stamps* magazine. He had a collection of Sanitary Fair stamps for sale for $295. We were on a train going to California at the time we read the ad and we contacted him upon our return to Chicago. Curiously this was the Jim Hamilton collection that Bob had seen at the Chicago Philatelic Society meeting!

It was some months later that Elmer Stuart, a Chicago dealer, agreed to part with his holding. He remarked at the time that Elliott Perry, somewhere in the east and unknown to us at the time, had a collection as well.

A telephone call to Mr. Perry in Westfield, New Jersey elicited the information that he was at the time advanced in age and was becoming more interested in local stamps. Since he had been able to do very little with adding to his collection because of the paucity of material, he might consider selling. At the time Perry was 79 years of age, spry of spirit and quick of mind. We made a trip east and then spent some time with Mr. and Mrs. Perry in their home, where we bought the collection on April 18, 1963. The Perry Collection, as he told us, was made up of the earlier collections of John Walter Scott, Hiram Deats, Charles Gregory, Charles Severn, George Sloane, Harry Konwiser, Percy Mann, Percy Doane, W.L. Babcock, H.L. Lindquist, and Dorsey Wheless.

Over the previous 125 years, collectors of importance have also included George Wray, A.B. Slater, William W. Steele, Dr. Ludwig Simon, Sidney Barrett, Honorable J. William Middendorf II, Howard Lehman, Alvey Adee, Vincent Domanski and H.C. Needham, who had sold his collection to Senator Ernest Ackerman in 1920. Elliott Perry served as Ackerman's philatelic secretary and buyer. While all these names have been included as collectors of these issues, in reality there have been no more than five or six really major collectors of these stamps because of their scarcity. We can give no satisfactory explanation as to why all the doyens of stamp collecting at the turn of the century sought after these issues. Perhaps the Civil War had touched their lives in some way as it was more of their time and memory; perhaps the scarcity of material piqued them; perhaps it was the fashion of the time. In all that span of time, however, except for the C.E. Severn book *The Sanitary Fairs and Their Issues*, published in 1911, little was accomplished except for an occasional article here and there. On October 8, 1918, Elliott Perry had written Vincent Domanski that the first reference to Sanitary Fair stamps in a catalogue was a list given in A.C. Kline's *Stamp Collector's Manual* in 1865.

At Rompex in Denver in 1965, S.A.V. Letkemann approached us and asked us if we would be interested in a small but important collection that he had put together. In addition to this Letkemann acquisition, there was Dr. Ludwig Simon's Collection (1965), William W. Steele's (April 6, 1964), J. William Middendorf's (October 6, 1967), and then Vincent Domanski's (1973).

Meanwhile we were adding much background material aside from the regular philatelic sources. Our Sanitary Commission library grew and the Library of Congress requested that a bibliography be prepared of all Sanitary Commission material. These references appear at the end of this book. Autograph dealers were a source for letters pertaining to the fairs, dealers in vintage newspapers contributed fair papers and contemporary news accounts, and print shops were culled for old prints and lithographs of the time. We were able to locate the youngest daughter of Dr. Henry Bellows, the founder of the Sanitary Commission; she was then an elderly lady living in Walpole, New Hampshire. She was most gracious, as was everyone else we contacted, professional or otherwise, in furnishing information or material.

The last Philadelphia Fair stamp on cover added to the collection was acquired as recently as 1984 at the American Philatelic Society annual meeting in Dallas. To the best of our knowledge that was the last stamp on cover with a fair cancellation not recorded, although one spurious cover exists of two stamps on a cacheted Philadelphia Fair cover, postmarked with a fraudulent fair cancellation.

The updated information in the *Scott Specialized Catalogue of United States Stamps* is largely the result of this mass of information. Scott numbers are used throughout this book and due credit is given to Scott Publishing Company, a division of Amos Press. The original Scott information was prepared by H.M. Konwiser and Dorsey Wheless, and it can be assumed that a number of the stamps pictured in this book were at one time examined by them.

All dates of the fairs were checked carefully with newspapers or other sources of the time for verification and a portion of the information covered is the result of Elliott Perry's study; his knowledge and information was rarely faulted even when checked against source material.

While it can only be assumed that the information and photographs are all the known covers with fair stamps, it may be presumed, based on the years of accumulating the material, that in some other areas the material is finite and in still others the covers are a good representation of what the advanced collector may be able to find. The Sanitary Fair stamps on cover with a fair cancellation, it is believed, comprise all the recorded examples of these very scarce pieces. The blocks of stamps are probably the largest known and are displayed so that future collectors can properly identify these elusive stamps.

The covers and corner cards from the various fairs serve to show the widespread participation of communities during the war years. It is estimated that once the idea of fairs caught on after the first Chicago Sanitary Fair in 1863, many more communities had fairs of their own. Few of them, however, issued stamps. When you consider that it was only 16 years after the United States first issued stamps that the concept of a semi-postal for charity came into being, you begin to realize how innovative were the early organizers of the fairs. It is true that local stamps had their beginnings in 1844, yet they were issued as part of profit-making ventures for the promoters of the different posts, and by the Act of 1861 all except Boyd's and Hussey's were put out of business. From these early fair stamps came the concept of Christmas Seals and that idea, with changes, of providing a benevolence in the carrying of our mail through these seasonal adhesives exists to this day.

The effort to prepare this book has been a dual one. The writing and research was largely done by Bob. The editing, further checking to make sure of accuracy, selection of covers, spelling, and everything else that goes into the preparation of a book was the work of Margie. The book was started in 1977 and this year represents 14 years in preparation. It has taken effort. While the stamps are enchanting, the research took us off in avenues of reading that were often dull because the style of writing in the 1860s was itself dull, verbose, and in some cases wrought with personal assessments that were vain and self-serving efforts.

The other benevolent activities detailed give further flavor to the collection and properly should be included since they have never been discussed in philatelic writings before except in passing. The hospital covers, both North and South, naturally fit into the subject since much of the efforts of the commissions, Sanitary and Christian, were concerned with hospital activity. Hospital construction, sanitation, provisioning, and the operation of the hospitals were major concerns of the Sanitary Commission.

Almost every phase of philately is covered within the four to five years of existence of the Sanitary Commission—stamps, rates, envelope corner cards, franks, foreign and domestic usage, postage dues, prisoners' mail, soldiers' mail, medals—all come within the province of the Sanitary Fairs and that may be the fascination of the entire subject.

Most of the original manuscripts covering the day-to-day operations of the Sanitary Commission were given to the New York Public Library when the Commission ceased its operation. At the library, packed in boxes, unclassified, accumulating dust, reposes the majority of material to this date! No attempt was made here to delve into this mountain of source material since a history of the Sanitary Commission would have succeeded in only adding another volume to other War Between the States histories that have gone before. Our chief concern here has been confined to philately. Experts within the field of sociology and medicine can better assess the efforts of the Commission, and they have. Divinity students and those interested in the early history of the Young Men's Christian Association (YMCA) can find its development in the work of the United States Christian Commission. No stamp collector interested in the Civil War period can fail to observe that while colorful patriotic envelopes give glamour to any collection and are a good reflection of the period, there also was the seamy side of suffering, disease, misery, agony, anguish of the wounded, the neglected, the lonely, the abandoned, the widows and orphans, and by contrast the munificent response of the caring people at home who arose to ameliorate these conditions. This is that story as told in stamps and covers.

Before we delved into the fairs and their stamps, we prepared a history of the United States Sanitary Commission and the United States Christian Commission so that this background would aid in a better understanding of the philatelic material at hand. The fair chapters are in chronological order as the fairs occurred. Following this is a section on soldiers' letters since the Sanitary Commission was so involved in forwarding the letters. Many soldiers' letters originated in hospitals and this section then follows. Lastly is the ephemeral material connected with the fairs and the two commissions.

For the purposes of definition, because frequent reference is made to "fairs", it may appear that this material would logically fall within the ken of topical collectors of fairs and expositions philately. But the fairs of the Civil War period were primarily bazaars at which goods, services, and products were sold in order to raise funds in support of the United States Sanitary Commission and Christian Commission as well as local Sanitary Commissions. One of the problems faced in writing this book was deciding what should be included and what material should be omitted in order to produce a concise, yet comprehensive reference work. Some interesting covers with unusual postmarks may have been omitted and only those that give a good representation have been included. All fair stamps on covers have, however, been included to give an extensive overview of the subject.

While we attempted to limit anecdotal material, we could not help but include it when there was a good story to tell. Part of the pleasure of collecting the stamps and covers of the period is the fact that the Civil War is so well documented with so many different sources of information that we were able to add material that enhances our story. For example, the short but relevant information that the sutlers, while in constant contact with the troops, never carried stamps with them because it was contrary to regulations to sell stamps at a profit. Certainly a sutler could make a larger profit selling a soldier the ubiquitous frying pan than a stamp at face value. How much simpler it would have been to have permitted the sale of stamps at even modest profit and thus avoid the countless nuisances and petty handling that was involved in moving mail where post offices and stamps did not exist!

Of necessity there is some overlapping of subjects. Many of the soldiers' letters originated on either Sanitary Commission or Christian Commission stationery but it was our feeling that soldiers' letters are of such interest and diversity that a separate chapter on soldiers' letters was necessary. The reader should refer to the index from time to time as subjects may be duplicated under several listings. At the end of the book under the bibliography will be found the sources that were used.

Where stamps were issued at a fair, a chapter has been devoted to the stamps of that fair, first because an attempt has been made to go into the subject of that fair's stamps in depth, and second, to indicate the importance of each one of the fairs. Keep in mind always that the stamps and covers had to be picked up in person or if the envelope was mailed at the fair, the prescribed government postage had to be prepaid. Attendance was largely local. This in itself was a limiting factor and these stamps have had to survive a century and a quarter.

I

INTRODUCTION TO SANITARY FAIRS AND THEIR STAMPS

1. Appendix I—Order of the Secretary of War, approved by the President, appointing the Sanitary Commission.

On June 13, 1861, President Abraham Lincoln signed the document that had been prepared on June 9th by Secretary of War Simon Cameron, giving the Sanitary Commission a semi-official status.[1] He neglected, however, to provide the funds needed to carry on its work. While the citizenry had provided sons and husbands as soldiers, those left at home could do little to overtly express their patriotism. The fairs provided an outlet and at the same time contributed funds for the Sanitary Commission to carry on its work, which by 1863, the time of the first fair, covered most of the battle areas and influenced medical services behind the lines.

Most fairs were held in the winter when the ground was frozen, making transportation easier, as roads were still unimproved. One of the main means of transportation during the winter was the sled because ruts and a muddy quagmire would stop all except the heartiest traveler. Furthermore, it was easier to heat a building then than to cool one. Time devoted to the fair during the winter months would not be time taken away from the farm. In general, there was more leisure time for all during the winter. Then, too, there was less disease during the winter months than in the summer. Measles, poliomyelitis, scarlet fever, and typhoid were all uncontrolled at the time, with smallpox only recently controlled by inoculation.

The fairs were gala events planned many months in advance. After the selection of a site, a building was constructed and then filled with exhibits, industrial wares, and booths of goods and services; the halls were decked with battle flags and other paraphernalia suitable for the event. It was not unusual for farmers to bring in their produce which would later be distributed to troops in the field. Such non-perishables as sauerkraut, dried fruits, and other sources of the then-unknown vitamin C were packed in barrels and shipped to ameliorate scurvy and other diseases associated with poor nutrition. An interesting feature of some of the fairs was the sale of autographs and works of literature by well-known persons of the time. Of particular interest to stamp collectors are the post offices and the stamps that were issued at eight of these fairs or bazaars.

Occupying less than a prominent location within a fair building, the post office always proved to be an attraction, with its young women tending the booths. Upon payment of a small sum, they would hastily write a note or poem, address it, and sell a stamp, a Sanitary Fair one, to complete the missive. While these young ladies may have performed an act of social graces as well as fund raising, it is also likely that they wrote many a letter for illiterates attending these fairs since in the 1860s the number of persons who could read and write was much less than today.

An eyewitness account of attendance at a fair was written by J.H. Houston in 1889 for Vol. 3, No. 4 of *The American Philatelist*:

> Sirs: I have read with pleasure Mr. J.W. Scott's paper on the Sanitary Fair Stamps, in the December "American Philatelist". I was a boy fourteen years old at the time some of these fairs were held in Washington, D.C., during the war of the rebellion, and attended some of them, but was not a collector at that time. If I remember rightly, some five or six different kinds of stamps were used. Did we not bless the Girls' Fair! As soon as you entered the fair, there came a group of little girls with letters addressed to you, and they charmed out fractional currency from the boys in good style. It was good in Uncle Sam to print it, as coins were seldom seen and postage stamps were as good as gold or silver, except for the premium which was paid by jewelers and speculators. Happy days were those that are past. I have often wondered what became of all the stamps, and I am glad to see that they are being resurrected.

J.W. Scott, writing in the *American Journal of Philately* in January 1889, was among the first to comment on the stamps of the Sanitary Fairs. In his article "Stamps of the United States Sanitary Fairs" he noted:

> In conversing with non-philatelic friends, we are frequently taunted with the assertion that stamp collecting teaches nothing, commemorates no important events, and, in fact, has none of those claims to recognition which are conceded to the older science of numismatics. I wish to call your attention to a neglected series of United States stamps, a collection which will fully vindicate the assertion that stamps do commemorate national events, and in that respect are not one whit behind their venerable competitors, coins...The stamp before you has, for its principal design, the American Eagle, the bird of all others selected by our forefathers to represent the country...he is now firmly established as the national emblem, and we must take him with all his faults and invest him with sufficient virtues for his honorable position. The bird as represented clasps three arrows in his right and an olive branch in his left claw; above is inscribed "Brooklyn Sanitary" and below "Fair Postage". Unfortunately, the value is not given, but perhaps this was intentional. The stamp is produced by lithography, and printed in green on white paper.

Further on Scott noted that "you could post a letter to any part of the world, provided you placed the necessary number of Uncle Sam's stamps on it, and one of the fair's labels to take it to the general post-office."

Elliott Perry, a Sanitary Fair authority, preferred to call letters posted at the fair post offices "drop letters" and the payment of fair postage as being for "carrier service". He was of the opinion that Sanitary Fair stamps occupy a position midway between semi-official carriers and private locals. (Locals are stamps issued by private companies having no official connection with the U.S. Post Office Department; they are called locals because their use was confined within the limits of a large city or town.) Perry made the distinction here between locals and semi-official "carriers":

> Broadly speaking then, local stamps are those issued by privately owned and operated express companies or posts and particularly for the prepayment of fees charged for carrying mail in competition with the government carrier service, or in the absence of the latter, in communities where the population was great enough to make such service remunerative...It is

2. *Scott's Monthly Journal,* January 1927, p. 322, Elliott Perry.

unlikely however, that more than a small fraction of the revenue of the local posts was derived from "drop letters" or other mail deposited at their offices to be called for by the addressees. Their customers used the facilities of these posts principally to secure quick and frequent *delivery* of mail to the addressee at the latter's residence or place of business.[2]

Carriers' stamps performed the same function as locals but the term "carrier" is used to designate a letter carrier employed by the United States Post Office Department or a stamp used to pay the fee of such a carrier. There is a definite connection between carriers' stamps and the post office. This connection does not exist with "local stamps".

The primary difference between the Sanitary Fair stamps and the semi-official carriers is in the method of their use. The carriers' stamps were available for paying the carrier fee to or from the post office within the city, and the fee covered only this service. According to Perry, "Purely 'drop letter' usage by which no service to the sender or to the addressee was performed *outside* the post office was not contemplated in the reasons for issuing carrier stamps and such 'drop letter' use, if it occurred at all, was irregular."[3]

3. Ibid.

Sanitary Fair stamps appear to have been intended for drop letter use at the fairs and bazaars. This service for drop letters was exactly like that for which the 1¢ U.S. general issue postage stamps were frequently used for many years. From and after July 1, 1851, letters deposited in any U.S. post office where no delivery was maintained or where they were to be picked up by the addressee were charged 1¢ each. So, too, letters left at a Sanitary Fair post office to be called for by the addressee were held until picked up and "postage", usually amounting to 5¢, 10¢, or 15¢, was charged for the service. Mr. Perry was of the opinion that "the stamps were used to pre-pay this postage, or perhaps to indicate the amount of 'postage due' when the charge had not been pre-paid."

The evidence, in the form of covers with Sanitary Fair stamps, seems to show that the charges for the Sanitary Fair stamps included a fee for carrying letters from the fair post office to a street letter box or to a post office outside the fair. Such use is exactly the service of a local and may explain the three values used at the Philadelphia Fair and two at each of the Brooklyn Fairs.

The main difference between the Sanitary Fair stamps and the stamps of the local posts lies in the fact that "local" stamps were purely private and were issued without the authority or consent of the United States Post Office Department and had no connection with the United States government. They were never encouraged and only tolerated during the period of their use and eventually were suppressed altogether.

There is ample indication that some fair post offices and stamps had the approval of the Post Office Department. For example, the Chairman of the Post Office Committee and assistant postmaster at the Great Central Fair in Philadelphia was C.A. Walborn, at the time postmaster of the United States post office in Philadelphia. It is unlikely that he would have permitted the use of his office or name without the approval of his superiors in the Post Office Department in Washington.

There is every reason to believe that the stamps were used to pay a fee for drop letter service within the fairs in the same way that drop letter service was in use in United States post offices. The sender of the letter delivered, or dropped, a letter in the fair post office; it was then handed over to the addressee when he called for it there. If the stamps were sold only as curiosities or souvenirs, it is not likely that they would have been canceled. It is also unlikely that the fairs would have been supplied with and able to use dated handstamps for postmarking or canceling at the fair post offices.

Very few fair covers are known. Only eight fairs, beginning in December of 1863 in Brooklyn and ending in Springfield, Massachusetts in December of 1864, issued stamps, all of them with gum. Those postmarked stamps seen from Philadelphia, which was the largest and best run of the fairs, are properly postmarked with the day of use and the postmark used as a cancellation. While the use of the postmark as a canceling device was prohibited by the Post Office Department on March 3, 1863, this same prohibition obviously did not apply to the non-official fair post offices. Canceling postmarks were used at Stamford and in some instances at Brooklyn as well as Philadelphia.

A reason for not recognizing the Sanitary Fair stamps as local stamps is that they were issued by private post offices to raise funds for charitable purposes rather than for the primary purpose of providing a postal service. The fact still remains, however, that in a limited way a service was performed for the public and a fee paid for that service. This is not much unlike the souvenirs issued by the United States Post Office Department beginning with the 1938 Philatelic Truck sheet and the many cards that followed. In the 20th century, however, revenue accrued to the P.O.D.

It is the opinion of the authors as well as earlier students that Sanitary Fair stamps occupy a place between semi-official carriers' stamps and the purely private local posts' stamps. Like the carrier stamps that were not officially issued under the direct authority of the U.S.P.O.D. but upon direction of an Act of Congress, the fair stamps had the consent and approval of that department. Like local stamps, though they were not used for postage within the U.S. mail service, their use outside the official post office channels was tolerated. The fair stamps performed a service in the fairs exactly analogous to that performed by a government stamp in post offices across the land. Elliott Perry stated:

> From the philatelic standpoint no group of stamps ever issued anywhere is more worthy of the adjective "clean" than are the Sanitary Fairs. None of them bear the slightest taint of speculation and not one of them was issued for philatelic purposes.[4]

4. Ibid.

For the collector of Christmas Seals the stamps of the Sanitary Fairs have a very special interest. In the *American Red Cross Bulletin of 1909*, page 69, there appears the article "Origin of the Christmas Stamp". It notes that while Christmas Seals were first used in Denmark, Iceland and Sweden in 1904 to aid in the fight against tuberculosis, the question is often asked as to where the whole concept of Christmas Seals originated. At a Tuberculosis Congress a Swedish report was published giving credit to the origin of their charity stamps to those first stamps known as the Sanitary Fairs 41 years before the first Christmas Seals. The Swedish report says, "The honor of having invented the Charity Stamps must be given to America—that land of inventions." The concept was adopted in Europe in 1892 when Portugal produced the first charity stamps (private stamps for the Red Cross Society). So to the many areas of interest and romance of the Sanitary Fair stamps should be added the fact that the many millions of Christmas Seals sold each year and their contribution to medical research have their origin with Sanitary Fair stamps.

Most of the stamps described herein are scarce, some very scarce, others rare, and others unique. Rarest are the stamps of the Stamford Soldiers Fair. Seen the most often, but never in profusion, are those of the Philadelphia or Great Central Fair. Should any stamps be found attached to a cover, then that piece is of the utmost rarity. While counterfeits do exist, these will be fully described and should prove no problem even to the beginning collector as they are readily identifiable. As a matter of fact, even the counterfeits are of interest and add to the charm of collecting these issues.

It has been estimated that two Union deaths resulted from disease for every single combat loss, while in the Confederacy the rate was three to one. It appeared to the doctors of the time that there was some connection between sanitation and disease, but sanitation was an elementary science at the time. Water, if it had no noticeable odors, was thought to be safe. The soldier had everything working against him except his native toughness. Thus, there arose the cry for a United States Sanitary Commission fashioned after the British Sanitary Commission of the Crimean War. Originally concerned only with the sanitary aspects of field operations and care of the injured, as the war progressed and the character of the war changed, so too did the Commission and its objectives change. These objectives were:

1. collecting supplies
2. support of 25 soldiers' homes
3. hospital directory
4. hospital inspection

5. transportation of the sick
6. supplying fresh food
7. battlefield services
8. relief for discharged soldiers

While the Commission had the approval of the Secretary of War and the President of the United States, no appropriation was authorized for its operation. Instead, the funds were obtained from an aroused citizenry, who in the early days of the war were most generous. As the war dragged on, contributions waned. The Commission next turned to insurance companies for funds on the premise that fewer deaths made for fewer death claims. In time, as casualties increased, the need for additional funds made this source wholly inadequate and as a result the United States Sanitary Commission turned once again to the people of the North. Various schemes and ideas for raising funds were tried, one of the most successful being a fair or bazaar. The fair concept was an immediate success and across the country in thousands of towns fairs were held in support of the Commission.

The first fair was held at Lowell, Massachusetts on February 24, 1863. It was, however, the fair in Chicago in October 1863 that popularized the fairs as vehicles for raising funds for the Commissions. Other fairs followed, some with stamps and special cachets, and that is what our story of the Sanitary Fairs and a philatelic study of the Civil War organizations is all about.

What had begun as a force to bring sanitary requirements up to a needed level of performance changed in character as needs of the period changed. It was the Commission that was largely responsible for developing the pavilion type hospital, the orderly evacuation of the wounded from battle areas, an ambulance service, and a new concept of field hospitals for quickly ascertaining medical needs of troops. As the war progressed, other changes in Commission activities took place. The proper feeding of troops to eliminate scurvy and other nutritional deficiencies was provided for and resulted in the establishment of diets and even central messes to supplant the system of each soldier cooking his own food. The influence of the Sanitary Commission and that of the Christian Commission were pervasive and all-encompassing, almost down to the smallest detail, in providing for the welfare of a soldier.

By and large the Sanitary Commission and the Christian Commission were helpful in getting women out of the home and gave them new interests in what had previously been a closed world to them. The Sanitary Commission also was instrumental in securing changes in postal requirements for soldiers who often had restricted access to stamps. Without its help in securing the forwarding of letters, the amount of Civil War correspondence available for collectors would be seriously limited. Finally, based on the experiences of the United States Sanitary Commission, the real merit of establishing a Red Cross was realized, and the United States eventually joined this international body of benevolences. (See Chapter II for more detail on this aspect.)

It is interesting to note that 24 years after the Civil War ended the Sanitary Fair stamps began to appear at philatelic auctions. Some representative descriptions of lots and prices realized are given here. R.R. Bogert & Co. was among the first to offer these stamps to collectors. In their 10th auction on January 28, 1889, the firm of R.R. Bogert & Co., Geo. Leavitt & Co. in Lot #100 first made mention of Sanitary Fair stamps. This leading house of the time noted the following: "U.S. Sanitary Commission, Central Fair Postage stamp 10, 20, 30 estimated $3.00." The lot realized $2.85. Within the same sale was Lot #34: "1847 5 & 10 used, est. $2.00", which realized $2.00. In their sale #12 of March 18, 1889,

Lot #59, described as "Central Fair 20 green & 30 black, est. $2.00", realized 90¢. On April 29, 1889 in Lot #51, three Philadelphia stamps were estimated at $3.00 and realized that figure.

In sales of December 2nd and 3rd of 1889, Lot #79 was described as follows: "Sanitary Fair 10, 20, 30 perforated, Sailors Fair 10 (Boston), Soldiers' Fair Stamford & Springfield, Bazaar P.O. blue, black & red (Albany) est. $9.00." These rarities realized only $1.35; compare that with the following lot in the same sale: "1869 90¢ unused fine, rare, est. $1.00." The realization was $4.50.

On March 7, 1896, appeared a fourth offering of Sanitary Fair stamps by R. R. Bogert & Co., Geo. Leavitt & Co. This lot #84 in sale #58 was described thus: "Central Fair Postage 20¢ Blue, unperforated, *unused ($5.00)** est. 1.00." The realization was $1.05 for what probably was a proof, of which there are relatively many known. The $5.00 in parenthesis advises the collector that in Europe this same stamp was sold for that amount in American money.

The final mention of Sanitary Fair stamps in the firm's catalogues was on June 6, 1896 in sale #64. Lot #243 is described as "Cent Fair 10, 30¢ postmarked, fine est. $2.00." The two used Philadelphia stamps realized only 70¢. In the same sale a used 5¢ 1847 did even more poorly and while it was estimated at $1.00, it realized only 55¢.

Viewed within the context of contemporary American society with its jingoism and Hearstism, spoiling for a conflict which was soon to explode with the sinking of the *Maine* and the Spanish-American War in February of 1898, the uncertainty of the times gave rise to the uncertainty of prices for stamps as well as other collectibles. Gold from the Klondike was beginning to pour into the American economy. The depression of 1893 was only dimly impressed on the minds and pocketbooks of collectors, but this too must have influenced the poor showing of stamp values in 1896, the time of the last entry of R. R. Bogert.

BEFORE THE BATTLE.

WV1 WV2
WV3
WV4 WV5
WV6 WV7
WV8 WV9 WV10
WV11 WV12 WV13
WV14
WV15

Plate 1:

Plate 2: Leeds and Franklin patent envelope

Plate 3: California Branch of the Sanitary Commission

Plate 4: Sanitary Commission, used in England

Plate 5: Christian Commission Soldiers' Relief Fair

Plate 6: Brooklyn Sanitary Fair stamp (black) with Brooklyn City Express Post

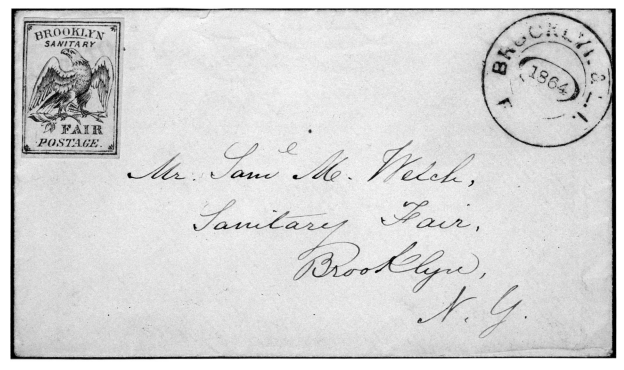

Plate 7: Brooklyn Sanitary Fair stamp (green), fair postmark

Plate 8: Albany Relief Bazaar

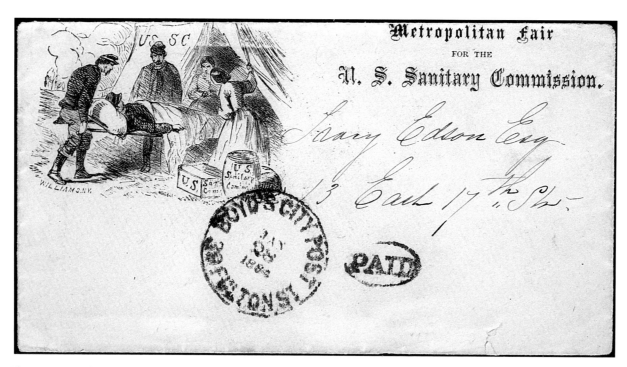

Plate 9: Metropolitan Fair with Boyd's City Post

CENTRAL FAIR LETTER-BOX.

The Postmistress directs the special attention of visitors to the CENTRAL FAIR to these *Letter-Boxes*, as a great convenience to all desiring to correspond with visitors to the Fair, as well as for letters to be delivered throughout the City, or at the Post Office for mailing.

Frequent collections are made throughout the day and evening of all letters deposited in these boxes, by carriers detailed for the service, and any person using the CENTRAL FAIR BOXES may rely on having all letters promptly transmitted to their destination.

ALL letters deposited herein, whether for delivery in the Fair or by the regular Post Office carriers, must have a "CENTRAL FAIR POSTAGE STAMP" attached.

Letters intended for delivery within the FAIR BUILDINGS DO NOT require any U. S. POSTAGE STAMP in addition to the CENTRAL FAIR STAMP.

Letters intended for mailing at the Post Office, or for delivery in the City, must have the requisite *U. S. Postage Stamp* attached in addition to the CENTRAL FAIR STAMP.

Parties desiring to communicate with any of the various Committees of the Fair, will find these boxes the proper medium.

RATES OF U. S. POSTAGE.

Letters for delivery within the City, 2 cts, for each ½ oz. or fraction thereof.
do.   addressed to any part of U. S. 3 do.   do.   do.   do.

E. D. GILLESPIE, Postmistress
CENTRAL FAIR

Plate 10: Instructions for posting a letter at the Great Central Fair

Plate 11: Mailed at the fair, with a fair postmark

Plate 12: Three values on cover, fair postmarks

Plate 13: Colored cachets from the Great Central Fair in Philadelphia

Plate 14: Soldiers' Fair (Springfield, Mass.)

Plate 15: Northern Ohio Fair (Cleveland), to Brazil

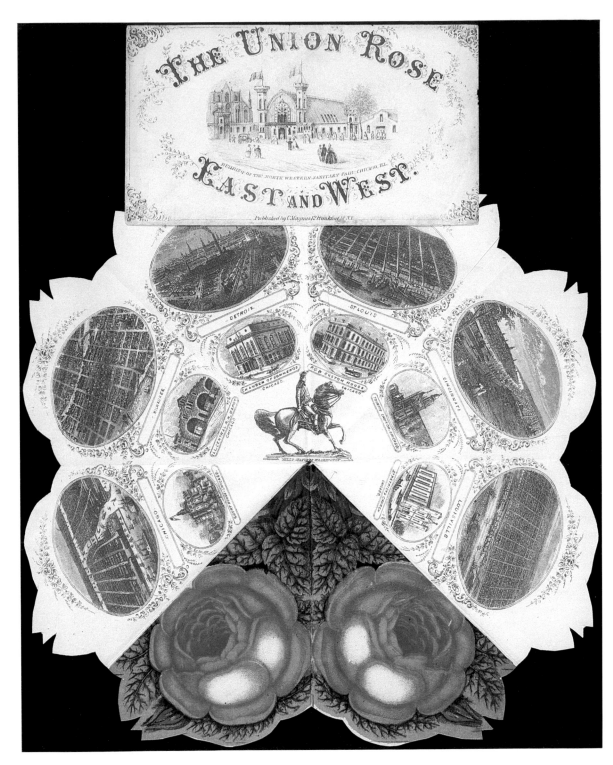

Plate 16: Union Rose, East and West (Chicago)

Plate 17: Postage paid by the Sanitary Commission

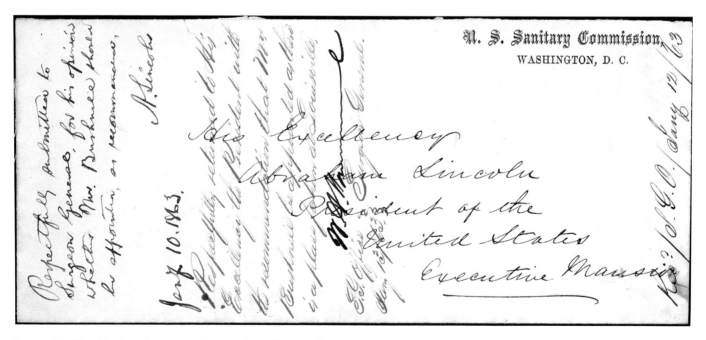

Plate 18: President Lincoln endorsement to Surgeon General Hammond

Plate 19: Patterson Park Hospital (used)

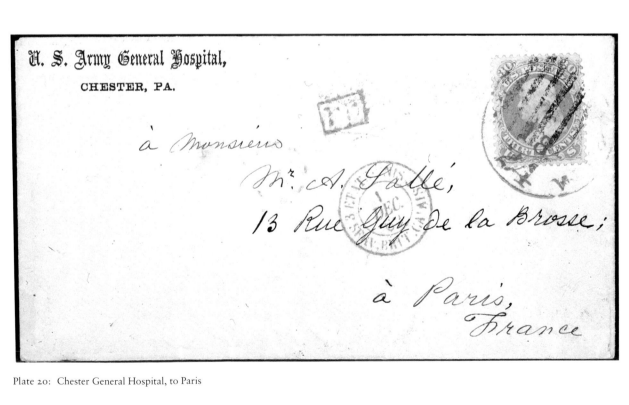

Plate 20: Chester General Hospital, to Paris

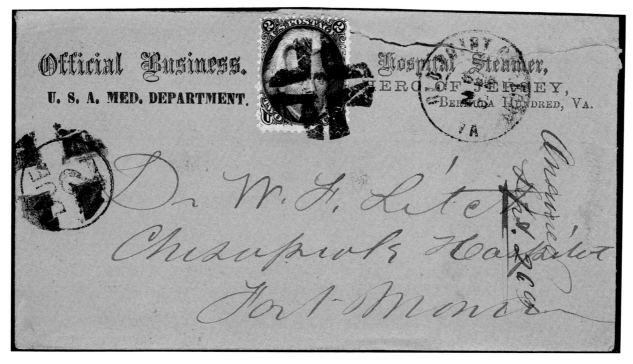

Plate 21: Hospital steamer "Hero of Jersey"

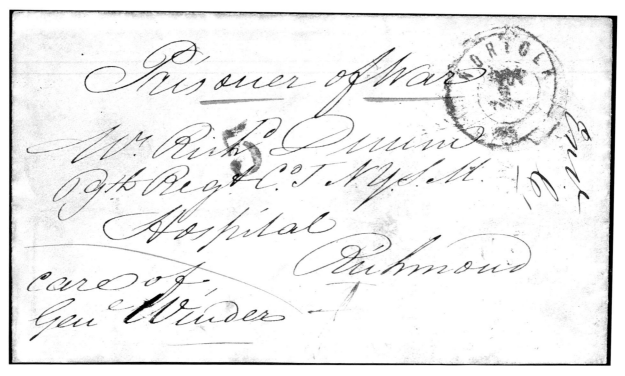

Plate 22: Inside Prisoner of War cover

Plate 23: Volunteer Refreshment Saloon in Philadelphia

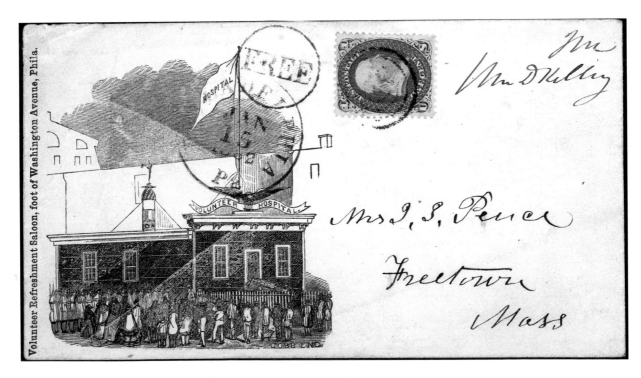

Plate 24: Franked Volunteer Refreshment Saloon cover

Plate 25: Union Volunteer Refreshment Saloon in Philadelphia

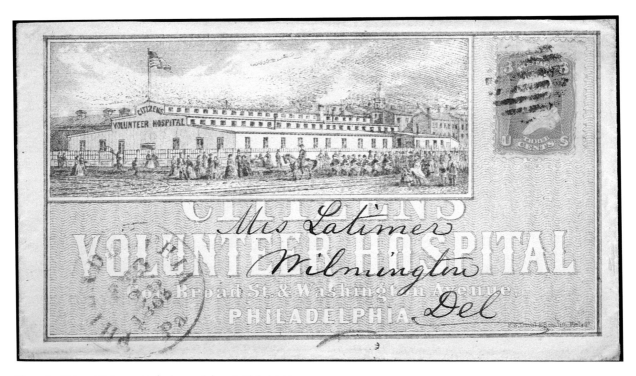

Plate 26: Citizens' Volunteer Refreshment Saloon in Philadelphia

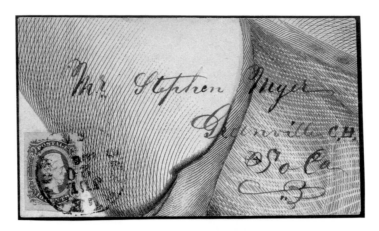

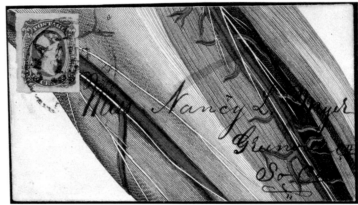

Plate 27: Two different Confederate stamps on adversity covers

Plate 28: Patriotic from France to the United States

II

UNITED STATES SANITARY COMMISSION — ITS ACTIVITIES AND AUXILIARIES

Dr. (of Divinity) Henry W. Bellows, president of the U.S. Sanitary Commission

5. "Woman's" and "Women's" Central Association of Relief were used interchangeably, with "Woman's" being the more acceptable.

Following the attack on Fort Sumter that had occurred on April 12, 1861, Dr. Henry W. Bellows, the founder of the United States Sanitary Commission, met in New York City with 91 of the most influential women of the city who were concerned with the health and well-being of the 75,000 troops that Lincoln had called upon to quell the rebellion. Meeting at the Cooper Institute, they drew up the constitution of the Woman's Central Association of Relief. Thus, on May 18, 1861, inspired by Elizabeth Blackwell, the first United States woman physician who later was instrumental in organizing field nurses during the war, the "Woman's Central Association of Relief for the Sick and Wounded of the Army"[5] was founded. Following this, "The Advisory Committee of the Board of Physicians and Surgeons of the Hospitals of New York" and the "New York Medical Association for Furnishing Medical Supplies in Aid of the Army" met and formed "The Commission of Inquiry and Advice in Respect of the Sanitary Interests of the United States Forces". The name was later shortened to the United States Sanitary Commission.

From the start the Woman's Central Association of Relief met with indifference and even hostility from the Army medical establishment. The Army Medical Bureau felt that in due time the Commission's enthusiasm would wane and the Army Medical could proceed as they had in the past — indifferent, lacking organization, with a medical department whose main endeavor had been alleviating minor medical problems encountered in frontier skirmishes with the Indians of the West.

General William T. Sherman made numerous observations regarding the structure and activities within the Army. One of his views was that the United States Sanitary Commission was not to be relied upon since it showed favoritism, giving supplies raised from a particular state only to soldiers from that state. He was also of the opinion that while mail

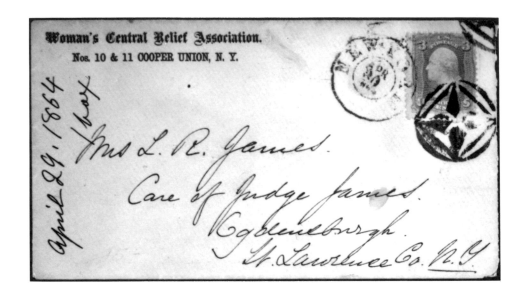

Fig. 1. Organized April 29, 1861, the Woman's Central Association of Relief along with two other groups combined to form the U.S. Sanitary Commission. Their objectives were the contribution of skill, labor, money, the preparation of lint and bandages, and the offer of personal services as nurses. SFI

to soldiers should be maintained, newspaper reporters were injurious to the prosecution of the war. He was aware that people back home were anxious for news and that a commander risked his own removal from command by barring journalists. (Fig. 1)

On June 9, 1861, Simon Cameron, Secretary of War, authorized the appointment of the Commission members. President Lincoln signed the order giving the government's approval on June 13, 1861. By June 16th the Surgeon General had ordered all medical officers of the Army and volunteers to "render every facility for such objects and to give the Commission admission when on visits of inspections, regimental, and general". The Commission's statement laid before the Secretary of War on its purposes and objectives read:

> The Commission would inquire with scientific thoroughness into the subjects of diet, cooking, cooks, clothing, tents, camping grounds, transports, transitory depots, with their exposure, camp police, with reference to settling the question how far the regulations of the army proper are or can be practically carried out among the volunteer regiments, and what changes or modifications are desirable from their peculiar character and circumstances. Everything pertaining to outfit, cleanliness, precautions against damp, cold, heat, malaria, infection; crude, unvaried, or ill cooked food, and irregular or careless regimental commissariat, would fall under their head.
>
> The Commission would inquire into the organization of military hospitals, general and regimental; the precise regulations and routine through which the services of the patriotic women of the country could be made available as nurses; the nature and sufficiency of hospital supplies; the question of ambulances and field services, and of extra medical aid; and whatever else relates to the care, relief and cure of the sick and wounded.

Afterwards, Cameron's order was reaffirmed by Edward Stanton, who had succeeded him as Secretary of War.

The Commission was given rooms in the Treasury Building in Washington and vested with full authority by the Surgeon General of the United States Army. Frederick Law Olmsted, that man of universal talent then and later on, was made secretary and general manager and with his ability and enthusiasm soon made the U.S. Sanitary Commission a viable and functioning entity. In his early days Olmsted had been a correspondent for the *New York Times* and had traveled in the South writing on the institution of slavery. Following the war he became one of the leading landscape architects, designing Central Park in New York. In 1876, he laid out the grounds for the Centennial Fair in Philadelphia. In 1892, he designed the grounds at the Columbian Exposition in Chicago. He was a talented and capable man who had much to do with the establishment of the Commission and its successes. His policies and ideas helped carry the U.S. Sanitary Commission through the early war years, though he resigned before the end of the war.

To a large extent the early sanitary reformers based their concern for the health and well-being of troops on the experiences of the British forces in the Crimean War (1854–1856) and the work of the British Sanitary Commission. It was Florence Nightingale at Scatari who had successfully brought the death rate down from a point where previously there had been more soldiers in hospitals than on duty. Her diligence and care of the troops had brought the disease rate down from 1,200 per 1,000 to a tolerable level where the British Army was no longer faced with replacing an entire army every ten months due to disease or battle casualties.

Three days after Simon Cameron had signed the order establishing the Commission, Dr. (of Divinity) Henry Whitney Bellows of Walpole, New Hampshire was elected president of the United States Sanitary Commission. A leader within the Unitarian Church of America, he had graduated from Harvard in 1837. Dr. Bellows served ably on the Commission from 1861 until it was deactivated in 1878.

George T. Strong, born in 1820, was treasurer of the Commission. He was a lawyer and trustee of Columbia University and, like Bellows, a founder of the Union League Club of New York. Alexander Bache was vice-president of the Commission and, like Mrs. Gillespie, postmistress of the Great Central Fair in Philadelphia, was a great-grandchild of Benjamin Franklin.

The board of the Sanitary Commission met in Washington once every six weeks. Later on they met quarterly, leaving the day-to-day operation to Frederick Law Olmsted. The meetings usually lasted four to five days. Eventually the day-to-day operation became so huge that standing committees were formed that met daily in New York. The Commission appointed a chief sanitary inspector for each division of the Army. The employees in the field were paid because it was felt that more efficient people could be recruited thereby. Salaries ranged from $5,000 annually for the general secretary down to two dollars a day plus subsistence for those in the relief services.

On June 21, 1861, a general appeal was sent out to the citizens of the North telling of the aims of the Commission and seeking their help.

> ...as a general rule, four soldiers die of diseases incident to camp life to one that falls in battle...sanitary measures, prudently devised and thoroughly executed will do more to economize the lives of our soldiers ...other subjects demand prompt attention...clothing, tents, hospitals, supply of nurses, drainage of camp sites...these demand investigation and action...members of the commission serve without fee or reward...funds will be needed for travel, printing and transportation...for obvious reasons there is reluctance to make application to Congress for an appropriation...rooms have been assigned it in the Treasury Building in Washington....[6]

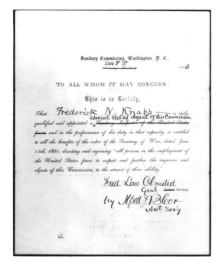

Appointment of Frederick N. Knapp as a special relief agent

6. *The Sanitary Fairs and Their Issues,* by C.E. Severn, p. 8.

The message was signed by Frederick Law Olmsted and Henry W. Bellows, with an added request that all donations be sent to George T. Strong at 68 Wall Street in New York.

Following the Battle of Bull Run on July 18, 1861, it became more apparent to the Surgeon General that there was a need for an overall plan to handle the sick and wounded. Soldiers wounded on the battlefield had been left to die of thirst or starvation, if not from their battle wounds. Others deserted the battle under the pretense of helping to remove the wounded. If a man was wounded and had to go to the rear, several comrades-in-arms would be all too ready to take him to the rear. These same comrades might encounter "extreme difficulty in finding their way back to the front".[7] There were few ambulances and those that were available were the torturous two-wheelers called "The Avalanche" because each step of the horse or any slight rut in the terrain resulted in a jolt or further injury to the soldier already in agony. Due to the low velocity of the bullets used and the rounded (rather than projectile) shape, each Minié ball was in itself a source of infection since insufficient heat was generated on the missile to sterilize or kill any bacteria on it. Uniforms were never laundered, and when a piece of clothing became impacted in the wound it provided an added source of major infection.

With few real facts on hand at the beginning of the conflict that was to occupy the next four years, the Sanitary Commission committee of five officers headed by Dr. Bellows laid before the Secretary of War its plans and recommendations, none of which were based on any legal authority. The official warrant creating the Commission made its work possible. It asked only the sanction and moral countenance of the government to permit its presence in the various theaters of operation.

The working plans of the Commission covered three distinctive departments of work and were prepared by Dr. Bellows, W. H. Van Buren, Dr. Elisha Harris, and Dr. Jacob Harsen. These were:

1. THE PREVENTATIVE SERVICE OR SANITARY INSPECTION. Within this department were persons hired as medical inspectors to visit hospitals, camps, and transports. They were to watch that troops were not overexposed to heat or cold and that adequate protection was furnished to protect them. The inspectors were to see that troops were not on unnecessary long and hard marches and that supplies of food and medicine were available at all times. If the supply methods then being used did not keep up with troop movements, then changes in logistics became a concern to the Commission. Statistics were to be kept and used as a basis for aiding troops and their supply. Medical tracts and sanitary bulletins came within the program, and some of the medical tracts were innovative in themselves since medical knowledge at the time was limited and unscientific. A long series of medical monographs written by the leading medical men of the time brought advances in the handling of medical problems that were of value not only to the soldiers but, as in most wars, provided technical advances that accrued to the civilian population as well.

2. THE DEPARTMENT OF GENERAL RELIEF. This branch took three-quarters of the time and effort of the Commission. Its duty was to supply food, clothing, bandages, hospital equipment, bedding, writing supplies, and postage for the sick and wounded in hospitals and soldiers' homes. These supplies, whether bought from basic supply houses or furnished as donations from the general population, were collected at 12 branches located in:

7. It reached a point that the clutter of deserting troops interfered with the war effort and left unaccounted these "lost troops". It was the Sanitary Commission that set standards of evacuation of troops and an agent of the Commission was usually present with cavalry pickets (the most feared and respected arm of the service) who insisted that these quasi-deserters "show blood" before they were allowed to go to the rear.

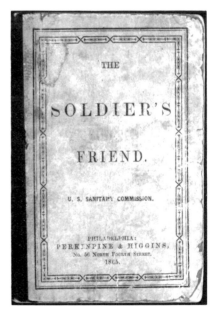

Handbook prepared by the Sanitary Commission

Boston	Columbus	Baltimore	Pittsburgh
Chicago	Philadelphia	Louisville	Cleveland
New York	Detroit	Cincinnati	Buffalo

Badge of a commission agent

Each one of these centers in turn generated local branches of the Sanitary Commission and subsidiaries numbering as many as twelve hundred local branches from one distribution point. While stores were distributed and used by Union soldiers regardless of the state that they hailed from, be it Maine or Missouri, some state Sanitary Commissions, like that of Indiana, limited their benevolences to soldiers from that state only.

3. THE DEPARTMENT OF SPECIAL RELIEF. This branch of the Commission concerned itself with strays and stragglers such as the wounded in transit or on furlough, convalescents, and others who were out of touch with the military system for one reason or another. The soldiers' homes came under the direction of this department. At one time eight such homes in Washington, Cincinnati, Cairo (Illinois), Louisville, Nashville, Cleveland, Columbus, and New Orleans gave food and lodging to over two thousand men every day.

Two years after the war ended and while Dr. Bellows was in Florence, Italy, a Mrs. Alexander inquired of him as to the purposes, objectives, and accomplishments of the Sanitary Commission. Here in his own words he tells of its achievements: (Fig. 2)

Florence, Italy
Dec. 14, 1867

My dear Mrs. Alexander,

You are kind enough to ask me to tell you two or three of the leading facts connected with the history of the U.S. Sanitary Commission of which I had the pleasure of being President, & indeed am so still.

We were present with our supplies & agents upon more than 500 battlefields. We supplied the extra wants of all the Hospitals, both general & regimental, & followed the several Corps of the whole army during five years, with incessant watchfulness & care. Seven thousand Soldiers Aid Societies furnished us with all the articles needed for the sick & wounded, & their gifts were estimated at a value of fifteen millions of dollars.

Besides this, we received five millions of dollars in cash from the American people, principally through *Fairs*, held by American women in the great cities. California & the Pacific Coast sent us, to the eternal praise of that remote & infant region, one million & a half of dollars!

The Commission had from two to five hundred men, with horses & wagons, constantly engaged in the relief-work; twenty great Lodges, at which nightly, it had an average of two Regiments of Soldiers, in its care for the whole war. This must suffice, my dear Madam,

& I remain
Your friend & servant
Henry W. Bellows
Prest of the U.S. Sanitary Comn.

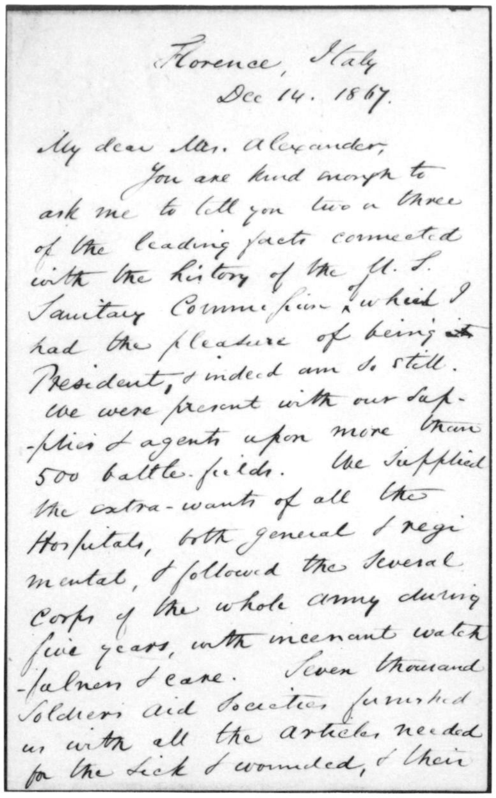

Fig. 2. Letter to Mrs. Alexander from Henry W. Bellows, president of the U.S. Sanitary Commission. SF3

Fig. 3. Each division was assigned a contingent of sanitary inspectors and stores. (Library of Congress)

The most successful methods of raising funds were the Sanitary Fairs. Records based on the Sanitary Commission archives reveal that $4,392,980.92 was raised by fairs across the nation. Of this total $2,736,868.84 was turned over to the Sanitary Commission, and the balance dispersed to local commissions, the Christian Commission, or local aid societies. (Fig. 3)

The circular from the Department of the South, dated September 9, 1863, by General Q.A. Gillmore, reflects the positive feelings of this officer toward the Commission. The war was to continue for another year and a half but the worth of the United States Sanitary Commission was recognized by this intuitive commanding officer. The enclosure originating from Morris Island, S.C., was written just two days after the fall of Morris Island on September 7, 1863. This important fort in Charleston Harbor along with Fort Sumter had been under siege by General Gillmore. (Figs. 4, 5)

Blacks played an important role in the Civil War with little of the glory or honor that they deserved and they, too, participated with fairs. Nearly ten percent of the Union Army was made up of blacks. These 178,985 enlisted men fought in 39 major campaigns, with 37,300 losing their lives. Twenty-one black soldiers were awarded the Congressional Medal of Honor, the highest award for gallantry "above and beyond the call of duty when confronted by the enemy".[8] Despite their numbers and valor, blacks were denied line officers' commissions in any great numbers. Of the only one hundred who received commissions, eight were surgeons commissioned as majors. Yet the black citizenry of Philadelphia, which numbered but 22,185 persons in the census of 1860, gave their money and time to aid the U.S. Sanitary Commission and became an auxiliary of the Commission on April 19, 1863. From the report of the Ladies' Sanitary Commission of the St. Thomas Episcopal Church comes the following comment:

8. The Congressional Medal of Honor was first authorized for the Army in 1862, the Navy the year before.

St. Thomas Colored Episcopal Church fair
announcement

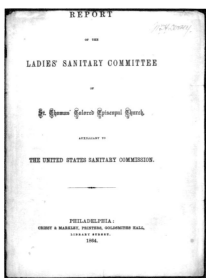

Fig. 4. Manuscript "U.S. Sanitary Commission, Morris Island, S.C." with enclosure. This important military objective adjacent to Fort Sumter had fallen only a few days before. Postmarked Port Royal (S.C.), Sep. 14 (1863). Port Royal also known as Hilton Head. SF2

Fig. 5. Post office at Hilton Head (Port Royal).

Fig. 6. (Top) Sanitary Commission, U.S. Govt., 3¢ 1857 #26 demonetized August 19, 1861, 20 days following this postmarked Washington cover dated July 30, 1861. An early use of a Commission cover. Quality of print indicates haste in preparing stationery. SF3

(Middle) Congressman Edward Haight of Westchester, N.Y. furnished his frank on this early "Sanitary Commission U.S. Govt." corner card to permit the letter through the mail without the required U.S. postage. Washington postmark dated Aug 6, 1861. SF2

(Bottom) Congressman Anson P. Morrill of Readfield, Maine supplied a frank that carried the letter. It was also necessary to prepay the carrier rate of 1¢. The stamp prepaid this. New York postmark cancel. SF3

Fig. 7. (Top) The early effort of the Commission to settle upon a satisfactory name: Sanitary Commission, U.S. Gov't. Full payment of postage is now evident. Postmarked Washington, Nov 18 (probably 1861). SFI

(Middle) Postmarked Washington, 1861 manuscript docket. As of this date the Woman's Central Association of Relief had not joined the national Sanitary Commission. Double rated. SFI

(Bottom) When Burt Van Horn, Congressman from New Fane, N.Y., franked this cover on Sep 3, 1862 from Washington, it was apparent that the Post Office Department looked upon the Commission as a quasi-governmental agency. SFI

One great drawback to our efforts and desires to assist and relieve the soldiers, as well as the efforts of their wives, children and friends, in the same direction is the refusal of the Directors of the City Passenger Railway cars to allow colored persons to ride, this rendering it obligatory upon all who visit to hire private conveyances, at exorbitant rates, spending money that could be, were it otherwise appropriated, to the benefit of the soldiers who went forth to fight the battles of their country, but have returned maimed, sick, and wounded, and in hundreds of cases, are deprived of seeing those near and dear to them in consequence of being unable to pay their carriage hire, and eventually passed from the busy scenes of life without an opportunity being offered of bidding a final adieu to wife, children, relations or friends…We intend holding a fair for the benefit of the association commencing on the 19th day of December, 1864 at Concert Hall, Chestnut Street.

At first the U.S. Sanitary Commission was not quite sure what to call itself. Even members of Congress were not certain whether the agency was an official arm of the government, and accordingly many of them readily and illegally took to franking envelopes in an attempt to save the group postal expenditures as well as to make personal contributions to the war effort. (Figs. 6, 7, 8, 9, 10, 11, 12)

Fig. 8. The 2¢ drop letter rate is consistent with a bank making the necessary trip to the post office to pick up its mail. SF3

Fig. 9. Although the enclosure has become separated from the cover, a notation indicated that the letter was written by a soldier from Lincoln Hospital in Washington, D.C. The penmanship and spelling for "inhast" would tend to confirm this. The 2¢ postage was insufficient; there should have been a "Due 2",—1¢ underpayment and 1¢ penalty. SF3

Fig. 10. Star killer cancel, Aug 9, Washington, D.C. postmark. According to Richard B. Graham both military and civilian mail passing through Washington might have had this cancel applied. SF1

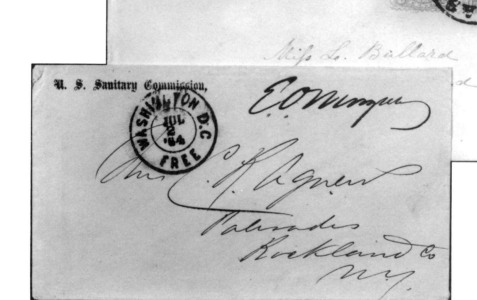

Fig. 11. (Top) Three 1¢ blues (Scott #63) paid postage on a cover that originated in Washington. SF3

(Middle) Pair of 3¢ rose (#65) prepaid double rated letter postmarked Washington, Apr. 20. SF1

(Bottom) On July 2, '64 from Washington, Senator Edwin D. Morgan of New York City franked the envelope for the Commission. Postmark added emphasis to its free passage. SF1

9. *Hampshire Gazette,* November 12, 1861, p. 2.

Outgrowing the space it first occupied in the War Department Building, the Commission moved to 244 F Street in Washington. (Fig. 13)

Based on information at hand and the apparent cooperation that seemed to exist between the Post Office Department and the Commission, as evidenced by the early "corner cards" on envelopes, the communication from Montgomery Blair, the Postmaster General, would seem to confirm this connection. This further advances the direct proof that the Sanitary Fair Post Offices and their stamps had the approval of the authorities in the United States Post Office Department. On October 15, 1861, the following communication originating at the P.O.D. was sent to the postmaster at Northampton, Massachusetts.[9] The same communication probably went out to many other postmasters. It reads:

POST OFFICE DEPARTMENT

Washington, October 15, 1861

To the Postmaster at Northampton, Mass.

Sir:– You are requested to take measures to effect an organization, if none exists, among the women of your district to respond to the accompanying appeal of the Sanitary Commission.

The Executive Government here very much desires to obtain the active co-operation of the women of America for the holy cause of the Union in this appropriate mode, and relies upon you to make known this wish to them and aid as far as possible in securing its accomplishments.

Yours respectfully,

M. Blair, Postmaster General.

Fig. 12. Alfred Bloor, signer of this acknowledgment for stores, served as Assistant Secretary of the Commission. William B. Allison, of Iowa, Member of Congress, franked the letter postmarked Washington D.C. Feb 12, 1864. SF2

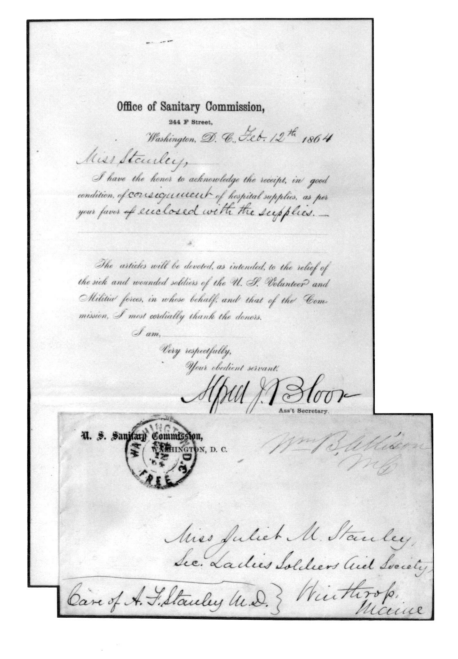

Fig. 13. Three examples of Commission covers that originated at the Commission headquarters on "F" Street. SFI

It would almost be expected that the Sanitary Commission, ever so concerned with making the soldiers more comfortable than the minimal government efforts provided, would take it upon itself to give the soldiers the one great morale-builder—mail from home. Early in the war, on August 1, 1861, the executive committee of the Sanitary Commission addressed themselves to supplying soldiers with a means for them to write home. A resolution was passed at the meeting that evening as follows:

> Resolved: That it be recommended that in each hospital, the Stewart, Ward-master, or intelligent convalescents,…in accomplishing this work; that to one of them be specially committed a store of stationery, marked with the stamp of the Commission, and either franked, or furnished with postage stamps, if the use of the congressional privilege is not preferred by the soldier. That this agent be required to make a daily record of every letter written, and of every hour of reading (letters) done, and make a weekly report of the same to the Inspector.

FORWARDED BY...

A major problem arose with insufficiently prepaid letters addressed to soldiers or those requiring forwarding fees. Existing post office regulations required that such letters be returned to the sender. The family of a soldier or one soldier writing to another soldier might find that the addressee had subsequently moved on. Thus, once again the United States Sanitary Commission found it necessary to make a change in the handling of mail to the military. At their morning meeting on Wednesday, July 13, 1864, this motion was offered:

> Resolved: That the proper officers of the Commission be instructed to pay the necessary postage on letters to soldiers in the field or in hospital, which, under existing usage of the Post Office Department, are obstructed in their transmission, and that the matter of distribution of letters to soldiers be referred to the General Secretary, with power. Each letter thus forwarded to bear the stamp of the Commission.

Letters so stamped with the imprint of the Commission did not require the necessary soldier's endorsement since postage was prepaid. World War II experience with soldiers' mail proved that with a backlog of mail, endorsing by chaplains or field grade officers only delayed its movement because of its sheer volume. In the hospitals of the Civil War it was the chaplain who normally would endorse the letters. This could be a time-consuming task, particularly when the chaplain had so many other duties to perform. In addition, the chaplain would only be available in a hospital, and the soldier in the field would be confronted with mailing a letter without any field post office or place to buy a stamp. (Figs. 14, 15, 16, 17, 18) (Fig. 19)

Fig. 14. (Top) Type Ia on reverse with offset on front — U.S. postage stamp furnished by U.S. Sanitary Commission. Where postage was furnished, letters were required under the rules of the Commission to be so hand-stamped. (39mm) SF3

(Bottom) Type Ib — Although the letter was stamped "Forwarded by . . . ", the local agent neglected to affix U.S. postage. The Post Office Department then stamped "Due 3" to be paid by the recipient. Without the handstamp there could have been a due 6¢. The letter enclosed mentions Lincoln's inauguration the previous day. (40mm) SF3

Fig. 15. (Top) Type Ic — Shield of Sanitary Commission, front handstamped "Forwarded by the U.S. Sanitary Commission". (40mm) SF3

(Bottom) Type Id — Dash after "y" in Sanitary. Handstamped front & reverse, fleuron similar to Washington handstamp. Postmarked Martinsburg, W.Va., Nov.; Martinsburg, in western part of former Virginia, was a base of operations for the Shenandoah Valley. Field offices of the Sanitary Commission were called "Shebangs" for their many services — "the whole Shebang." (39mm) SF3

Forwarding handstamps

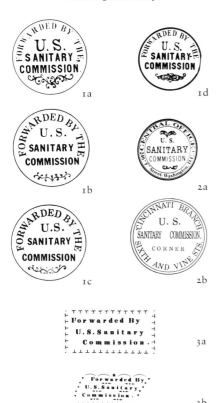

Types of U.S. Sanitary Commission Handstamps:

Type	Size	Description
1a	39mm	"Forwarded by the U.S. Sanitary Commission", 24mm filigree (at bottom of circle), comma after "the"
1b	40mm	"Forwarded by the U.S. Sanitary Commission", 21mm ornamentation (13 balls)
1c	40mm	"Forwarded by the U.S. Sanitary Commission", 20mm ornamentation, wider space between "SANITARY" and "COMMISSION"
1d	39mm	"Forwarded by the U.S. Sanitary Commission", 19mm filigree; dash after "y" in Sanitary

2a	35mm	Double circle, around the rim appears "Central Office". Center "U.S. Sanitary Commission".
2b	37mm	Double circle, inside circle appears "Cincinnati Branch U.S. Sanitary Commission corner Sixth and Vine Sts."
3a	50x23mm	Rectangle bordered with T's. Inside figure appears in three lines "Forwarded by U.S. Sanitary Commission". Stenciled.
3b	42x22mm	Parallelogram-shaped stencil. Straight line. Words "Forwarded by U.S. Sanitary Commission" are underlined.

Fig. 16. (Top) Type 2a — Although the word "Forwarded" is not part of the handstamp, it may be assumed, based on other examples in the collection, that this handstamp was evidence that the Commission prepaid the postage. The handstamp reads "Central Office-244 'F' Street, Washington, D.C., U.S. Sanitary Commission." (35mm) SF3

(Bottom) Type 2B — Handstamp of Sanitary Commission on a Christian Commission corner card, "Cincinnati Branch-Corner Sixth and Vine Sts.". Cincinnati postmark. (37mm) SF3

One of the strangest and most unusual of the philatelic associations with the United States Sanitary Commission is found in the survival of a few examples of the patented "Leeds Envelope" of the 1860s (also known as Leeds & Vaux and Leeds & Franklin). In an era of fertile inventive minds, no object of everyday use was beyond their scope, including envelopes and other types of stationery as well as stamps themselves. These had been in general use for just slightly more than a decade when the Civil War broke out and there was great concern about both the reuse of stamps and the separation of the envelope from the correspondence it enclosed.

Fig. 17. (Top) Type 3a(U35) — "Forwarded by" in box with border of T's. The envelope being an entire, it was unnecessary to affix a postage stamp so the Commission applied its rubber stamp on government stock. (50mm x 23mm) SF2

(Bottom) Type 3a — Backstamped with Commission handstamp. Congressman S. (Samuel) F. (Franklin) Miller of New York used his frank, contrary to postal regulations. The envelope is postmarked Washington, D.C. May 21, '64 Free. Perhaps concerned that the illegal use of the frank would not be honored by the post office, the Commission then added its handstamp. The envelope is addressed to New Hampshire. SF2

Fig. 18. Type 3b straightline — Parallelogram-shaped handstamp. It appears that this style and the previous one are the only ones that exist in straightline format. (42mm x 22mm) SF2

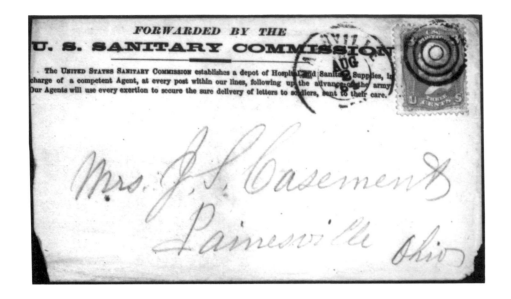

Fig. 19. Nashville Aug 2, 1864 postmark, imprinted "Forwarded by the U.S. Sanitary Commission... Our Agents will use every exertion to secure the sure delivery of letters to soldiers, sent to their care." SF3

Whereupon entered one Lewis Leeds, a heating and ventilating "engineer" who, on the side, dabbled in such "inventions" as a special envelope to meet these concerns. His brother, Barclay, and Barclay's associate, Calvert Vaux, came into contact with Frederick Law Olmsted, general secretary of the Sanitary Commission, through Olmsted's concerns with ventilation of Sanitary Commission facilities. Olmsted also had the prerogative to buy other supplies, including envelopes, from any source he thought best. Thus it was that in November 1862 the Sanitary Commission bought 29,500 of the Leeds envelopes for $185.75.

What distinguished the Leeds envelopes? This story was detailed by E. Tudor Gross in 1942–1944 in various issues of *The Collectors Club Philatelist* (see bibliography) under the title "The First 'Window' Envelope". Surprisingly little has been added to philatelic knowledge of the subject since that time and because so few of the envelopes have survived, most collectors are entirely unaware of them. The following facts are drawn from the Gross study:

As the title of the Gross study implies, he set out to determine when the first window envelope, as we know it today, was introduced. His sleuthing took him back to Civil War days and a strange type of envelope that indeed had "windows" cut into it but not for the conventional address area. These envelopes had die-cut geometric designs where the stamp and postmark would normally be located that could be described as a cut-out, lattice-type pattern in the stamp area.

It seems that the Leeds concept was built on the idea of an earlier patentee named Morison whom he had bought out. It was to provide, as quoted by Gross, "an envelope with one or more openings through which, by use of the postage stamp, the letter and envelope are sealed fast together, and when the letter is removed from the envelope, the postage stamp and postmark placed on them remain adhering to the letter."

Thus, the sender would insert the letter into the patent envelope and apply the stamp over the opening, thereby fastening it to the strips or lattice in the die-cut design and through the openings to the enclosure as well. The recipient, in order to remove the enclosure, had to slit open the envelope and push the stamp down through the hole to break its connection with the envelope. The stamp then remained on the enclosure as evidence of time and place of mailing, *if* it bore the postmark and year date. (Fig. 20, Plate 2)

Fig. 20. (Top) Apparently William Bullard, the son of C.C. Bullard, a sanitary agent, did not understand the intended use of the patented Leeds and Franklin envelope. Instead of placing the stamp *over* the lattice cut-out, the stamp was placed to the left of it. In the enclosed letter he mentions the New York draft riots, which would date it as 1863—the riots having taken place beginning July 13. SF5

(Bottom) Correct positioning of the stamp on the letter portion after the letter had been folded and sealed. The use of the "PAID" stamp partially illustrates the purpose of the patent *except* it appears here that the lattice work was removed before the "PAID" canceling. The stamp, while affixed to the letter, reveals no lattice work remnant. The "PAID" was used instead of a date cancellation. SF5

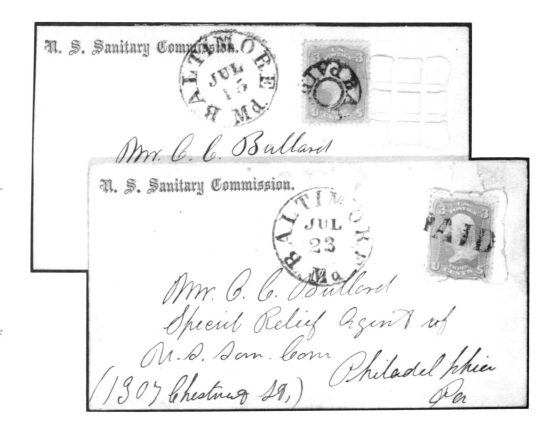

But up to this time, postmarks did not commonly use year dates and the government favored the newer type obliterating devices which were attached to the postmark so that the latter fell on the envelope and the "obliterator" or "killer" cancel on the stamp. Without postal cooperation the Leeds envelope could not succeed, and indeed, it quickly failed despite the undoubted advantage of rendering a stamp unfit for reuse.

Section 178 of official postal regulations reads:

> The use of the office rating or postmarking stamp as a canceling instrument is positively prohibited, inasmuch as the postmark, when impressed on the postage stamp, is usually indistinct, and the cancellation effected thereby is imperfect. The postage stamp must, therefore, be effectually cancelled with a separate instrument.

While this prohibition was not promulgated until 1866 when the new regulations were published, it appears that in September of 1862 Mr. Skinner of the Post Office Department wrote to the postmaster in Brooklyn that a new regulation was about to be adopted that would prohibit the practice of using a postmark as a canceling device. Apparently the order to this effect had been issued on July 23, 1860, but few knew of its existence or paid too much attention to the regulation.

As of March 3, 1863, the notice was stated once again: "The use of the office dating or postmarking stamp as a canceling instrument is prohibited and a separate instrument must in all cases be used." As a result of this order there was a proliferation of the duplex canceling devices and the end of the Leeds and Franklin patent and the further use of their envelopes. It can be assumed that the Sanitary Commission destroyed their stock on hand since so few of the covers with their imprint remain.

E. Tudor Gross believed that 18 of these patented envelopes were extant at the time of his articles. Of this number at least four to six of them have some connection with the Sanitary Commission. The two Sanitary Commission covers shown here are good examples of the use for which the envelopes were intended as well as their misuse. The 1c blue stamp "postmarked" Leeds and Franklin demonstrated how the patent could be used and was probably intended as an advertising piece. (Fig. 21) The July 15 cover has the stamp to the left of the lattice opening, thus serving no special function.

Fig. 21. Overprinted "Leeds and Franklin" on #63, perhaps intended as an example for buyers explaining the method for its use. SF2

AUXILIARIES OF THE U.S. SANITARY COMMISSION

BOSTON (NEW ENGLAND WOMEN'S AUXILIARY) — SANITARY COMMISSION

The efforts of the New England Women's Auxiliary Association were confined primarily to Maine, New Hampshire, and Massachusetts. There were over 1,050 auxiliaries within the area. (Figs. 22, 23)

Fig. 22. (Top) Alexander Hamilton Rice, of Boston, member of the United States House of Representatives, franked the cover for the Sanitary Commission offices in Boston. The faint Boston postmark is overshadowed by the bold Fitzwilliam, New Hampshire one dated Dec 31. The correspondence had been addressed to Mrs. Gaylord in Fitzwilliam. The addressee had moved, necessitating that the letter be forwarded. The Fitzwilliam postmaster handstamped "Forwarded" along with a "Due 3" as the franking would pay only the first mailing and not the forwarding. SF2

(Bottom) 1¢ Franklin and 2¢ Jackson for a 3¢ rate, postmarked Boston Apr. 13. SF3

Fig. 23. (Top) Three-cent rose (#65). SF1

(Middle) In December of 1863 a fair was held by the New England Women's Auxiliary. It raised $146,000. No stamps were issued for this fair. It was not until the next year in Boston that a National Sailors Fair was held and a stamp issued. Offices located on West Street. SF1

(Bottom) Offices moved to 22 Summer Street. SF1

Procession of the Sanitary Sack

CALIFORNIA—SANITARY COMMISSION

Lincoln had anticipated a short-lived skirmish to put down the rebellion. But as the war dragged on into months the need for funds burdened the Commission. California was the first to send funds to the Commission to insure its continued operation. Throughout the war California raised more money in support of the Sanitary Commission than any other state.

While no fairs were held in California there is the story of the flour sack that captured the imagination of those who served at home. Mark Twain in his essay, "Roughing It", describes the story of a simple flour bag in California that was bid upon at auction, resubmitted, bid upon again and again until it raised a total of $150,000—all for the Sanitary Commission. (Figs. 24, 25) (Fig. 26, Plate 3)

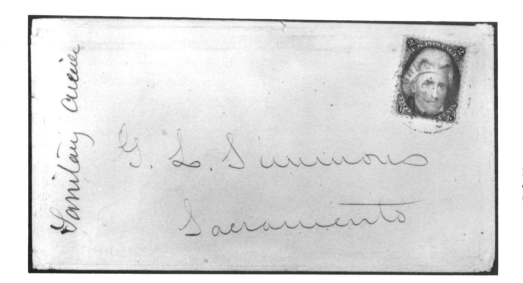

Fig. 24. San Francisco to Sacramento, 2¢ circular rate with enclosure and with a manuscript docket. SF2

Fig. 25. Printed Sanitary Commission corner card with San Francisco postmark dated Aug 16, 1864. California uses are scarce. SF2

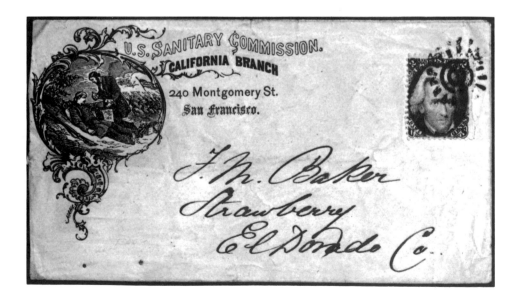

Fig. 26. U.S. Sanitary Commission, California Branch on Montgomery Street corner card. Canceled with San Francisco cogwheel. Two-cent circular rate. The cogwheel was in use between 1864 and 1865. SF5

CHICAGO — SANITARY COMMISSION (Fig. 27)

The Chicago Sanitary Commission was formed on October 17, 1861, a time when the city had a population of approximately 200,000. Mark Skinner was the president. From the start it acted as a branch of the United States Sanitary Commission. Towns and cities around Chicago sent supplies and were generally in tune with the same efforts and directions as those of the Chicago center. To eliminate confusion of names, all local societies merged under the name of Soldiers' Aid Society with the name of the city then following. Recognizing the contributions from the Iowa Branch, the Wisconsin Branch, and the other local Soldiers' Aid Societies, the Chicago Sanitary Commission officially changed its name to the Northwestern Sanitary Commission in January 1864.

Fig. 27. The home of The Chicago Branch of the United States Sanitary Commission in the McVicker's Theatre, Madison and State Streets. (Chicago Historical Society)

The Chicago Sanitary Commission, like local commissions elsewhere, was concerned with the problem of scurvy and made major efforts to supply the troops with anti-scorbutics, i.e., Vitamin C, in the form of either fresh produce in summer or preserved foods in the winter. There were more casualties as a result of scurvy than battlefield injuries. A soldier weakened by scurvy would become a serious battlefield casualty if wounded because he was incapable of fighting off the ravages of the disease and infection that accompanied almost every break in the skin. (Fig. 28)

Toward the middle of 1863 the Chicago Branch moved to the basement under the McVicker's Theatre at 66 West Madison Street (later 25 West Madison Street). I.H. Burch donated the use of the McVicker's Theatre for its activities.

All railroads entering Chicago carried express free of charge when addressed to the Commission or "The Sanitary", as it was called at that time. Like the national organization, this local group concerned itself not only with furnishing supplies to the troops, but with inspections of hospitals, campsites, and even the prison camp at Fort Douglas. The field of operations covered Wisconsin, Illinois, Indiana, and Ohio, with stores being shipped all along the rivers contiguous to this area. Cairo, Illinois became a main shipping point for

Fig. 28. (Top) Chicago Sanitary Commission, forerunner of the Northwestern Sanitary Commission. SF2

(Upper middle) Docketed "Mrs. D.P. Livermore", organizer of the first Chicago Sanitary Fair along with Jane Hoge. SF2

(Lower middle) In January 1864 the name Chicago Sanitary Commission was officially changed to the Northwestern Sanitary Commission to reflect the efforts of all surrounding regions. SF2

(Bottom) One of the local aid societies that came under the aegis of the Northwestern Sanitary Commission was the Illinois Sanitary and Relief Agency. Postmarked Chattanooga, Tenn., Feb 1, 3¢ 1861 stamp, harp cancellation. January 31, 1867 letter enclosure. SF3

battle areas to the south along the Mississippi River. The Ohio River provided still another avenue of shipment. The railroads, already taxed, carried what they could. Pressed into service to carry stores was *The City of Memphis*, a river boat with sufficient speed to rush supplies wherever needed in the western theater.

It was with this branch that the whole concept of fairs was developed as a massive fund-raising event.

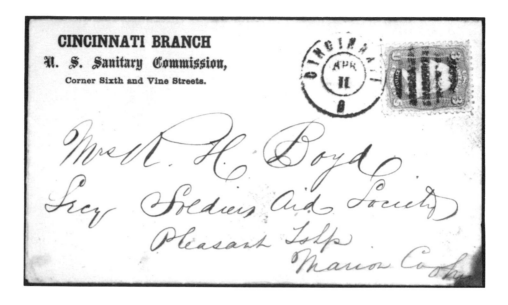

Fig. 29. Cincinnati Branch. SF2

CINCINNATI — SANITARY COMMISSION (Fig. 29)
The Cincinnati Branch of the U.S. Sanitary Commission was organized on November 27, 1861, with Robert W. Burnet as its first president. A Central Ladies Soldiers' Aid Society was formed for purposes of securing supplies for the troops. Inspections and relief services for camps and hospitals in the area were carried on by the Commission. From this group originated the Great Western Sanitary Fair where $235,406.42 was raised.

Soldiers' Home at Cincinnati

DEPARTMENT OF KENTUCKY — SANITARY COMMISSION
The Kentucky Branch began with the establishment of the Soldiers' Home in February of 1862. During the first years of the war, due to its proximity to the front, Louisville, in western Kentucky, became one of the main transfer points for supplies and stores. Twenty-one hospitals located in Louisville were supplied through this branch as well as hospitals in the interior of the state. A hospital directory was also established here.

Robert Mallory of LaGrange, Kentucky served in Congress from 1859 to 1865, placing the use of the franked cover shown within the period of our concern. George N. Malpass, a philatelic student and writer, listed only two publishers of Civil War patriotic covers from Louisville—L.A. Civill as in the cover pictured here, and F. Madden.

The cover is addressed to "Hon. Joseph Holt" whose career during this period is of interest and major importance. He had served under President James Buchanan as Postmaster General and as Secretary of War. He was a strong supporter of Lincoln and denounced the policy of neutrality of Kentucky. His ability as a lawyer and his vigorous support of the President brought about his appointment as the first Judge Advocate General. (Fig. 30) Upon the assassination of President Lincoln, President Andrew Johnson on May 1, 1865 directed that General Holt should conduct the trial against the perpetrators of the crime.

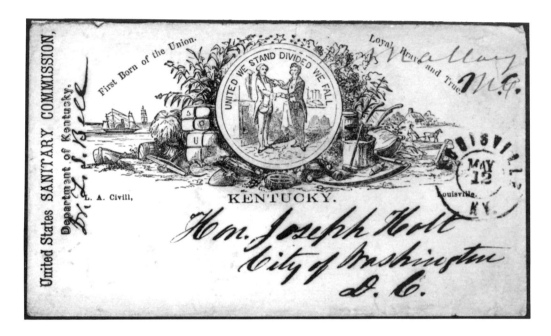

Fig. 30. Department of Kentucky of the United States Sanitary Commission. Addressed to "Hon. Joseph Holt", first Judge Advocate General. SF3

Sanitary Commission tent at City Point

Sanitary Commission at Brandy Station

NEW ORLEANS (DEPARTMENT OF THE GULF)—SANITARY COMMISSION
New Orleans was occupied by General Butler in April of 1862 and the establishment of the Department of the Gulf soon followed. Under General Butler's and later General Banks' administration of the territory, vigorous hygienic measures were instituted to forestall any outbreaks of disease among troops never before exposed to southern maladies, particularly yellow fever. This branch of the Commission took an active part in the exchange of prisoners in that region as well as establishing a soldiers' home in New Orleans. It was the Department of the Gulf that, in addition to seeing that troops in the delta were furnished with foodstuffs, also was responsible for sending vegetables to the outlying island forts from Key West to Mobile. (Fig. 31)

NEW YORK—WOMAN'S CENTRAL ASSOCIATION OF RELIEF
The "Woman's Central Association of Relief" was the forerunner of the United States Sanitary Commission. On June 24, 1864, it voluntarily offered to subordinate itself to the Commission. Situated in New York with its voluminous correspondence, it gave rise to more covers than most other branches. Miss Louisa Lee Schuyler, whose name appears on

Fig. 31. (Top) By January 9, 1864, C.C. Bullard, to whom the Leeds and Franklin covers had been addressed, was transferred to New Orleans. In writing to Mrs. Bullard he overweighted a letter and neglected to add the extra 3¢. Mrs. Bullard then had to pay 6¢ — the 3¢ overweight and 3¢ penalty. SF2

(Bottom) By the time Bullard had written the letter of January 15, (18)64 he had taken steps to correct the insufficient postage. SF2

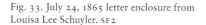

Fig. 32. Woman's Central Association of Relief, Cooper Union, New York. (Museum of the City of New York)

many of the covers, was in charge of the correspondence out of this office. Besides regular letter writing, there were many requests for the publications of this branch to be filled, generating even more correspondence. Late in 1862 a hospital directory was opened at Number 10, Cooper Union. (Fig. 32)

The Woman's Central Association, under Miss Schuyler, also took upon itself quantity buying for local agencies that were too impoverished to buy stores themselves. The Sanitary Commission in turn would then assist the Central Association to help defray this added expense burden. For four years this agency purchased hospital supplies and sent them where needed. Express companies provided freight handling without any charge. Following the war, on July 7, 1865, the Woman's Central Association was disbanded. (Fig. 33)

Fig. 33. July 24, 1865 letter enclosure from Louisa Lee Schuyler. SF2

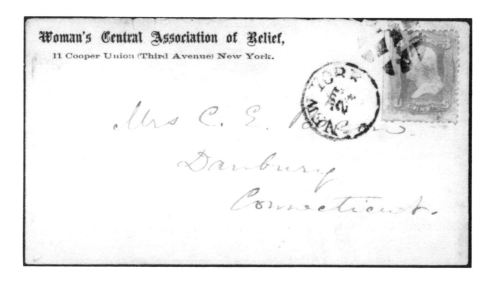

NEW YORK—SANITARY COMMISSION

As just noted, in New York the work for army relief had already been started by the Woman's Central Association of Relief. Its officers soon became aware that the interests of the soldiers could best be served by their associating themselves with the United States Sanitary Commission. They made application for this and for recognition as one of the branches. The City of New York and northern New Jersey functioned as a unit under the direction of the Commission. It did not subordinate its autonomy until June of 1864. (Figs. 34, 35)

Fig. 34. (Top) Oct 2, 1862 postmark on the circular corner card (31mm) dates the location of this office of the Commission. Cover is backstamped with a blue oval imprint. SF3

(Middle) The U.S. Sanitary Commission occupied offices apart from the Woman's Central Association of Relief. Triple-rated letter to Washington, D.C.; crinkled edges and depression on right confirm overweight. New York cancellation. SF2

(Bottom) The Act of March 3, 1863 to take effect July 1, 1863 created a uniform postage rate regardless of distance. Double rated circular. SF2

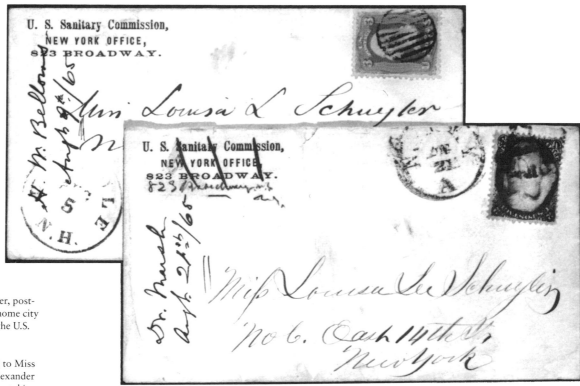

Fig. 35. (Top) To Louisa Lee Schuyler, postmarked Aug 5, Walpole, N.H., the home city of Dr. Henry Bellows, president of the U.S. Sanitary Commission. SF2

(Bottom) Much mail was addressed to Miss Schuyler, great-granddaughter of Alexander Hamilton. In 1872 she was instrumental in establishing the first nurses school at Bellevue Hospital. Dr. Marsh, whose name appears on the docket, was a sanitary agent. SF3

PHILADELPHIA — SANITARY COMMISSION

Collections of money and supplies at first were slow in accumulating in Philadelphia. To hasten and simplify collections from Pennsylvania, Delaware, and Western New Jersey, the ladies in the area formed the "Women's Pennsylvania Branch". Throughout the war the women were active in their endeavors and successful in establishing more than 350 auxiliary groups. They were primarily concerned with supplying the army operating in the east. Over $1,500,000 was raised for the war effort by this group of ladies who were directed by Robert M. Lewis. (Figs. 36, 37)

WESTERN DEPARTMENT — SANITARY COMMISSION

The St. Louis Branch under the Sanitary Commission became operational early in the war with the Northern seizure of Cairo, Illinois on April 24, 1861. A detachment of men was secretly brought to the area by the Illinois Central Railroad just in time to thwart rebel plans to seize this strategic area at the junction of the Mississippi and Ohio Rivers. Asked to join with the United States Sanitary Commission on September 23, 1861, the St. Louis Sanitary Commission, after due consideration, chose to be independent and ally itself with the Western Sanitary Commission and to assume full responsibility for all troops quartered or on duty west of the Mississippi. (Fig. 38)

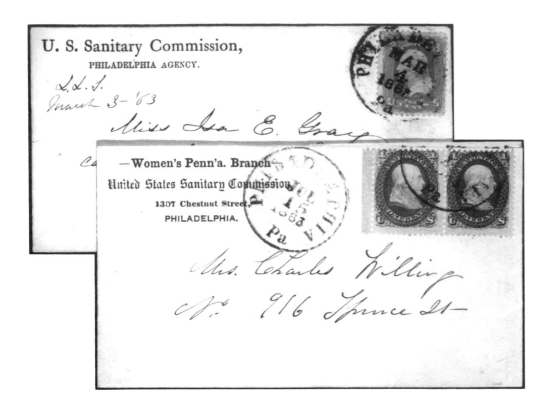

Fig. 36. (Top) Philadelphia, Mar 4, 1863 postmark. SF1

(Bottom) Two 1¢ stamps prepaying 2¢ drop letter rate from the Women's Pennsylvania Branch. SF2

Fig. 37. (Top) Double rated Philadelphia, Nov. 1863. Women did much of the collecting and packing of stores for the battle zones. SF2

(Middle) Oval U.S. Sanitary Commission corner card over embossed American flag. Postmarked Philadelphia, target cancel. SF1

(Bottom) Another example of an oval Commission corner card from Philadelphia. Postmarked Washington, May 25; cork cancellation. SF2

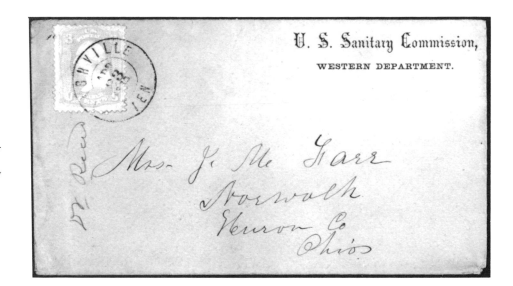

Fig. 38. The Western Department was under the direction of Dr. John S. Newberry of Cleveland. The functions of the U.S. Sanitary Commission were carried out in the west by this department, its concern directed primarily for the western theater of operations of the northern armies. Postmarked Nashville, Ten., Apr 23, 1863. SF3

OTHER STYLE CORNER CARDS — SANITARY COMMISSION

Being autonomous, local auxiliaries preferred to print their own corner cards. Examples of their design resourcefulness are many. (Figs. 39, 40)

The "Soldier's Shield" — The field of 34 stars representing the 34 states of the Union in 1861, North and South, was a popular motif. (Fig. 41, Plate 4)

Fig. 39. (Top) Ornate style imprint of "U.S. Sanitary Commission" addressed to Dr. Agnew, a member of the Commission. Postmarked Louisville, Jun 1, '64. SF2

(Bottom) A fancy cancellation of the period. Originating from Brattleboro, Vt. on September 2, 1864. SF2

Fig. 40. (Top) On October 17 (1865), after the war, Frederick N. Knapp, a special agent, wrote Louisa Schuyler at her home in Dobb's Ferry, N.Y. The Commission was still in operation at the time processing war claims and would continue to do so for a few more years. SF1

(Middle) When a letter could not be delivered, rather than sending the letter to the "Dead Letter" office, regulations provided that a notice could be advertised in a local newspaper indicating that a letter was on hand. To claim the letter it was necessary to pay 1¢ for the advertising fee. SF3

(Bottom) U.S. Sanitary Commission corner card with second line "The Soldier's Shield". It is not quite clear what the Commission shielded but the same theme is repeated with a shield or escutcheon on other covers. The shield could either be allegorical or it was intended as a shield against disease and illness. SF1

Fig. 41. (Top) Postmarked Gallatin, Ten., target cancellation. "Carrier" postmark dated May 29, 7 A.M. on reverse. SF3

(Middle) Two-cent circular rate, Boston, Mass., Paid, Dec 12 (1864). SF4

(Bottom) U.S. Sanitary Commission, London to Liverpool, forwarded to Leicester. Manuscript "1", "to be called for" and "not called for". Embossed "Cincinnati Branch—U.S. Sanitary Commission" over the shield. There was strong support of the Commission in England. SF4

ENGLISH BRANCH — SANITARY COMMISSION — AND THE RED CROSS
CONNECTION (Fig. 42)

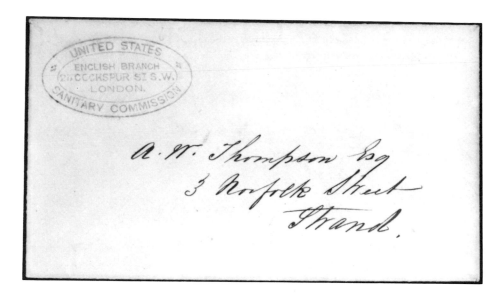

Fig. 42. Letter originating at the English Branch of the U.S. Sanitary Commission. Hand carried. SF2

The English branch of the United States Sanitary Commission was originally presided over by E.C. Fisher, later on by Dr. (of Divinity) John McClintock. Its purpose, at first, was to "interest Americans in England in the welfare of those fighting for our national integrity" and especially in winning the "sympathy of agents in England for the loyal side in this struggle." Dr. Bellows was very enthused about the establishment of a European branch of the Commission and in a ten-page letter to Dr. John McClintock, the chairman, he went to great lengths about the Commission, its aims, and its association with Dr. Henri Dunant, the future founder of the Red Cross. He then went on to mention the Metropolitan Fair in New York. The letter dated December 23, 1863, is as follows, with deletions:

> Rev. Dr. John McClintock
> Chairman of the European Branch
> of the U.S. Sanitary Commission
>
> Dear Sir,
>   The standing Committee of the U.S. Sanitary Commission, entrusted with the full powers of the Board in its vocations, receives with great gratification the announcement through your sec'y Mr. W.B. Bowles...of the establishment of a European Branch of the U.S. San y Com n...From China & Chili from India and the Sandwich Islands, from all the great & all the little Kingdoms of Europe, our fellow citizens...have sent us munificent testimonies of their hearty self-sacrificing devotion to the Cause & especially to our noble soldiers directly suffering in it.
>   ...having received almost by the same mail which brought the news of your existence...a document containg [sic] the full Report of an International Congress, held at the close of October at Geneva, Switzerland of the...chief powers in Europe, to consider what could be done to improve the *Sanitary Service of Armies in the field*!...

Strange today, not a reference to the existence of an Institution which would flood all their speculations with light, is made in this International Congress, two years & a half after our operations had become matters of universal observation in America…You would not know indeed from reading the Book that a War was still waging in America in which larger numbers of Hospitals & of sick & wounded men had existed than ever before in any Historical Record and in which vastly greater, more systematic and more successful attempts to alleviate suffering both governmental & popular, had been made than ever before. I notice, too, that the Delegates recommend that their future sessions should be confined wholly to European counsellors!…We should at any rate have put into their hands Documents that would have modified…their whole discussion—& we should have been able to prove that America…knows more of the subject matter of their Congress than all Europe!

…We hope you will write to M. Dunant, at Geneva—Secretary & get from him all the Documents necessary for the information of your Branch touching the operations of that new and Humane Body, & also inquiring to whom it is desirable in all countries to send our Documents. We believe that America can *lead* in this good work; can teach Europe a practical lesson, which will astonish, if it does not delight her, & we look to you to undertake this necessary & honorable work for us.

…It does seem judicious to forward, a portion of your funds in the shape of *good Brandy*, which it is almost impossible to procure except at ruinous prices. Besides that article I can mention no other as acceptable as money.

Allow me to mention one other mode of interesting your Constituents & serving us. We are to have a great Metropolitan Fair; in behalf of the San y Commission, in New York—to open about Easter week…

Commend me to each & every American citizen working with you in this European Branch, & accept for yourself & them, the grateful thanks of the U.S. Sanitary Commission, happy & proud to welcome its first foreign-born child.

> I have the honor to be
> very cordially & Respectfully
> Yours
> Henry W. Bellows
> Pres t. U.S. San y Com n.
> (Fig. 43)

Later on it was these same American agents in England who made direct contact with M. Henri Dunant of the International Red Cross. On May 23, 1864, Dunant, Secretary of the Comité International de Secours les Militaires Blessés of Geneva, had sent out an invitation to all civilized nations including the United States to attend the Geneva Convention on August 8, 1864. The resolutions of the Swiss organization were precisely those that the United States government had been operating under and would be asked to ratify and would refuse. Briefly, these resolutions involved a common insignia, noncombatant status for those wearing a white band with a Red Cross (the reverse of the Swiss flag) on it, and neutrality extended to all associated with the organization. It can unequivocally be stated that the liaison of the United States Sanitary Commission and the Red Cross ultimately resulted in the United States joining the International Red Cross on March 16, 1882 and signing the Geneva Convention at that time. By then Clara Barton and others had overcome

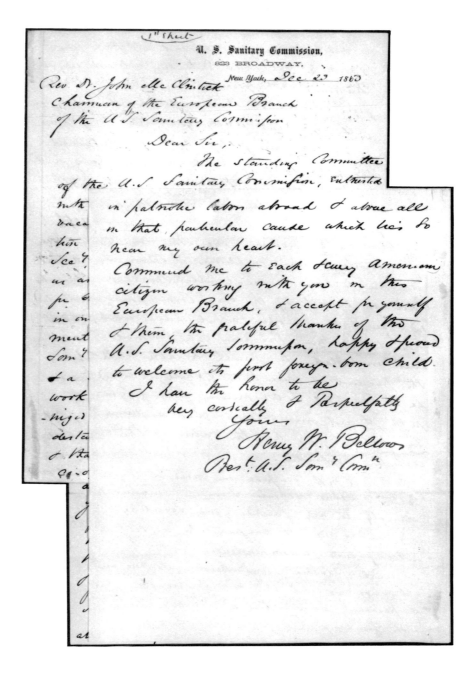

Fig. 43. President Bellows' letter to the Chairman of the European Branch of the U.S. Sanitary Commission.

the objection of the isolationists who were afraid of foreign entanglements should America join the convention.

For her unfaltering efforts much credit must also be given to Clara Barton. Despite the fact that she had never been a member of the Commission, she had seen all the misery and cruelty to the wounded on the battlefields. Throughout the years following the war Clara Barton almost single-handedly carried on the fight for ratification by the United States of the Geneva Treaty until it was eventually signed by President Chester A. Arthur. The experiences and events of the United States Sanitary Commission convinced her of the worth of an international organization to ameliorate the suffering of the wounded. Surely the U.S. Sanitary Commission provided the example of beneficence and charity that resulted in the establishment of the American Red Cross. It took educating the public about the genuine value of the organization and that was Clara Barton's real contribution, since the Red Cross had already established its merit with the victims of the war.

OTHER SANITARY COMMISSION ACTIVITIES (Fig. 44)

As the war progressed and a need to assist the wounded and helpless increased, so did the activities of the special relief service of the Commission located in Washington. "The Soldiers' Home" provided its headquarters. It supplied food and housing for soldiers in transit without sufficient funds to provide for their own care and communicated with a soldier's regiment in order to secure his discharge papers and the benefits from having these papers. It acted as an agent for the enfeebled or severely wounded to secure their claims, furnished money for soldiers' transportation back home, secured railroad tickets at a reduced rate for the afflicted, made the wounded clean and sanitary before they left for their homes, and contacted the necessary authorities to make sure that a malingerer was not a deserter or endeavoring to avoid active duty.

Fig. 44. (Top) "The Home" provided interim care between release from a hospital and a medical discharge or medical furlough. Postmarked Alexandria, Va., Sep 11, '64. SF2

(Middle) Soldier's Home at Nashville, postmarked Nashville. SF1

(Bottom) Soldier's Home at Nashville, postmarked Lexington, Ky., Mar 9, 1865. SF1

At first the soldiers' homes were vigorously opposed by the Sanitary Commission as it was felt that placing disabled veterans in these homes would institutionalize them and place them on regular doles instead of helping them find their place within an emerging America.

Dr. Bellows, president of the Commission, as early as 1862 did not wish these helpless masses of disabled soldiers to become political pawns as had every other group touched by the war. He strongly fought for not only the prompt payment of pensions and widows benefits but also for greater government generosity. Later, in 1866, one of those opposing the use of soldiers' homes, Samuel Gridley Howe, a Sanitary Commission activist, stated: "Better have 500 maimed veterans stumping about…than shut up in the costliest and best structures that art could plan or money build."

Similar homes were established in other theaters and transfer points where necessary and where indigent soldiers were congregated. Forty such homes were maintained by the Commission. In Nashville over 200,000 men were cared for in 1864 alone.

PENSIONS, CLAIMS, BONUSES — SANITARY COMMISSION

The full name of this department was the Pension Bureau and War Claim Agency. The Agency was created on February 10, 1863 and was active until January 1, 1866. It appeared that every soldier who passed through the homes had some type of claim against the government for pay, bounty, or pension. Evidence was necessary to establish claims from soldiers, many of whom could not read or write or were too badly injured to comply with the requests of the government. So pervasive was the need for pay and the number of claims so numerous that the Commission established one of its offices right across the street from the Army paymaster. As the war went on, the claims became even more numerous. By the end of the war the Claim Agency was active in 24 states and had 108 branches. (Figs. 45, 45A, 46)

It was not unusual for offices within this Agency to use different names for their departments, as illustrated by the letter to Alonzo Brown originating from the Army and Navy Claim Agency. The envelope was postmarked Jan. 12 (1867) in Washington.

Washington, D.C. Jan 10, 1867

Sir:

In reply to your letter of Dec 5, 1866 relative to the case of John Hein, a deceased soldier, I have to inform you that the records of this office fail to show that any claim on account of said soldier has ever been received. And as we ceased to receive new applications on the 1st of Jan. '66, we do not see how this claim could have been filed through this office so recently as last June. We are unable to give any information in the matter.

Respectfully yours,
W.F. Bascom
Gen. Agt.

Alonzo Brown Esq.
Garnaville
Clayton Co. Iowa.

The Protective War Claim Agency began operations on April 8, 1863 in Philadelphia. Its purpose was to expedite soldiers' claims against the government for pay and disability benefits. As the Sanitary Commission did not favor institutionalizing soldiers as a result of their injuries or their inability to adjust to civilian life, these welfare assists were left to private agencies and to the states. The Commission, should it have subscribed to confining veterans to homes or hospitals, would have had to continue its services long after the war had ended. (Figs. 47, 48)

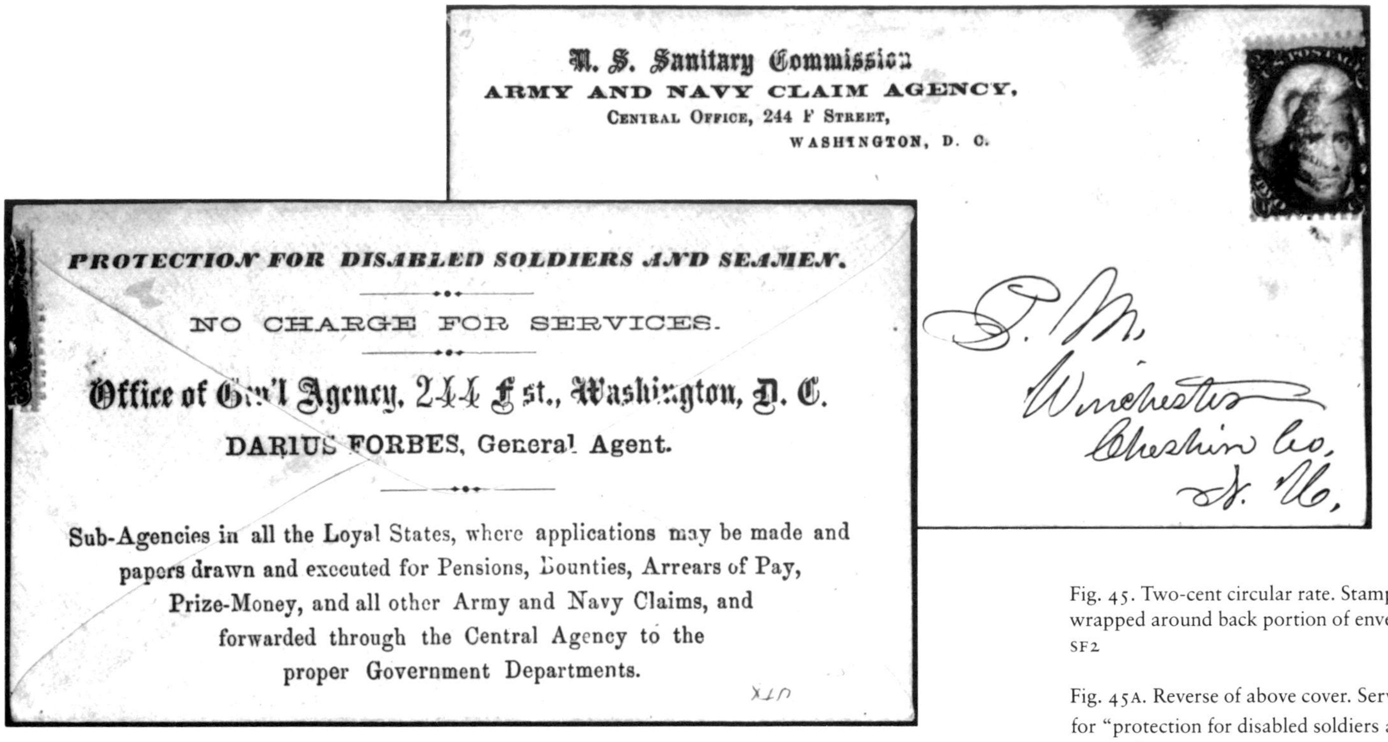

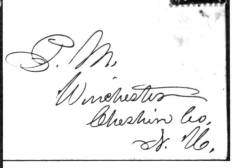

Fig. 45. Two-cent circular rate. Stamp wrapped around back portion of envelope. SF2

Fig. 45A. Reverse of above cover. Services for "protection for disabled soldiers and seamen".

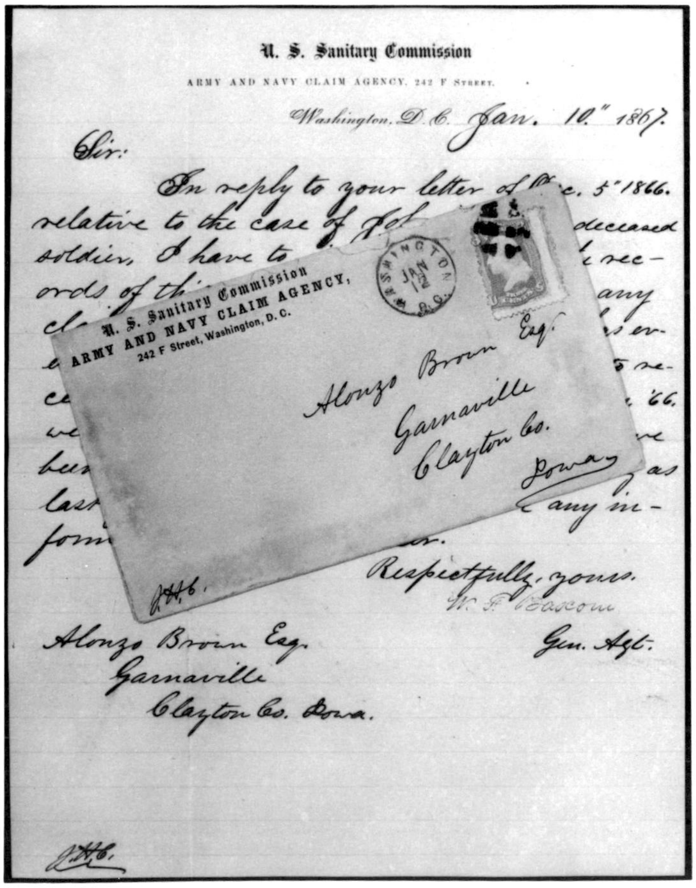

Fig. 46. Claim of Alonzo Brown of Iowa. Reply dated January 10, 1867 by Mr. W.F. Bascom, general agent of the United States Sanitary Commission at the Office of the Army and Navy Claim Agency. SF2

Fig. 47. (Top) (#U58) entire, postmarked Washington, Jul 21. SF1

(Middle) U.S. Sanitary Commission, Protective War Claim Agency corner card, 2¢ circular rate, postmarked Philadelphia. SF3

(Bottom) Three-cent rate, postmarked Philadelphia, Aug 11 from the Protective War Claim Agency of the U.S. Sanitary Commission. SF2

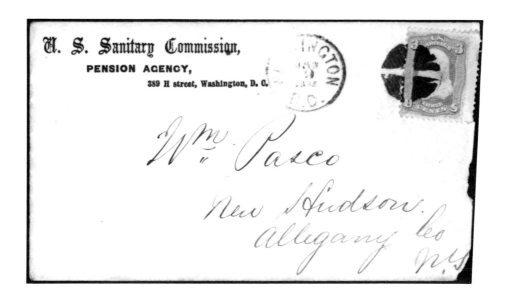

Fig. 48. The prime purpose of the Pension Agency was to secure pension rights for survivors and their dependents. SF2

HOSPITAL DIRECTORY — SANITARY COMMISSION

The central office of the Hospital Directory was opened in Washington on November 27, 1862. Originally a part of the Special Relief Department, the demands placed on it were such that a special directory bureau was established. In this bureau were kept the names and locations of patients in hospitals. There were 230 general hospitals reporting this information to directory services in Washington, Philadelphia, Louisville, and New York — all this in the days before computers, modems, and memory banks. Besides securing this information, the directories answered inquiries in regard to soldiers. Records of more than 600,000 soldiers were kept as to their current condition and location. Not content with obtaining this information from the hospitals alone, agents of the directory bureau walked the battlefields soon after a battle, reassuring the recently wounded that their families would be notified in short order about their condition and whereabouts. (Fig. 49)

Fig. 49. (Top) Hospital Directory Bureau in New York. Docket indicates location at 10 Cooper Union, original location of the Woman's Central Association of Relief. Docketing dates Feb. 5 and 6, 1864. Two-cent drop letter rate. SF3

(Bottom) Hospital Directory at Louisville, one of the four branches of this information service. Postmarked Louisville, Oct 17. "Missent" handstamp acknowledges that letter was sent to Peoria, Ill. instead of Finileer in Peoria County. SF3

HISTORICAL BUREAU — SANITARY COMMISSION

On July 27, 1866, John Blatchford, then general secretary of the United States Sanitary Commission called a meeting to discuss suggestions for the storing of the archives and preparation of the history of the Commission. It was stated at the meeting that the archives were to include letters, responses, instructions, reports, memoranda, records of the Hospital Directory, financial accounts and vouchers, statistical studies, and *The Bulletin* and other publications. The mass of material generated which required classification and preparation for publication was apparently too great since no comprehensive history of the Commission was published following cessation of all its activities on May 14, 1878. Charles Stillé's *History of the Sanitary Commission* had been printed in June of 1866 and had reported events only up to that date which was previous to the meeting. Blatchford suggested moving the mountain of material to a fireproof storage place in New York and this was done. At the end of the Blatchford report appears a series of questions regarding what should be included in the history, all of which have been answered by present day researchers. (Fig. 50)

Fig. 50. With the war's end it was necessary that a repository be established for the myriad correspondence, reports, schedules, monographs and all printed material of the Commission. The office was opened at 21 West 12th St. in New York. Eventually all historical material was transferred to the New York Public Library, where it remains today. Double rated letter, postmarked New York, pair and single of the 2¢ stamp. SF4

III

UNITED STATES CHRISTIAN COMMISSION

From a preliminary meeting in April 1861 of members of the Young Men's Christian Association (YMCA — founded June 7, 1854) evolved the United States Christian Commission and the vast network of its branches. It was not, however, until November 16, 1861, that plans were finalized at a meeting in New York. The object of the Commission was to promote the spiritual and temporal welfare of the officers and men of the United States Army and Navy, in cooperation with chaplains and others. A corollary of this was "to arouse the Christian associations and the Christian men and women of the loyal states to such action towards the men in our army and navy, as would be pleasing to the Master; to obtain and direct volunteer labors, and to collect stores and money with which to supply whatever was needed, reading matter,[10] and articles necessary for health not furnished by government or other agencies, and to give the officers and men of our army and navy the best Christian ministries for both body and soul possible in their circumstances."[11]

Frequently they tried to do that with such zeal and fervor that often the end never justified the means. Most agents of the Commission were uncompromising, lacking in compassion, tactless and taciturn. Yet they served a real function in not only furnishing certain material accouterments but in filling the spiritual needs of soldiers away from home, most of whom were unprepared to meet their Maker. Fear, ignorance, filth, suffering, pain, and demeaning circumstances were the lot of the soldier in the Civil War.

Walt Whitman, author of the poem preceding the Preface, had attended his wounded brother in Washington. He conceived the idea of writing *The Wound Dresser* some 12 years after the war and after having read Louisa May Alcott's *Hospital Scenes*. Whitman himself had a commission as a Soldiers' Missionary in the Christian Commission. For the over one million men of the North that served in the Civil War the Christian Commission

10. To its credit it was the Christian Commission that initiated the traveling library for soldiers. The idea was first offered by Joseph Conable Thomas, chaplain of the 88th Illinois Infantry, who tackled the problem that all armies faced, namely boredom. Chaplain Thomas laid out a system of portable libraries and then went to the Christian Commission for help in distributing these to the different regiments. The Commission, not entirely enthusiastic since it interfered with the distribution of their religious tracts, nonetheless relented and had their agents assist. By the time the Civil War ended there were more than 400 of these traveling libraries in general hospitals, permanent posts, and forts, on naval vessels, and in army installations where the Christian Commission had their agents.

11. *The Tribute Book*, by Frank B. Goodrich.

published 12 million religious tracts and publications—many for each soldier. Their determination to distribute this literature was not always well received. Whitman commented, "You ought to see the way the men as they lie helpless in bed turn away their faces from the sight of these Agents, Chaplains, &…[commissioners] (hirelings as Elias Hicks would call them—they seem to me always a set of foxes & wolves)."[12]

The Commission also established diet kitchens for the wounded who were unable to eat regular hospital fare. While the religious tracts rated high priority in their printing budget, the next most important printed pieces were the envelopes that were furnished to the troops. There is no evidence that the Christian Commission ever forwarded soldiers' mail or paid the postage for letters as did the Sanitary Commission.

In December of 1862, Frederick Law Olmsted, general secretary of the United States Sanitary Commission, issued an order to all inspectors of the Sanitary Commission which set the matter of the relationship of the Christian Commission and the Sanitary Commission in its proper perspective. The competition between the two groups, as to funds, the public perception of each, and even their activities in the field made this statement of basic policy necessary. In the order, Olmsted instructed the Sanitary Agents that the Christian Commission was a body designated to supplement the Chaplain Service in the Army and Navy, as the Sanitary Commission did to the needs of the Medical Service. In reality it was from the same agents of the Christian Commission that the Chaplain Corps of the Army and Navy evolved.

The Christian Commission was the first of the major relief agencies to cease operations. This occurred officially on February 10, 1866. In the final report of its activities the Christian Commission advised that it had supplied 7,066,000 envelopes and 7,067,000 sheets of writing paper.

12. *Walt Whitman—A Life*, by Justin Kaplan, p. 280.

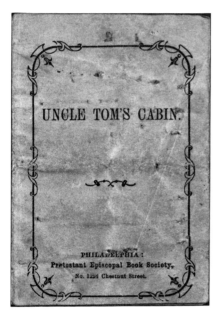

Tracts distributed by the Christian Commission

CHRISTIAN COMMISSION AND SOLDIERS' RELIEF FAIR IN WASHINGTON, D.C.
The Christian Commission and Soldiers' Relief Fair in Washington, D.C. was held in the Patent Office Building. (Fig. 51, Plate 5)

Fig. 51. Christian Commission and Soldiers' Relief Fair in Washington D.C. First postmark dated 16 (July). Two-cent circular rate. Nondeliverable, it was then forwarded to Hanover, N.H. The 3¢ with Washington D.C. postmark prepaid the forwarding fee. A Christian Commission Fair was also held in Baltimore in the spring of 1864 and in Buffalo, New York in the same year. SF5

SCROLL DESIGN

The scroll and pigeon designs along with other corner cards show the diverse areas where the presence of the Christian Commission was felt.

The convention on Prussian closed mail was signed in Washington on July 17, 1852 and in Berlin on August 26, 1852. It provided for an international rate of 30¢ per half ounce — 5¢ United States inland postage, 18¢ sea and British transit, 2¢ Belgian transit and 5¢ Prussian inland postage. The bags were made up in New York or Boston and at Aix-la-Chapelle (Aachen) in Prussia. The unopened bags moved through Great Britain and Belgium without either country applying a postal marking. Prepaid letters from the United States were marked at Aachen with handstamps reading "Franco" or "Aachen". (Figs. 52, 53)

Fig. 52. (Top) Albany, July postmark, Albany Branch, addressed to the president of the Soldier Relief Society. SF2

(Bottom) Alexandria, Va. postmark used as cancel; authorized target cancel appears to the right. SF1

Tending the wounded

Tracts vs. Pound Cake

Fig. 53. (Top) Scroll type corner card, post-marked Fort Laramie, Dakota Territory, Dec 6, 1866. Wyoming became a territory on July 29, 1868 and a state on July 10, 1890. SF2

(Bottom) Foreign usage, Washington D.C., Feb 6 to Aachen (Prussia) via New York, 30¢ due, German marking of 45. SF3

Christian Commission tent (Library of Congress)

CARRIER PIGEON DESIGN (Fig. 54)

Fig. 54. (Top) Baltimore, Jun 27 postmark "Due 3" for unpaid soldier's letter. SF2

(Middle) Soldier's letter with "Due 3". Old Point Comfort, Jul 29 postmark. Endorsed by the "Asst Surgeon U.S. Army in Charge Hospitals". SF2

(Bottom) Soldier's letter postmarked Old Point Comfort, lacking proper endorsement. "Due 6" handstamp, 3¢ for postage due and 3¢ for penalty. SF3

OTHER CHRISTIAN COMMISSION CORNER CARDS (Figs. 55, 56, 57, 58)
Since each branch had the option of printing envelopes as it saw best, the designs were generally the same but in many different type styles and settings. Some corner cards appear to have been prepared by hand in a cottage print shop. (Figs. 59, 60, 61)

The enclosure with the Michigan Branch cover is most informative and interesting. As of June 30, 1865, the date of the enclosure, there were 20,000 troops in Kansas, Nebraska, Idaho, Montana, Colorado, New Mexico, Utah, and the Indian Territories. The enclosure states, "They [the troops] are yet calling loudly, not only for greater supplies of vegetables, but for spiritual rations—asking for more religious books and papers, and for stationery, housewives and clothing, and other articles supplied by the Christian Commission...We need now large quantities of pickles, krout and grated horse radish. Many hundreds die for the want of them. [These ascorbics helped prevent scurvy.]...Housewives are most gladly

Fig. 55. (Top) Point Lookout, Md. postmark. Rev. Hartsough's name imprinted on a Baltimore cover. sf2

(Bottom) Baltimore postmark dated Jun 22, '64. sf1

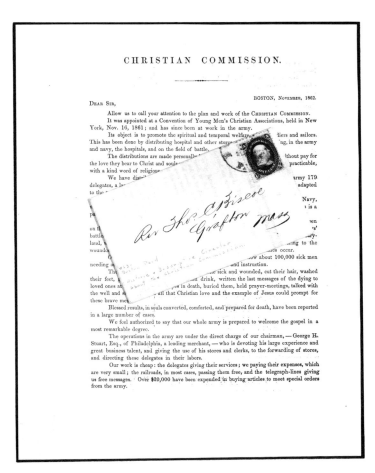

Fig. 56. 1¢ (#63), circular rate, "Boston Paid" cancellation. The aim of the Christian Commission was stated in this circular. sf2

received by the soldiers. Send them, friends, well filled with thread, yarn, needles, pins, buttons, combs, soap, towels, and handkerchiefs, and 'kind words to the soldier.'"

E.C. Walker, the chairman of the Michigan Branch, advised that all energies and supplies were to go only to their *own Michigan* troops. (Figs. 62, 63, 64) (Fig. 65) (Figs. 66, 67)

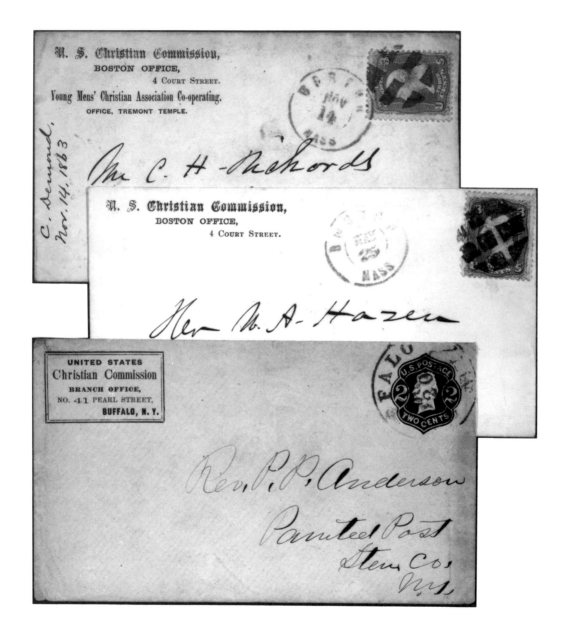

Fig. 57. (Top) U.S. Christian Commission and Young Men's Christian Association Co-operating corner card. Nov 14, 1863 docket. The YMCA had been founded only nine years earlier on June 7, 1854. From the YMCA grew the vast network of Christian Commission branches. To this day the YMCA renders a moral force for good without regard to race, creed or color. Its aim is to give young people a healthy outlook on life through physical fitness and mental training. SF3

(Middle) The corner card for Boston changed and the Christian Commission set its own course. SF1

(Bottom) Christian Commission Branch Office, Buffalo, N.Y., 2¢ circular rate (#U46). Buffalo postmark used as cancellation. SF3

Fig. 58. (Top) Cairo, Ill. at the junction of the Ohio and Mississippi Rivers had been of strategic importance ever since its first fortification on June 1, 1861. It was a major transfer point of troop movements north and south. SF1

(Bottom) Paducah, Ky., May 6, '65 postmark on a corner card originally from Cairo, Illinois. Paducah was seized early in the war. SF1

Fig. 59. (Top) Chattanooga branch, postmarked Nashville, Ten. SF1

(Middle) Handset type Chattanooga straightline postmark. SF3

(Bottom) Cincinnati Branch of the Christian Commission. Cincinnati was one of the most patriotic and active cities during the Civil War. SF1

Fig. 60. (Top) Old Point Comfort, Jul 29 (1864), Ft. Monroe; letter enclosure. SF2

(Middle) Double rated, Harper's Ferry branch, Harper's Ferry postmark, April 6, 1865 letter enclosure. A Commission agent was assigned to each military unit. SF2

(Bottom) Little Rock, Jan 22, '65 postmark. Little Rock fell to northern forces on September 10, 1863. SF1

Fig. 61. (Top) Louisville postmark dated Mar 27, '64 with target cancel. March 25, 1864 letter enclosure. Kentucky was a border state. SF3

(Middle) Ann Arbor, Michigan postmark. Michigan Branch of the U.S. Christian Commission. The general state agent was located in Ann Arbor. SF4

(Bottom) U.S. Christian Commission for the Army and Navy corner card, New York postmark. SF1

Fig. 62. (Top) Savannah, Apr 29 (1865) postmark on New York Branch, 30 Bible House corner card. Savannah surrendered to Sherman on Dec. 21, 1864. SF2

(Bottom) Phila., Mar 18, 1865 postmark, 3¢ rose (#65). SF1

Fig. 63. (Top) Postmarked Jefferson Barracks, Mo. Two 2¢ (#73), one-cent overpayment. SF4

(Middle) Jefferson Barracks octagonal postmark used as cancellation. SF2

(Bottom) Christian Commission corner card listing roster of officers. St. Louis postmark with target cancel. SF1

Fig. 64. (Top) Fort Leavenworth, Kan., Aug 4 postmark. SF2

(Bottom) Soldier's letter endorsed by the major of the 7th Indiana Cavalry. "Due 3" for nonpayment of postage, postmarked Austin, Texas. These units of the cavalry arrived in Austin on November 4 and were stationed at Seiders Springs, 2½ miles north of Austin. The regiment was mustered out of service February 18, 1866. SF3

Fig. 65. Dove or homing pigeon-type Christian Commission corner card. Postmarked St. Louis, May 1 with target cancellation. Interesting letter enclosure about Andersonville. SF3

April 30th 1865

Dear friend Lewis,
I thought I would writ (sic) you a few liens to let you no that I am well and hope this letter will find you the sam. I have not much to do to day so I shall mail a few letters home. I am just out of prison from Andersonville, Ga. Lewis I shall be at home in a month or two then I will tell you of prison life wich I spent in the Confederacy which I spent 27 months of Sufring, wich any mortal bing never saw or never will see. In one years time's 13900 men have dider in Andersonville Ga. with Starvation. Lewis send my best respects to all of the boys and girls. So good bye.

From your friend
G.M. Tripp
Seg. Major.
Mercantile Battery
Chicago

(The official name of the Mercantile Battery was Charles G. Cooley's Independent Battery.)

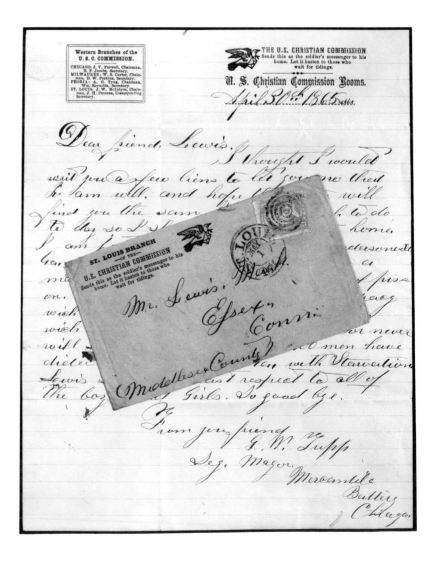

Fig. 66. (Top) New Orleans, May 15, '65 postmark. Vicksburg up the Mississippi had fallen to the North on July 4, 1863, New Orleans much earlier in the war. "Envelopes and Stationery on our writing tables…It's all a gift, from those at home who are prayerfully anxious that you be true, noble men, turning your backs upon every sinful indulgence." SF2

(Middle) Soldier's letter postmarked Washington D.C. Only the "D" appears for "Due"; either 3¢ or 6¢. Endorsement not completed as required by regulations. SF1

(Bottom) Washington D.C. postmark, 2¢ circular rate. SF3

Fig. 67. (Top) With Washington D.C., Jun 23 postmark. Within one branch different style corner cards were used. SF1

(Middle) Nashville, Jun 14, '64 postmark. Nashville and its environs had always been a center for both northern and southern military activity. Northern troops had first occupied Nashville on February 25, 1862. SF1

(Bottom) Philadelphia Station C postmark, dated Sep 3. SF1

Christian Commission in the field

YOUNG LADIES LOYAL LEAGUE
OF SOUTH BROOKLYN BAZAAR

Brooklyn, New York–December 1863
WV6–5¢ Black
WV7–10¢ Green

AND IN THE WAR…*As the fighting of the fall season comes to an end, the longer winter nights give both sides time to reflect on their victories and defeats. On the military front, events tip toward the North. The resolve of the North has not been broken. Fort Sumter still has not fallen and is a thorn in the side of the South. President Lincoln issues his Proclamation of Amnesty and Reconstruction to those implicated in the war if they now sign the oath of loyalty.*

Fig. 68. The majority of known 5¢ black on rosy buff Young Ladies of Brooklyn stamps. SF3

The Young Ladies Loyal League of South Brooklyn is more often referred to as the Young Ladies of Brooklyn to differentiate this group and their stamps from the stamps of the Brooklyn Fair. There is little documented evidence about this fair but it is known that there was indeed such an event; the stamps attest to that. In the *History of the Brooklyn and Long Island Fair* is a reference that "The Young Ladies Loyal League of South Brooklyn held a fair at the Athenaeum near the close of December, the funds resulting from which were handed over to the [Sanitary] Commission."

The stamps are rare at best, the 10¢ being scarcer than the 5¢. Both are typeset, with the 10¢ being printed in green ink on white paper and the 5¢ printed in black on rosy buff paper. In their sale of November 6 and 7, 1889, auctioneer Messrs. Bangs & Co. of New York listed in their lot #626 "'Young Ladies of Brooklyn Bazaar Post Office,' 5¢, used, *very rare*. Little Wanderers' Aid Society, (Boston) Post Office, 10¢, *very rare*. 2 pcs." (Authors' note: The Young Ladies of Brooklyn 5¢ used is probably the copy in the authors' collection with a contemporary pen cancellation but has not elsewhere been recorded since

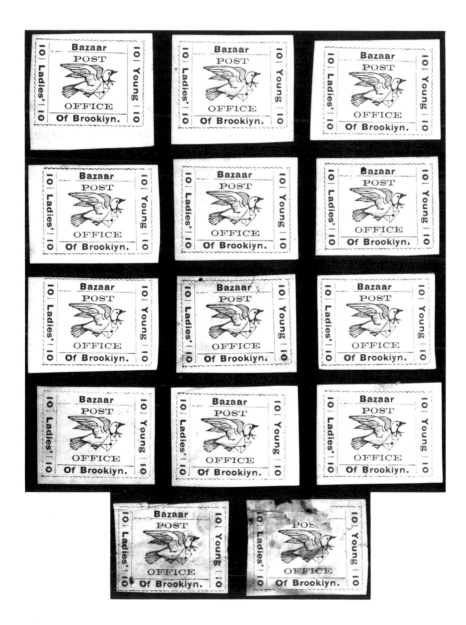

Fig. 69. The majority of known single copies of the 10¢ green Young Ladies of Brooklyn stamps. SF3

there is no other substantiating information. The latter stamp described in the lot probably originated with S. Allan Taylor.) Perry in his letter of April 14, 1930 reported that he could trace only about 12 copies of the 5¢ rosy buff and about 20 copies of the 10¢. More have come to light since that time. Shown here are the majority of known copies of these elusive Sanitary Fair stamps.

The 5¢ (WV6) eagle design measures 23mm x 29mm. Since there is no individual variation on the stamps, it would appear that they were printed one at a time. There may be individual differences in the color of the paper but that would seem to be more the result of natural causes such as fading or deterioration. (Fig. 68)

The 10¢ (WV7) measures 34mm x 27mm. The pigeon-carrying-a-letter design was repeated often on envelope corner cards and truly represented one method of sending information during the war. The telegraph was the favored method of the military but most farm boys, now soldiers, could relate to the carrier pigeon. (Fig. 69)

Tête-bêche pairs of this stamp are rare. Three are known to exist—two of which are shown here; the other is pictured in the catalogue of Christie's September 10, 1981 sale. It would appear that the stamps were printed in this arrangement rather than another type of format, although there is no firm evidence for this assumption. It also follows that the singles were all trimmed since the distance between the tête-bêche stamps is greater than any borders on the singles. (Fig. 70)

There are no known used copies of either of these two Young Ladies of Brooklyn stamps. Neither are there any known counterfeits.

Fig. 70. Two of the three known tête-bêche copies. SF5

V

BROOKLYN AND LONG ISLAND FAIR

Brooklyn, New York—February 22 to March 8, 1864
wv4—Green
wv5—Black

AND IN THE WAR...*Lincoln approves an act to pay a slave owner $300 for each slave released from bondage who subsequently enlisted in the army. The volunteer is then to be set free. The same act provides that those who refuse to bear arms for religious reasons should be assigned noncombatant duties with freedmen or serve in hospitals. Andrew Johnson is confirmed as Federal Military Governor of Tennessee. President Lincoln designates the western boundary of Iowa as the starting point of the Union Pacific Railroad. At Americus, Georgia, federal prisoners of war are arriving at a prison camp known officially as Camp Sumter but known to history as Andersonville.*

View of the Academy of Music from the stage at the Brooklyn Fair

Originally the ladies of Brooklyn were to hold their fair with the women of New York City. When those in charge of the New York (Metropolitan) Fair wished to delay the opening for six weeks, the Brooklyn women decided not to wait and instead opened their fair on February 22 at the Academy of Music on Montague Street. (Figs. 71, 72)

In the *History of the Brooklyn and Long Island Fair* is the notation that "The price of postage was 15 and 25 cents."[13] "The fact [is] that the postage on every letter goes towards increasing the funds of the Sanitary Commission...".[14] An issue of the fair newspaper admonished that "some letters of an objectionable character...occasion of annoyance and

13. *History of the Brooklyn and Long Island Fair*, p. 39.

14. Issue No. 1, February 22, 1864, *The Drum Beat*, fair newspaper.

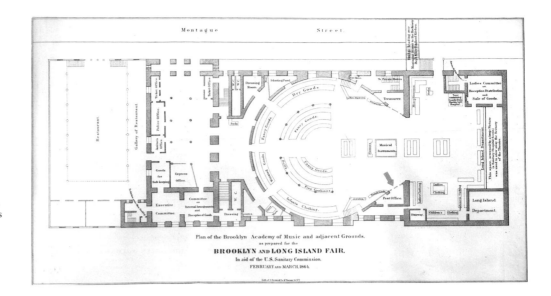

Fig. 71. "In one of the proscenium boxes was the Post Office, under the care of Mrs. J.P. Duffin and assistants. These ladies not only conducted the business of their bureau, but they wrote the letters too. The recipients paid fifteen and twenty-five cents postage, *according to bulk, perhaps, or else according to their being written in prose or verse.*" *The Tribute Book*, p. 193.

Fig. 72. A sketch of the Brooklyn Fair Post Office Booth by Winslow Homer from *Harper's Weekly.*

15. Ibid—Issue No. 12, March 5, 1864.

pain to those whom they reached…must have been expected, where four or five thousand letters were to be received and distributed."[15] The fair closed on March 8, 1864. The Post Office raised a total of $830.55, while $305,513.83 was raised overall for the benefit of the United States Sanitary Commission.

The stamp picturing an eagle with outstretched wings, clasping arrows within one claw and an olive branch in the other, measures 22mm x 31mm and was lithographed. It is believed that the green (wv4) was the 15¢ value and the black (wv5), the 25¢ value. Both are on white paper. The single sheet of ten shown herein is of the green stamp and has been reconstructed from a block of six and a block of four. Also shown are the only known pair and the majority of known single copies of the green fair stamp (WV4). One is known used with a portion of the fair postmark. (Figs. 73, 74)

Only two copies are known of the black stamp (WV5), including one on cover addressed to Henry M. Needham. (Fig. 75, Plate 6)

Fig. 73. (Top) Reconstructed sheet—largest known multiples, block of six and block of four of the green Brooklyn Sanitary Fair stamps (WV4). SF5

(Bottom) Only known pair of the green (WV4). SF4

There are three addressed and two unaddressed covers bearing the Brooklyn and Long Island Fair stamps in green. Of the three addressed covers the one formerly in the Luff Collection was sent to Mr. Sam'l M. Welch, Sanitary Fair, Brooklyn, N.Y. The postmark is struck in the upper right corner of the cover and the green "Brooklyn Sanitary Fair Postage" stamp is affixed in the upper left corner covering the word "PAID" previously handstamped there.[16] Elliott Perry indicated that although the stamp was not canceled, it was used on the cover and both the stamp and cover are *absolutely* authentic.

The other two addressed covers were in the Henry C. Needham collection as late as 1919, and the owner at that time claimed to have had them for many years. One is addressed to Mr. Henry M. Needham, believed to be the father of Henry C. Needham, at an address outside the fair. In the upper right corner the fair postmark appears, and adjacent to it is an uncanceled Brooklyn Fair stamp printed in black (WV5). In the upper left corner is affixed a copy of the "Brooklyn City Express Post" 1¢ local post stamp (#28L2) tied to the cover with a ring-shaped cancellation. Henry C. Needham had so little faith in the authenticity of the 1¢ Brooklyn City Express stamps that he stated in *The Philatelic Ga-*

16. The "PAID" would seem to indicate prepayment within the fair or, as in the case of the Needham cover, movement in the regular mails.

zette of May 1917 under the title "United States Local Stamps—A Concise History and Memoranda, Compiled by Henry C. Needham" the following:

> The one cent stamp, properly cancelled and showing authentic usage, would be a rarity—something we have never seen. We list both colors of this stamp, however, but without vouching for them.

Yet the Needham cover addressed to his father and authenticated by Robson Lowe, an authority on locals, at Anphilex in New York in 1971, appears to assure the genuineness of the presence of this stamp and its proper use on the cover.

Fig. 74. The majority of known copies (WV4). SF3

Only known green fair stamp (WV4) with a fair postmark. SF5

Fig. 75. The two known copies of the black Brooklyn stamp (WV5). On the Needham cover is the fair postmark and a 1¢ green Brooklyn City Express Post local. SF5

Fig. 76. (Top) Handstamped PAID under the no-value green Sanitary Fair stamp. Brooklyn and L.I. Fair 1864 postmark. SF5

(Middle) Addressed to Dr. Reese with one-cent blue (#63) stamp, the drop letter rate. Green fair stamp pen canceled. SF4

(Bottom) From the "Gentlemen's Executive Committee", no-value green, Brooklyn and L.I. Fair 1864 postmark. SF5

The other cover is addressed to a location outside the fair and bears a 1¢ U.S. postage stamp (Scott #63) canceled with the Brooklyn town postmark and a pen cancellation on the green Brooklyn Fair stamp. This cover does not bear any fair postmark. (Fig. 76, Plate 7) (Figs. 77, 78, 79)

It is possible to plate these stamps but not necessarily in order to determine their authenticity, as the counterfeits are easily detected. On the counterfeits, in addition to the overall difference in appearance, in the word "Sanitary" there is a heavy cross bar to the "T" and in the second "A" the left leg of the letter is longer than the right. The counterfeit is also roughly typographed without shading in the letters of the word "Fair". Compared with the genuine stamp, fewer imitations appear to exist. Most, it is believed, are the work of S. Allan Taylor, as at least one of the imitations was printed on a colored paper typical of the kind that he would have used. (Fig. 80)

Fig. 77. Brooklyn and L.I. Fair 1864 post-mark, three gentlemen's calling cards enclosed. (One of the enclosures) Fred Wells was "The gentleman without a moustache". SF5

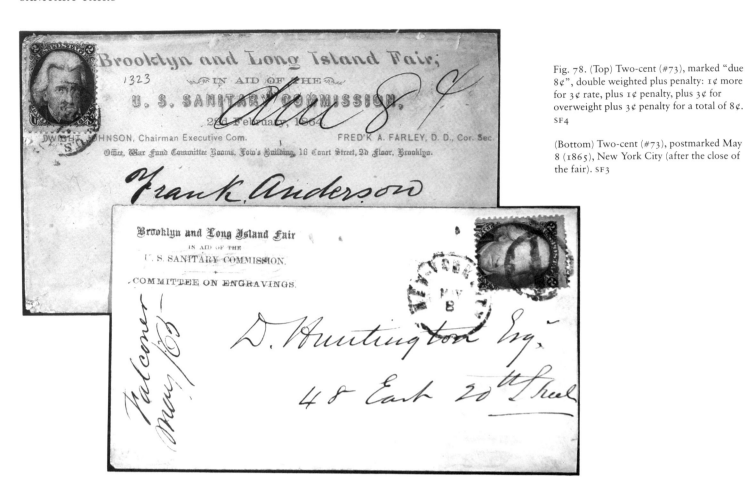

Fig. 78. (Top) Two-cent (#73), marked "due 8¢", double weighted plus penalty: 1¢ more for 3¢ rate, plus 1¢ penalty, plus 3¢ for overweight plus 3¢ penalty for a total of 8¢. SF4

(Bottom) Two-cent (#73), postmarked May 8 (1865), New York City (after the close of the fair). SF3

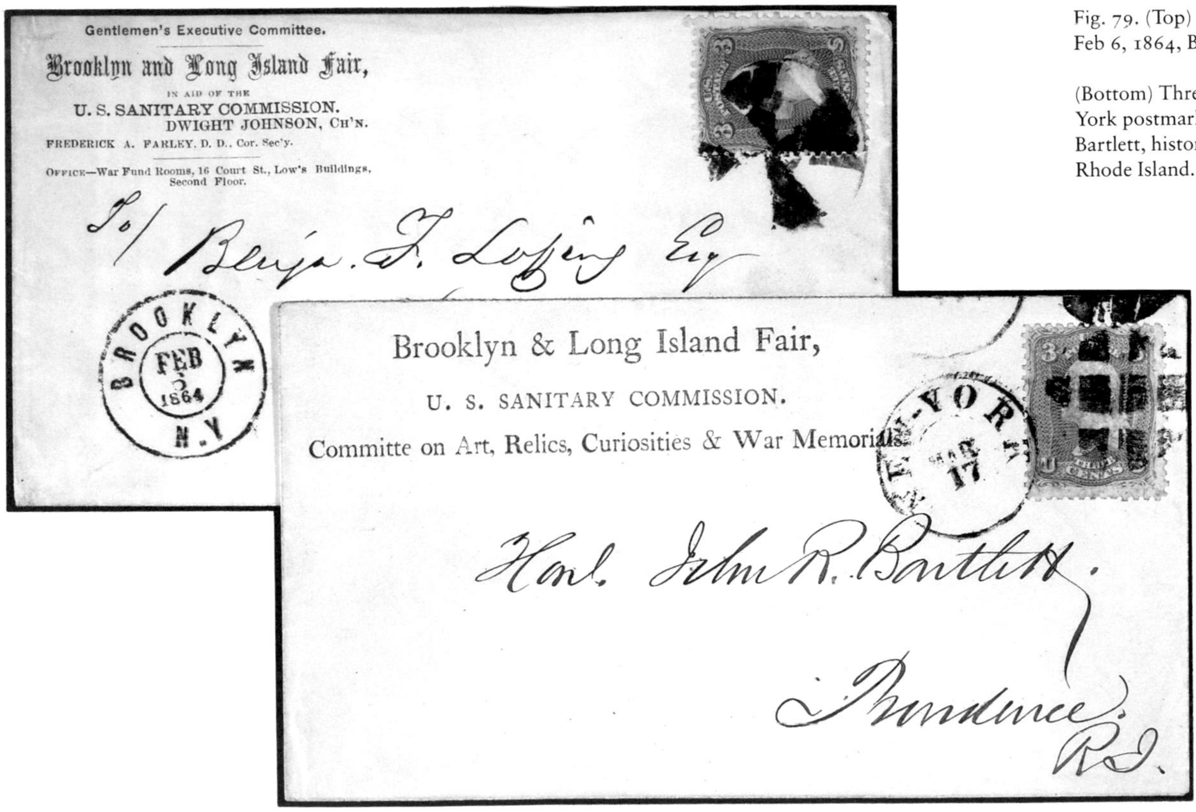

Fig. 79. (Top) Three-cent (#65), postmarked Feb 6, 1864, Brooklyn. SF3

(Bottom) Three-cent (#65), Mar 17, New York postmark, addressed to John Russell Bartlett, historian and Secretary of State of Rhode Island. SF3

Fig. 80. Counterfeit green Brooklyns.

VI

ARMY RELIEF BAZAAR

Albany, New York—February 22 to March 30, 1864
WV1—10¢ Rose
WV2—10¢ Black

AND IN THE WAR...*With the rank of Lieutenant General reactivated, Grant assumes command of Union forces under the title of General in Chief of the Army of the United States. Despite the lassitude brought on by the winter, guerrilla activity and armed patrols continue, and the noose on southern ports grows tighter. On the home front the doldrums set in. Fairs offer a respite. More fairs open on Washington's Birthday in other cities including Brooklyn, Buffalo and Cleveland.*

Postal staff at the Albany Sanitary Fair

On November 1, 1861, the women of Albany organized the Army Relief Association. By February 22, 1864, the citizens of Albany and Troy had organized, planned, and opened their fair called the Army Relief Bazaar. It raised a total of $80,000. Included were the proceeds from the sale of a copy of the Emancipation Proclamation. (The New York State Library has this preliminary draft of the Emancipation Proclamation. Lincoln had donated the Proclamation to the Albany Army Relief Bazaar where it was auctioned off to Gerrit Smith, an abolitionist, who in turn gave the Proclamation to the Sanitary Commission to sell to raise funds.

(The New York State Legislature, on April 28, 1865, appropriated $1,000 to purchase the Emancipation Proclamation for the State of New York. This receipt records the transaction. William Barnes, whose name is on the receipt, was chairman of the Albany lottery committee for disposition of the Proclamation. (Fig. 81)

(Lincoln's own holograph final draft had been given to the Northwestern Fair held in Chicago in October 1863, but was later destroyed in the Chicago fire of 1871. In 1911, the

New York State Library suffered a fire, but this important remaining preliminary draft of the Emancipation Proclamation was saved.

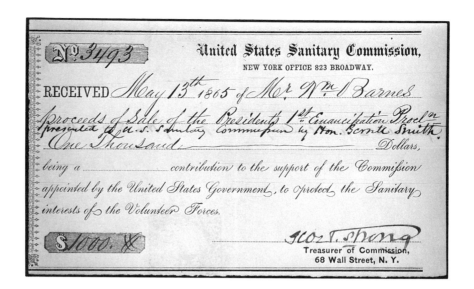

Fig. 81. Receipt for Lincoln's preliminary draft of the Emancipation Proclamation—previously in the authors' collection, now in the New York State Library, Albany, N.Y.

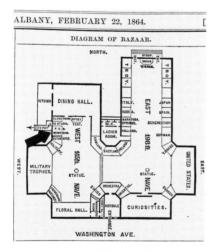

Fig. 82. Location of fair post office.

(The official copy of the Emancipation Proclamation, signed and sealed by Lincoln, is in the National Archives. There exist 56 versions of the Proclamation in various stages by different printers, all published prior to 1866. Forty-eight copies of one of these versions were prepared by Leland and Boker for sale at the Philadelphia Fair for $10 each; each was signed by Lincoln, Seward, and Lincoln's secretary, John G. Nicolay. Five of the copies left unsold were later sold at the National Sailors' Fair (Boston, 1864) and the few remaining copies were distributed to libraries. In the Sotheby Sale #5229 of October 1984 one of these copies sold for $297,000. This copy can be seen at Forbes Magazine Galleries in New York City.)

Buildings were erected in Academy Park of the city. Like most fairs there was a post office but unlike most, this one issued Sanitary Fair stamps. A contemporary floor plan of the booths delineates the post office booth. Evidence of the issuance of fair stamps, WV1 and WV2, at Albany for the Army Relief Bazaar is found in an advertisement in the February 25th issue of *The Canteen*, the fair newspaper:

Bazaar Postage Stamps
Can be procured at the Book and Music Stores and at the Post Office in
the Bazaar. All letters placed in the letter box must be prepaid.
Geo P. Ten Broeck, Secretary
(Fig. 82)

The stamps of the Bazaar were issued in two colors, the more common of the two in rose (WV1), and the other in the rare black (WV2). Both measure approximately 17mm x 22mm and were lithographed on thin white paper. According to Elliott Perry, it was John E. Gavit of Albany, brother-in-law of George Pomeroy of Pomeroy's Letter Express, who engraved both the Pomeroy Express stamp in 1844 and the Albany Bazaar stamp. On October 14, 1918, Gavit's grandson wrote to Perry and explained that his grandfather had formed Gavit and Company in 1842 in Albany. It was logical, then, that as a local craftsman he would be called upon to design this stamp. Later on Gavit served as president of the American Bank Note Company. Seven years after his death in 1872, the American Bank Note Company became the surviving name upon its merger with the National and Continental Bank Note Companies.

Apparently there were two printings despite the relatively small volume of sales amounting to a reported $126.64 within a seven-day period. There appears to be no satisfactory explanation for the fact that while the stamps sold for ten cents each the total for the week ends in an odd amount.

One printing was a pane of 12 stamps with a narrow spacing between the stamps. This is referred to as Setting A, which has a common cross line between the stamps both horizontally and vertically. In the other setting, Setting B, that was printed in sheets of 25, there is wide spacing between the stamps which each have their own extra outside line. (Figs. 83, 84, 85, 86)

Fig. 83. Army Relief Bazaar in Albany, New York. Pane of 12, blocks of four, setting A, narrow spacing, rose color (WV1). SF4

One pane is known of Setting A of WV1 and its scarcity may account for another printing having been made. At least three full sheets are known of Setting B. More may have been printed to satisfy the demand for additional stamps during the five-week life of the Bazaar.

A block of five is the only known multiple of the black Albany Relief Bazaar stamp (WV2) and is Setting A. In April 1930, Perry indicated that he could trace about 12 copies of the red but did not mention the black. Today there are at least 30 known single black stamps.

The Albany postmark tying the rose Albany (WV1) to the cover sent by Allen B. Durant to William H. Hale is from a cancellation die which had been retired by the United States

Fig. 84. Setting A, black, only known multiple (wv2). SF5

Fig. 85. Sheets of 25 of 10¢ rose, setting B, wide spacing. SF4

Fig. 86. Ten-cent rose, setting B. (Setting A is the scarcer of the two settings.) SF3

Post Office at Albany just three months previously and undoubtedly was loaned to the Albany Fair Post Office. This unofficial use and intermingling of the official post offices and the fair post offices prevailed throughout the fairs and further tends to confirm the semi-official status of these stamps. The letter enclosed discussed the Bazaar. (Fig. 87, Plate 8)

Durant in his letter to Hale not only made mention of the fair but also noted that Hale, having written to him previously, had taken the unusual step of writing a Sanitary Fair note as an enclosure when Durant thought that only women wrote the letters. This is the only known postmarked Albany on cover.

The Collin cover has the 3¢ 1861 with the fair stamp, though not tied but typical of the placement of the stamp at the Bazaar. It is postmarked February 26, 1864, on the fifth day of the fair. The word "typical" is used because there exists a similar placement on a cover (also with a 3¢ 1861) in the Albany Historical and Art Society that is addressed to Jas Pierce, Esq., Oswego, N.Y. and is dated February 23, 1864.

For the opening event at the fair, Alfred B. Street authored and read a poem "which was distinguished for great delicacy of thought, beauty of expression and fervid patriotism" according to Rufus W. Clark writing in *The Heroes of Albany*. While his poem was soon forgotten and passed into oblivion, his name continues to live on the cover addressed to him at the fair—marked "10" and displaying a railroad postmark. (Fig. 88)

Many counterfeits of the Albany Fair stamp exist. They were typographed in red, blue, black, or green on a thin white paper, on ordinary white paper, or on colored paper. The colored papers appear to be the work of S. Allan Taylor who for one reason or another took a fancy to these stamps since he made so many of the fair counterfeits.

Of the counterfeits, type (a) can be recognized with the eagle having a topknot. The stamps were printed in sheets of 30 (6 x 5). Flaws appear in individual transfers and the spacing is irregular.

Type (b) has the eagle without the shading around it and is the most common type. Perry believed that several different stones were used since there is a minute difference in the lengths and strengths of the ornaments and lettering.

Type (c) has a shading around the eagle but with a period instead of a circle in "C" of Cents, and the "Ten Cents" is smaller than on the genuine stamp. The shaping of the letters in the word "Post Office" also differs from the original. (Fig. 89)

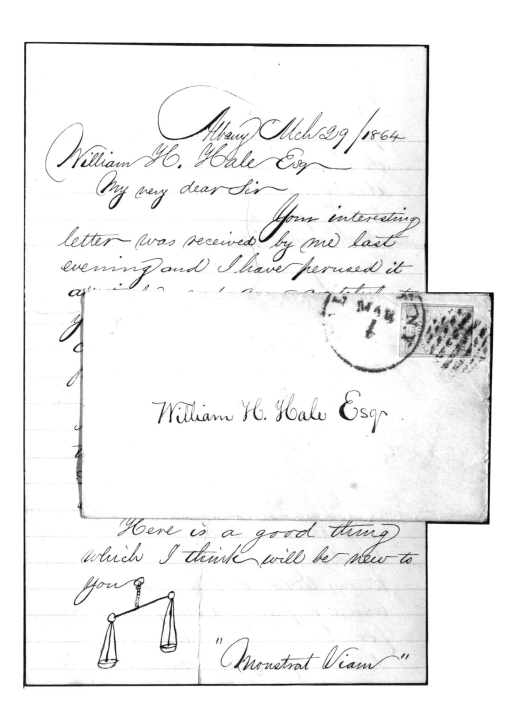

Fig. 87. Albany 10¢ rose tied to cover. Letter enclosed tells of the Bazaar. The postal marking device had been retired three months earlier by the United States Post Office. SF4

Fig. 88. (Top) Albany 10¢ rose on cover postmarked Albany, New York, Feb 26, (18)64 (fifth day of the fair). SF3

(Bottom) Addressed to Alfred Street at the Bazaar Post Office (author of poem read at the Bazaar dedication), railroad postmark, marked "10". SF3

Fig. 89. (Left) Counterfeit type (a) of the Albany stamps, (Center) counterfeit type (b), (Right) counterfeit type (c).

VII

METROPOLITAN FAIR

New York, New York–April 4 to April 27, 1864
wv8–10¢ Blue
wv9–10¢ Red
wv10–10¢ Black

AND IN THE WAR...*The war is not going well for the North. Anxious eyes are turned toward Virginia where Lee's Army of Northern Virginia confronts Grant with Meade's Army of the Potomac. Southern dissatisfaction with Jefferson Davis increases. On April 12 the Confederates capture Ft. Pillow, Tennessee. General Banks and General Taylor of the South are locked in battle in Louisiana, with Banks the loser.*

Museum of Arms and Trophies at the Metropolitan Fair

The Metropolitan Fair was originally planned for the 22nd Regiment Armory but it became obvious that more space was needed which was then provided with the construction of supplementary buildings on the adjoining grounds known as the Palace Garden.

This fair was one of the largest and best attended. It raised a total of $1,340,050.37, of which one million dollars was tendered to the treasurer of the United States Sanitary Commission.

On November 20, 1863, Edward Everett, the main speaker at the dedication of the cemetery at Gettysburg, wrote to Lincoln, "Permit me to express my great admiration for the thoughts expressed by you, with such eloquent simplicity and appropriateness at the consecration of the cemetery. I should be glad, if I could flatter myself that I came as near to

Sanitary Fair Post Office

17. *A Record of the Metropolitan Fair in Aid of the United States Sanitary Commission.*

Theodore Steinway's family donated $1,000 in lieu of a Grand Piano

18. *Report of the Treasurer of the Metropolitan Fair in Aid of the United States Sanitary Commission Held in New York City, April 1864 to August 1, 1864,* printed by John F. Trow, 50 Greene St., New York.

the central idea of the occasion, in the two hours, as you did in two minutes." He was, of course, referring to Lincoln's Gettysburg Address. At a later time Everett asked Lincoln if he would write out a copy to be sold at the Metropolitan Fair and Lincoln did so. That copy is slightly different than drafts one and two and now is owned by the Illinois Historical Library in Springfield.

(George Bancroft, the historian, asked Lincoln for another copy for the Baltimore Sanitary Fair and he once again obliged. Lincoln, however, had written this draft of the Gettysburg Address on the wrong-sized stationery and it could not be included in the album of contemporary letters of authors. The Bancroft family retained this copy which in 1929 was donated to Cornell University. In place of this odd-sized copy, Lincoln wrote still another one at Bancroft's request for the Baltimore Sanitary Fair. This draft is considered the official and correct one because it was the last one written. It is now in the Lincoln Room of the White House.)

According to George Wray, one of the early collectors of Sanitary Fair stamps, John E. Gavit of Albany, who engraved the Albany Relief Bazaar stamp, was also responsible for engraving the Metropolitan stamp. The original plate for the Metropolitan stamp was presented to the Collectors Club of New York in 1950 by Dorsey F. Wheless.

The prospectus for the fair, published in early 1864, advised that a "Post Office will be established, at the illegality of which it is hoped that the Honorable Postmaster-General will wink, if official dignity is capable of such an act and at the novel promptness and regularity of which it is believed the public will wonder."[17] The reaction of the postmaster is not known. However, using Philadelphia as an example where the postmaster looked the other way at the operation of the fair post office, it is likely, because of the intense rivalry which existed between the two cities, that the New York postmaster must have permitted the operation of the Metropolitan Fair Post Office in order not to be outdone or deemed less patriotic than his Philadelphia counterpart.

This fair lasted over three weeks and while the floor plan map indicates the presence of a post office, there are no Metropolitan Fair stamps on cover or canceled fair stamps off cover. This would tend to confirm the fact that while stamps were prepared for use at the Metropolitan Fair, none were ever used at the fair.

It may be conjectured that perhaps engraver Gavit, recalling his handiwork at the Albany Bazaar, called this fair a bazaar and as a result the stamps intended for a fair were rejected for use because of the misnomer. The inscription on the New York stamp refers to a bazaar post office, yet all letterheads and receipts use the title of *Metropolitan Fair*. Thus, it may be presumed that stamps, if used, would have borne a similar inscription. J. Walter Scott, writing in the January 1889 issue of the *American Journal of Philately* (page 22), maintained that the Metropolitan Fair stamp was prepared by Gavit "but that as the time drew near [for the fair to open] it was found impossible to have a supply [of the stamps] printed in time: the plate was accordingly laid aside and never used." (Fig. 90)

The fair newspaper, *Spirit of the Fair*, showed a floor plan for a post office. A final report on the fair published in 1867 by Hurd & Houghton stated that a post office was operational. It was located in booth No. 46 at the 17th Street side off 4th Avenue.

The paucity of stamps can best be accounted for by the fact that few stamps were actually sold. Within the final report of the Metropolitan Fair submitted to its treasurer by Mrs. Ellen R. Strong, who incidentally along with Augustus R. Macdonough headed the Post Office Committee, is a notation that the income from the sale of stamps on May 17, 1864 came to $13.80.[18] That would be 138 stamps. There was nothing within this same report to indicate that any person or any place made a donation of these stamps. Since even the smallest donation of any kind was noted, it can be presumed that if Mr. Gavit, the engraver, or the Albany Committee had made a donation, this would have appeared within the list of donors.

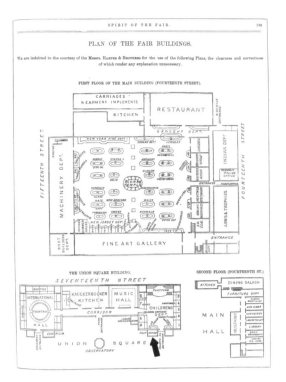

Fig. 90. Floor plan showing location of post office at the New York Metropolitan Sanitary Fair.

Fig. 91. Eagle Carrier stamp of 1851 from which the Metropolitan Fair stamp was copied.

The stamps were printed in a block of four, issued imperforate, and in three colors: blue, red, and black; the blue (wv8) is the most common. Dimensions are approximately 20mm x 25mm. Elliott Perry believed that the center eagle was transferred four times from the vignette for the "eagle" carrier postage stamp (LO2 of 1851 engraved and printed by Toppan, Carpenter, Casilear & Company), with the border and lettering engraved separately on each stamp. There are differences in the scroll work around "Post Office" and "Ten Cents" that tend to bear this out. (Fig. 91)

At least 50 copies of this blue Metropolitan Fair stamp are extant, with only the rose Albany and the three Philadelphia Sanitary Fair stamps being more common. Six sheets of four stamps each are known of the blue on thin white paper. (Fig. 92) There are no red sheets of four known, only two pairs of the red. Only one black single is known to exist.

To plate a sheet of the four Metropolitan Fair stamps the following differences should be noted:

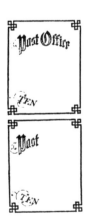

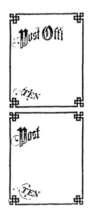

#1 One scroll ends under the foot of "T" of Ten.

#3 One scroll ends under the right serif of "T" of Ten.

#2 Dash over "t" of Post and "f" of Office.

#4 The double pair of curved dashes in front of Post is omitted.

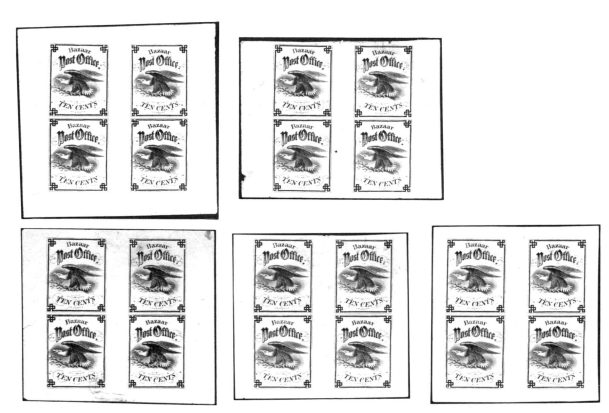

Fig. 92. Blue 10¢ (WV8)—only known sheets of four. SF3

Of the red (WV9), 12 singles and two pairs—one vertical and the other horizontal—are known. The horizontal pair is similar to positions 1 and 2 on the blue pane, and the vertical pair consists of positions 2 and 4. This red stamp was issued on thin white paper similar to the blue. (Fig. 93) Unique is the black (WV10) on thin white paper. (Fig. 94)

A black Metropolitan proof on yellow glazed card also exists. On October 8, 1918, Perry wrote to Mrs. Francis Gavit, widow of the designer of the Metropolitan stamp, to inquire about it. She could give little information but this proof showed up when the Vincent Domanski collection was sold.

The fairs were essentially dashing and cheerful events that lent themselves to color and the free spirit of a free people. Halls were decked with bunting and flags. The women appeared in their finery as the fairs were among the first adventures of the newly liberated sex. There were, in addition, many wounded soldiers all about. Families were touched with a son, brother, or husband in the service of their country. It is more than likely that a selection of a bright and cheerful stamp would be made. And rather than opting for black and its dreary and somber connotations, the red or blue symbolic of the colors in the flag would be selected for use.

While no stamps exist on cover, the fair did provide a pictorial corner card or cachet printed in black ink by Williams of New York City. Contrary to regulations the printer in producing the cachet placed the information on the right, necessitating that the stamp be affixed on the lower left.

The cover addressed to a Mrs. MacDonald is dated January 19, 18(64). In another letter, Mrs. MacDonald is invited to become a manager of one of the departments of the fair. The transcript of the letter, like others in this presentation, is included not only to reflect the charm but to suggest the ambiance and grace of the period.

Fig. 93. (Top) Red 10¢ (WV9). Majority of known single copies. SF3

(Bottom) The only recorded red 10¢ multiples. SF4

Fig. 94. (Left) Unique 10¢ black (WV10). SF4

(Center) Plate proof of 10¢ black on white card (WV10P). SF3

(Right) Plate proof of 10¢ black on yellow glazed card. SF3

Mrs. James MacDonald

Dear Madam

I have the honor to inform you that you have been appointed a manager of the "Metropolitan Fair". Will you not exert your influence in your neighborhood to draw out the interest of the people, & induce them to send contributions of every kind. We shall be happy to meet you or hear from you at our rooms No. 2 Great Jones Street any day between the hours of 10 A.M. & 4 P.M. . . .

It does not appear that Mrs. MacDonald accepted the appointment as the *History of the Metropolitan Fair* does not reveal her name as being a member of any committee. (Figs. 95, 96)

Fig. 95. (Top) Three-cent 1861, New York postmark. Battlefield scene in black as are all the corner cards from the Metropolitan Fair. Printer's name, Williams, appears below the stretcher-bearer on the left. SF3

(Bottom) Battlefield scene, double 3¢ rate, Feb 3, 1864, New York postmark, approximately two months before the fair opened. SF3

Fig. 96. (Top) Battlefield scene with receiving depot address–Feb 27, 1864, New York postmark. SF3

(Bottom) New York postmark with New York cancel. The receiving depot and the address of the Executive Committee are both noted. SF3

The Tracy Edson Esq. cover represents an independent mail service cover stamped with a black circular postmark of Boyd's City Post at 39 Fulton Street in New York. Adjacent to the circular Boyd postmark is a black oval handstamp "Paid". On the back flap is the notice "Send by either one of the Principal Express or Transportation Companies". (Edson was president of the American Bank Note Company.)

The 1¢ rate for carrying the Edson letter was established by William and Mary Blackham, successors to John Boyd, who had sold out his business in November or December of 1860. This rate was for carrying letters to the United States Post Office and also for delivery of circulars.

In 1862, the Blackhams had moved from the Boyd office on William Street to their new premises at 39 Fulton Street. It was in early 1863 that they introduced the new circular postmark that incorporated the address and omitted the word "Express". Boyd's from that point on became known as Boyd's City Post.

There is no satisfactory explanation how Boyd's and also Hussey's Posts were able to operate and continue business after the Act of 1861 suppressing locals. (Earlier in July 1860, to take effect on August 1, 1860, J. Holt, Postmaster General, had the following notice inserted in all New York newspapers: "…it is hereby ordered that all the avenues, streets, lanes, alleys, roads and highways in all the part of the city of New York lying south of and below 55th street including that street, be and the same are hereby established as

Fig. 97. (Top) Boyd's City Post, 39 Fulton Street, circular (30mm) postmark dated Jan 28, 1864, with oval "Paid" handstamp on Metropolitan Fair cover. SF4

(Bottom) Two-cent 1863 drop letter, Metropolitan Fair corner card from the Ladies' Executive Committee. SF3

postroads." Later on the same order applied to Boston and Philadelphia.) Blood and other local posts were compelled to quit business after the 1861 ruling. It is said that Boyd was able to continue after 1861 because of a charter granted by the State of New York. This, however, would be contrary to the principle that where any state law was in conflict with a federal law, the jurisdiction of the federal statute would prevail. It is more likely that Boyd would have fallen within the meaning of the law of 1861 and would have been forced either to go out of business or change the method of operation. The latter explanation seems more probably true, since Boyd continued in business under Blackham's ownership for another two decades, making use of a loophole in the law. (Fig. 97, Plate 9)

BOWLSBY PATENT

During this period one of the Post Office Department's concerns was the prevention of the reuse of postage stamps. The double penalty in effect for deficient prepayment only served to compound such fraudulent reuse. At the same time there was also a shortage of coins in circulation needed to purchase stamps. Further aggravating the situation were the poverty of the times and the large volume of mail that moved from home to the soldier in the field. Collectors are familiar with the use of "killer" cancellations, grills, etc., to prevent the reuse of stamps. The covers pictured illustrate one such attempt to devise a method that would thwart the illegal practice. (Innovative ideas and experimental methods were first tried on many Sanitary Fair covers during this 1861 to 1865 period. Earlier mention was made of the Leeds envelopes in Chapter II.)

An example of a patented device to prevent the reuse of a stamp was the work of G.W. Bowlsby of Monroe, Michigan, who was issued patent No. 51782 on December 26, 1865. An essay based on it was prepared by the National Bank Note Co. The examples illustrated are on a cover with a corner card of the Metropolitan Fair that had closed in April of 1864. In the patent application Bowlsby explained that:

> The nature of my invention consists in applying the adhesive substance to only a portion of the under surface of the stamp, so that when the stamp is attached to the letter or other mailable matter it will leave the remaining part, which is not made adhesive, projecting that is, not adhering to the letter.
>
> It also consists in the tearing off of the projecting part of the stamp by the postmaster before the letter is put into the mail, and so totally destroying the stamp past all further recovery and use.
>
> The object of this invention is to totally destroy the stamp so that it cannot be washed or otherwise cleaned and reused, as is now much done.

The three 1¢ G.W. Bowlsby "coupon essays" affixed to the unused Metropolitan Fair cover are listed by Scott as 63-E13, perforated all around and printed in both red and blue. The three on the cover are red and measure 20mm x 48mm. Obviously prepared after the fair, envelopes with the essays may have been used as examples for submission with the patent application or to show the quality of work of the bank note company.

The legend on the coupon portion reads: "Stamp of no value without coupon — coupon to be removed only by the postmaster". Upon its presentation, the postmaster would remove the coupon portion and then enter the letter in the mails. Obviously this cumbersome and time-consuming effort was never used by the Post Office Department.

The purpose of this patent was to eliminate the need for canceling the stamps; only the top portion of the coupon had to be removed. Some were perforated all around, some were grilled, some were left imperforate, and others were rouletted. The essays shown here are all unused except for the strip of three on a partial cover which appears to have been canceled. In *Stamps* of February 6, 1965, page 241, "The One Cent 1865 Coupon Essay" (and later in *Bakers' U.S. Classics*, pp. 243–246) this strip of three is shown on the cut cover. Since these essays were never accepted by the Post Office Department and the purpose of the patent was ignored, there does not seem to be any reason that these should have seen postal usage. Since the bottom half of the cover has been cut away, there is little other clue. (Fig. 98)

There are no known counterfeits of the Metropolitan Fair stamp.

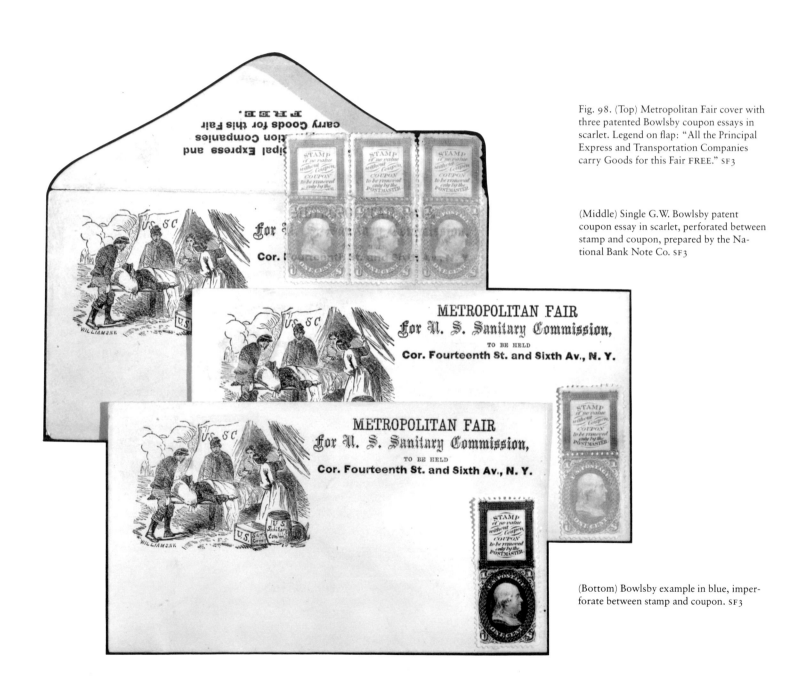

Fig. 98. (Top) Metropolitan Fair cover with three patented Bowlsby coupon essays in scarlet. Legend on flap: "All the Principal Express and Transportation Companies carry Goods for this Fair FREE." SF3

(Middle) Single G.W. Bowlsby patent coupon essay in scarlet, perforated between stamp and coupon, prepared by the National Bank Note Co. SF3

(Bottom) Bowlsby example in blue, imperforate between stamp and coupon. SF3

VIII

GREAT CENTRAL FAIR

Philadelphia, June 7 to 28, 1864
WVII—10¢ Blue
WVI2—20¢ Green
WVI3—30¢ Black

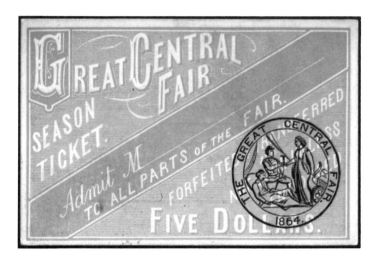

AND IN THE WAR...*The crises loom for the South as its territory shrinks and war supplies become even shorter. Sherman is marching through Georgia and Grant's Army of the Potomac moves to attack Lee's Army of Northern Virginia at Cold Harbor. Lincoln is nominated for a second term as the fair opens. One of the great sieges of the Civil War begins—the assault on Petersburg, gateway to Richmond. The U.S.S. Kearsage sinks the C.S.S. Alabama off the coast of Cherbourg, France on June 19. On June 27th, the day the fair closes, General Sherman suffers a defeat at Kennesaw Mountain, Georgia at the hands of the more experienced General Johnston. As June closes, Secretary of the Treasury Salmon P. Chase submits his resignation once again and this time Lincoln accepts it. Lincoln signs the bill repealing the Fugitive Slave Act.*

The Great Central Fair held in Logan Square in Central Philadelphia was by far the grandest of all fairs of the period. It was well-organized, well-financed, and well-planned. It is not surprising, then, that information, stamps, and memorabilia exist from this major effort to raise funds in support of the United States Sanitary Commission. While the fair was located in Philadelphia and is associated with that city, the effort also included the people of New Jersey and Delaware, and thus the name, Central Fair. Numerous descriptions of the fair exist that add romance to these stamps. Mrs. Hoge, one of the two organizers of the Chicago Fair which had been such a success, was invited to attend the early planning meetings. The experiences of the first fair in Chicago were a help in planning the different departments at the Philadelphia fair.

On February 11, 1864, the Union League of Philadelphia, itself an organization for mustering the patriotic feelings of the people of that city, passed a resolution to implement plans for a fair to open in June. The following fundamental principles were set: a) all classes of society were to be appealed to for assistance (this in a highly structured society such as Philadelphia's was indeed a step forward in a period when the concept of equality for all was being put to trial); b) all proceeds were to go to the central treasury of the Commission; c) the executive committee was to be placed in the hands of men, yet it was the women of Philadelphia who made this and the other fairs such successes; and d) the fair was to be an outstanding and brilliant spectacle. This was achieved. Captains of industry in each field were selected to head a committee, much as fund-raising committees are set up today. Among these committees were Trophy and Awards, Retail Dry Goods, Relics and Curiosities, Machinery, and Heavy Wheeled Equipment.

One of the fund-raising departments was the Post Office. Its chairman was C.A. Walborn, who also served as postmaster of Philadelphia at the time. Postmistress of the Fair Post Office was Mrs. E.D. Gillespie, granddaughter of Benjamin Franklin, our first Postmaster General. She remarked, "Generous friends of the cause we were working for, instigated by Mr. Joseph R. Carpenter (a member of the Post Office Committee and of the firm of Butler and Carpenter, the engravers and printers of the Philadelphia Sanitary Fair

Mrs. E. D. Gillespie, postmistress of the Fair and Benjamin Franklin's granddaughter

Fig. 99. Great Central Fair Buildings in Logan Square in Philadelphia. The mammoth flag in the center floated on a staff 216 feet high and was a gift to the fair from the ship carpenters of Philadelphia.

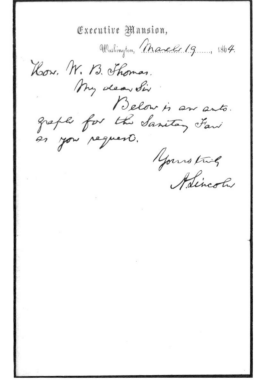

Fig. 100. Autograph letter signed by President A. Lincoln acknowledging a request for his autograph, written on White House stationery on Saturday, March 19, 1864. SF5

stamps), provided the post-office with beautiful stamps for ten cents, twenty cents, or thirty cents, according to the value of the lines within."

The fair building was constructed solely for the fair. Where most other fairs had utilized existing structures, this fair had the advantage of a structure designed large enough to accommodate the anticipated crowds. It is estimated that over one hundred thousand people attended this gala event. Union Avenue was the walkway that went through the center of the fair compound. It was 540 feet long and 64 feet wide, and the highest point of the central arch reached 51 feet above the ground. The building was an imposing sight in Logan Square. (Fig. 99) This, and other attractions, helped to make the fair as well attended as it was. Now, a century and a quarter later, we can recall the events of a civilian populace supporting the efforts of a nation at war.

Despite doubts, the building was completed in time for the opening and except for the mishap of the grandstand collapsing on opening day, everything went well. Of the $1,135,343.50 raised at this fair the Post Office Committee accounted for $1,083.40 of that total. As visitors entered the fair building through the 18th Street entry, on the right and halfway down they found the post office booth attended by young ladies who, upon payment of a postage fee, would write a ditty or poem, the length depending on the denomination of the stamp purchased. Also on sale at the booth was one of the first limerick books ever published. Called *The Book of Bubbles*, it was followed shortly by a second, *The New Book of Nonsense*.

In *Forney's War Press* newspaper, dated Saturday, June 11, 1864, and headlined Philadelphia, there is this reference to the post office at the Great Central Fair: "There is a very neatly arranged little house with four large windows, wreathed with evergreens — Those wishing to send a love missive to their inamoratas, can do so by buying and affixing thereon either a ten, twenty, or thirty cent stamp, the price of the stamp to be used depending on the sender's estimate of the value of his letter. There are already four thousand love notes in readiness for the onset..."

While the post office was one of the minor attractions, one of the major departments at the fair was the autograph booth. Notables across the North were solicited to furnish their autographs and even poems for sale at the fair. Autograph collecting in the 1860s was different than today in that the collector preferred a complete collection of either writers, poets, or signers of the Declaration of Independence. These autographs were then bound in a book or "tipped in"; this accounts for many historic manuscripts and documents having hinge remnants or gluing along the edge.

The Lincoln autograph letter signed, dated March 19, 1864, was addressed to Col. William B. Thomas, the Collector of Customs at the Port of Philadelphia who served as a member of the Fair Military Goods Committee. (Fig. 100) Lincoln penned:

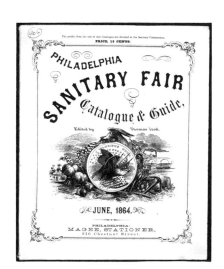

Catalogue and guide for the Philadelphia Fair

> Hon. W.B. Thomas
> My dear Sir
> Below is an autograph for the Sanitary Fair as you request.
> Yours truly
> A. Lincoln

This letter was written just one day after the close of the Sanitary Fair in Washington. (No stamps were issued at the Washington Fair.) The President said on that day in his closing statement, "If all that has been said by orators and poets since the creation of the world in praise of woman applied to the women of America, it would not do them justice for their conduct during this war."

Eleven days later General U.S. Grant, writing on Great Central Fair stationery, also sent an autograph to the fair. Grant wrote:

March 30, 1864

Liberal patronage for the benefit of the sick and wounded soldier is respectfully solicited.

U.S. Grant
Lt. Gen. U.S.A.

At the time of this writing Grant was in Washington, as he had been formally appointed Lieutenant General on March 9, 1864, three weeks before. With this appointment, the new designation of rank, Grant was subordinate only to his Commander-in-Chief, President Lincoln. (Fig. 101)

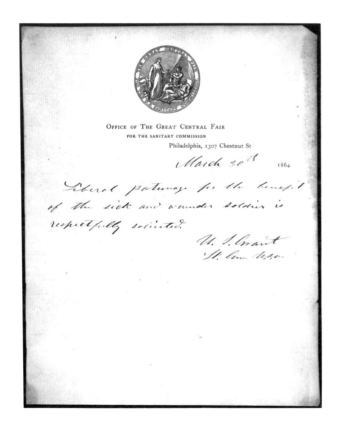

Fig. 101. The newly appointed Lt. General Grant submits his autograph for sale at the fair. sf5

On May 21, 1864, Lincoln once again directed a communication to the committee at the fair. On Executive Mansion (White House) stationery he had his secretary, John Nicolay, write Charles Richardson the following:

My dear Sir

I have the honor to acknowledge the receipt of a photographic copy of your allegorical sketch, together with your letter asking me to accept it at the close of the Fair to be held in Philadelphia.

I thank you very sincerely for your kindness but respectfully request that instead of being sent to me as suggested, the picture be sold for the benefit of the Fair.

I am very truly
Your Obt. Servant
A. Lincoln

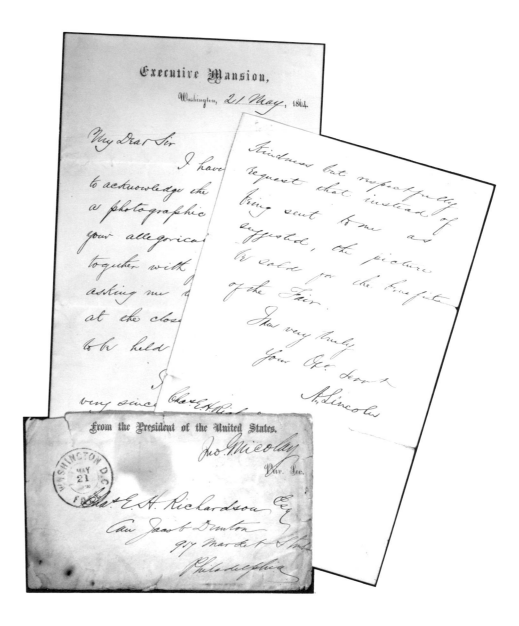

Fig. 102. Letter signed of President Abraham Lincoln with frank of his secretary, John Nicolay. Cover postmarked Washington, D.C., Free, May 21, '64. SF5

The letter was signed by Lincoln and sent in an envelope franked by John Nicolay. The cover bears a Washington, D.C. "Free" postmark dated the same day as the dating on the letter. (Fig. 102)

On June 16, 1864, President and Mrs. Lincoln appeared at the fair where he made a speech. Both were so enthusiastically greeted that their safety was in jeopardy. As a result of this experience, Mr. Lincoln declined all future invitations from fairs. This is what he had to say at the fair that day:

> War, at its best, is terrible, and this war of ours, in its magnitude and in its duration, is one of the most terrible…it has carried mourning to almost every home, until it can almost be said that the 'heavens are hung in black.'
>
> Yet the war continues, and several relieving coincidents have accompanied it from the very beginning which have not been known…in any former wars in the history of the world. The Sanitary Commission, with all its benevolent labors; the Christian Commission, with all its Christian

and benevolent labors; and the various places, arrangements, so to speak, and institutions, have contributed to the comfort and relief of the soldiers. You have two of these places in this city—the Cooper Shop and Union Volunteer Refreshment Saloons. And lastly, these fairs, which, I believe, began only last August, if I mistake not, in Chicago, then at Boston, at Cincinnati, Brooklyn, New York, and Baltimore and those at present held at St. Louis, Pittsburg, and Philadelphia. The motive and object that lie at the bottom of all these are most worthy; for, say what you will, after all, the most is due to the soldier who takes his life in his hands and goes to fight the battles of his country. In what is contributed to his comfort when he passes to and fro, and in what is contributed to him when he is sick and wounded, in whatever shape it comes, whether from the fair and tender hand of woman, or from any other source, it is much, very much. But I think that there is still that which is of as much value to him in the continual reminders he sees in the newspapers that while he is absent he is yet remembered by the loved ones at home. Another view of these various institutions, if I may so call them, is worthy of consideration, I think. They are voluntary contributions, given zealously, and earnestly, on top of all the disturbances of business, of all the disorders, of all the taxation, and of all the burdens that the war has imposed upon us, giving proof that the national resources are not at all exhausted, and that the national spirit of patriotism is even firmer and stronger than at the commencement of the war.

How well Lincoln put the benevolences of the fair in focus! At the same time he was using the fair to advise the Confederacy that the resolve of the North would continue undiminished. Lincoln could now speak with confidence as his armies were on the move with the northern armies numbering close to one million men under arms while the South could only match this number with their estimated six hundred thousand troops.[19] The territory under the southern states had shrunk dramatically and Jefferson Davis was now forced to defend his conduct of the war, much of the criticism coming from his former staunchest supporters.

In the fair newspaper *Our Daily Fare* appeared a reference to the post office worthy of a direct quotation since it clearly projects the fair stamps into a position as semi-postals between a carrier stamp and a regular issue:

> The Post Office has a tasteful little edifice close by the great flagstaff, and is in the full tide of successful operation. A regular postal system is established throughout the Fair buildings. Letters may be safely deposited for the U.S. Post Office or the Fair Post Office, in any of the boxes distributed through the different departments. The Post Office also receives from the U.S. Office all letters addressed to the Central Fair, and delivers them to their proper departments. (Fig. 103)

Ten covers addressed directly to the fair exist. Covers also exist with a postal rate of 1¢ or 2¢ with local Philadelphia addresses. It appears that these letters with a fair cachet may have been addressed and/or mailed at the fair and the carrier payment of 1¢ was not necessary since the fair post office performed the function of the carrier. The broadside pictured and quoted herein more fully explains the function of the fair post office.

19. Actual numbers of troops that served in the Federal and Confederate armies cannot be accurately determined. Only educated guesses are possible. Probably as many as two million served at one time or another in the Union Forces with about one million being on duty at any one time. Figures for the Confederates are even in more dispute but it is generally assumed that six hundred thousand served under the Stars and Bars. Including northern black troops, the Confederates, it is estimated, were outnumbered about three to one.

Fair ribbon of the Post Office Committee

Fig. 103. Ground plan of the Great Central Fair showing post office location.

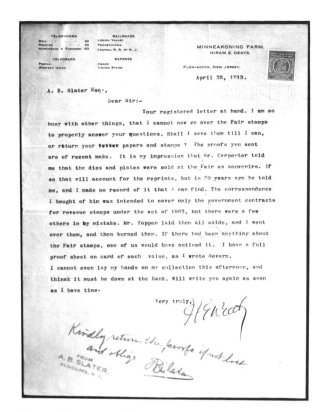

Fig. 104. Deats' letter to Slater.

CENTRAL FAIR LETTER-BOX.

The Postmistress directs the special attention of visitors to the CENTRAL FAIR to these Letter-boxes, as a great convenience to all desiring to correspond with visitors to the Fair, as well as for letters to be delivered throughout the City, or at the Post Office for mailing.

Frequent collections are made throughout the day and evening of all letters deposited in these boxes, by carriers detailed for the service, and any person using the Central Fair Boxes may rely on having all letters promptly transmitted to their destination.

All letters deposited herein, whether for delivery in the Fair or by the regular Post Office carriers, must have a "CENTRAL FAIR POSTAGE STAMP" attached.

Letters intended for delivery within the Fair Buildings DO NOT require any U.S. POSTAGE STAMP in addition to the Central Fair Stamp.

Letters intended for mailing at the Post Office, or for delivery in the City, must have the requisite U.S. Postage Stamp attached in addition to the Central Fair Stamp.

Parties desiring to communicate with any of the various Committees of the Fair, will find these boxes the proper medium.

RATES OF U.S. POSTAGE.

Letters for delivery within the City, 2 cts, for each ½ oz. or fraction thereof. do. addressed to any part of U. S. 3 do. do. do. do.

E.D. GILLESPIE, Postmistress
CENTRAL FAIR

(Plate 10)

The question might arise as to why there exists today, comparatively speaking, a greater number of Philadelphia stamps when sales at the fair were as modest as they were, slightly over one thousand dollars, while the stamps from other fairs are rare. The existence of proofs and essays can be partially explained by the association of one Ernest Schernikow with them (see section on Schernikow below). The explanation for the relative great numbers of the Philadelphia stamps is a bit more circuitous. As noted previously, Joseph Carpenter served as a member of the post office committee under Mrs. Gillespie. None of the other members of the committee appeared to have any connection with the actual manufacturing of stamps and served probably because of their position in Philadelphia society at the time. Carpenter, on the other hand, was knowledgeable; he not only prepared stamps for the fair but he had an association with the security printing firm of Butler & Carpenter.

Among the articles left for disposal some months after the fair closed, besides the trophies, manufactured articles, handicrafts, art works, and all the army artifacts that had been collected for sale, were the dies for the Sanitary Fair stamps. On April 25, 1913, in reply to a letter from A. B. Slater of Slocums, Rhode Island, an early Sanitary Fair collector, Hiram E. Deats wrote a letter from his Minneakoning Farm in Flemington, New Jersey:

April 25, 1913

A.B. Slater, Esq.

Dear Sir,

Your registered letter at hand. I am so busy with other things, that I cannot now go over the Fair stamps to properly answer your questions. Shall I save them till I can, or return your papers and stamps? The proofs you sent are of recent make. It is my impression that Mr. Carpenter told me *that the dies and plates were sold at the Fair as souvenirs* [authors' emphasis].* If so that will account for the reprints, but is 20 years ago he told me, and I made no record of it that I can find. The correspondence I bought of him was intended to cover only the government contracts for revenue stamps under the act of 1862, but there were a few others in by mistake. Mr. Toppan laid them all aside, and I went over them, and then burned them. If there had been anything about the Fair stamps, one of us would have noticed it. I have a full proof sheet on card of each value, as I wrote Severn. I cannot lay my hands on my collection this afternoon, and think it must be down at the Bank. Will write you again as soon as I have time.

Very truly,
H.E. Deats

*Refer to page 137 concerning Schernikows.

And then at the bottom Slater penciled in, "Kindly return the proofs if not lost, and oblige. A.B. Slater". This letter may partially explain the relative abundance of the stamps. (Fig. 104)

It appears that Carpenter bought the dies and plates and then perhaps printed more of the stamps and sold them, still riding the tide of the popularity of the fairs. Or he might have used the stamps as samples of his firm's work since they were so beautifully engraved and printed. Several revenue stamps duplicate the designs of the Philadelphia stamps, notably the so-called "Match and Medicine" stamps.

The design, particularly the ever-popular American Eagle theme, was copied a number of times for these private proprietary stamps manufactured as a result of the Revenue Act of 1862. For example, the revenue stamp of the New York Match Co. (Scott RO137b) at first glance could easily be mistaken for a Philadelphia Sanitary Fair stamp. With modification of the frame, the Zisemann, Griesheim & Co. 1¢ (RO185) in similar colors of black (Fig. 105), green, and blue might also be confused with the Philadelphia stamps. The James L.

Fig. 105. 1¢ James L. Clark Match and Medicine revenue stamp (#RO62). Similar in design to the Philadelphia stamps. SF1

Fig. 106. 10¢ Blue (WV11), 20¢ Green (WV12), 30¢ Black (WV13). The sheets of stamps were printed 14 x 9, a total of 126 to the sheet. SF1

Fig. 107. A 10¢ Philadelphia Great Central Fair stamp on a New York Metropolitan Fair envelope with a 3¢ 1861, postmarked at New York in 1864. The cancellation is the same on the 3¢ stamp and the fair stamp. SF3

Clark revenue (RO62) retained only the central eagle vignette. An obvious variation is the Park City Match Company proprietary stamp (RO142).

The Sanitary Fair stamps of Philadelphia were issued in three colors and three denominations—10¢ blue (WV11), 20¢ green (WV12), and 30¢ black (WV13). They were engraved and printed by Butler and Carpenter who were then producing revenue stamps for the Treasury Department at their plant in Philadelphia. The stamps measure 24mm x 31mm and are printed on thin wove paper. Of all the fair stamps, these were the only ones issued perforated (12) and are the most professional looking of any of the fair postage. The workmanship is superb and the design ornate and eye-appealing. Once seen, it is unlikely that the design will ever be forgotten. The 34 small stars in the background are for the 34 states in the Union prior to the outbreak of the Civil War and represent northern and southern states. (Fig. 106)

In the January 1889 issue of the *American Journal of Philately*, J.W. Scott stated that the Great Central Fair stamps were from the Metropolitan Fair but there is no solid proof that this is the case, and we must conclude that Mr. Scott was in error. There is no substantiating material linking one fair to the other or a cover postmarked to verify the Philadelphia stamps being bought at New York two months earlier. The cover with the Metropolitan Fair corner card and the 10¢ Philadelphia stamp pictured here may have contributed to the error in Scott's statement. At the time of the Metropolitan Fair the New

From the governor of New Jersey   From the governor of Massachusetts

Yorkers were having their own problems attempting to secure stamps in time for their fair and each city was in competition with the other to raise the largest sums in support of the United States Sanitary Commission. (Fig. 107)

It is known that one of the major exhibits at the fair was a huge steam press that stamped out the Great Central Fair medals. There may have been a printing press for printing the stamps also, but there is no recorded evidence of this fact. It may be, too, that the promoters of the fair had anticipated the sale of many more stamps than actually took place and those existing today are the remnants or leftovers.

It has been suggested by Percy Mann[20] that one die was used for all three of the stamps. He further indicated that a slug was used for the three different values and that for the spelled-out denomination on the ten-cent stamp a star was inserted before and after the words "ten cents" to justify the space of the "twenty" and "thirty" that are exactly six letters each. Where a slug was removed or changed, ink colors were also changed for each of the three values. However, a careful examination of the 20¢ reveals so intricate a design that a slug insert would be out of register with the adjacent area. Keeping in mind that the se-tenant $^{10}/_{30}$ value on the original die proof is one piece, it is more likely that the 10¢ value and 30¢ value were made on one die and then transferred to the transfer roll. The 20¢ and "without value" were on another transfer roll.

Of the 10¢ blue a number of mint copies exist, while only eight are known canceled with a fair postmark. Four blocks of four are known. Four covers have been reported with the 10¢ blue and a fair postmark, including one cover also with a 3¢ 1861 stamp and the Philadelphia postmark. (Fig. 108)

Of the 20¢ green ten blocks of four, two blocks of six (one with the Butler & Carpenter imprint), and two blocks of 12 are known (one with the Butler & Carpenter imprint). Five singles on cover with the fair postmark and ten singles used off cover with the fair postmark are also known.

One position on the sheet of 126 (14 x 9) has a strong double entry. According to Elliott Perry, it exists in the fourth horizontal row and either in the first, second or third stamp. (Fig. 109)

20. "Was the Plate of the 20-Cents Sanitary Fair Stamps Used for the Experimental Work of the American Bank Note Co.?", Percy Mann (editor), *Philadelphia Stamp News*, August 1, 1914, p. 345.

Fig. 108. Blocks of four. Largest known multiples of the 10¢ blue (WV11). SF2

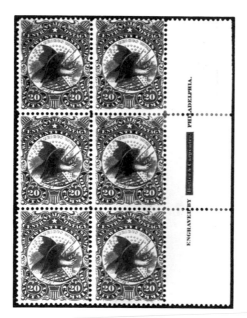
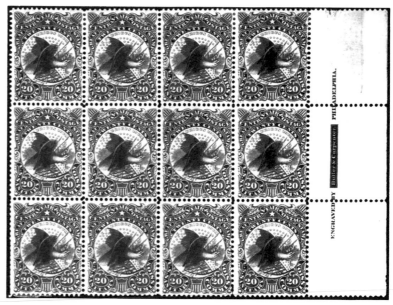

Fig. 109. (Top left) Block of six 20¢ green (WV12), Butler and Carpenter imprint. SF2

(Top right) Block of twelve 20¢ green (WV12), Butler and Carpenter imprint. SF3

(Bottom) Block of twelve 20¢ green (WV12). SF3

Of the 30¢ black (WV13) 11 singles are known off cover canceled with the fair postmark and seven on cover similarly marked. One block of six and five blocks of four are also known. (Fig. 110) All recorded blocks of the 10¢, 20¢, and 30¢ are unused.

(Fig. 111)

Among the scarcest of all patriotic stationery are the envelopes or cachets prepared at the fair with the Great Central Fair stamp tied to the cover with a fair postmark. Of the 4,000 letters reported by Forney in his newspaper of the day before the fair opened plus additional covers prepared during the fair, only the 14 covers pictured here are known today. While J. Walter Scott reported the Sanitary Fair stamps in an early issue of the *American Journal of Philately* and some early catalogues listed them as post office issues, it was not until Hiram Deats and A.B. Slater each formed collections of these stamps in the first decade of this century that the stamps began to be collected widely. These few covers are the survivors of this period of the Civil War in Philadelphia.

(Fig. 112, Plate 11) (Fig. 113, Plate 12) (Figs. 114, 115, 116, 117, 118)

One counterfeit cover is shown here for comparison purposes although others may exist. The "fake" was originally submitted to a collector by an eastern dealer. There is a break on the left side of the outside circle of the fair postmark. The genuine fair postmark has in each case a well-defined circle with no breaks. Overall the postmark does not have the "right" look when compared with a genuine strike. The ink is not of the same intensity and this gives rise to further suspicions. (Fig. 119)

Fig. 110. (Top) Blocks of four 30¢ black (WV13). SF2

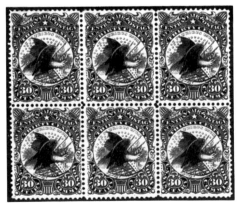

(Bottom) Block of six. Largest multiple known of the 30¢ black (WV13). SF3

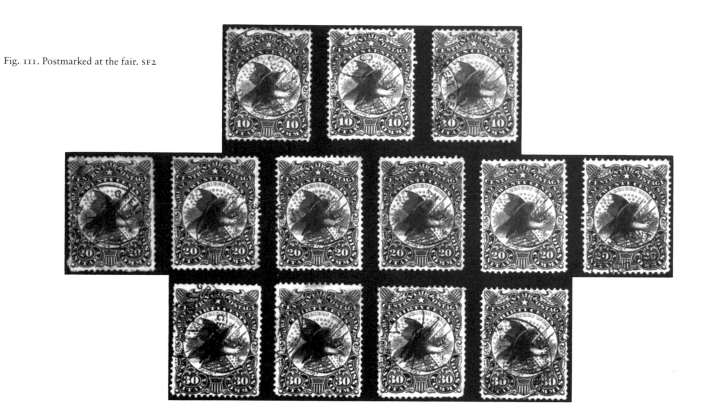

Fig. 111. Postmarked at the fair. SF2

Fig. 112. The rarest of all Philadelphia Sanitary Fair covers. Red corner card with a fair stamp (10¢ blue—fair canceled on June 15, 1864) and also a 3¢ 1861 with duplex cancel. Fair stamps were only valid within the fair or as a carrier and it was necessary to affix the 3¢ postage for the letter to go through the mails to Boston, Mass. SF5

Fig. 113. (Top) 10¢, 20¢, 30¢ values—double strike June 11, 1864 fair postmark. SF5

(Middle) Cover reverse—triple strike June 18, 1864 fair postmark tying 10¢, 20¢ and 30¢ Great Central Fair stamps. SF3

(Bottom) Ten-cent blue with double strike fair postmark dated June 14, 1864. Fair postmark used to cancel stamp. Script "Prepaid". Addressed to Miss Hettie M. Logan, "P.O. Dept. San. Fair". SF4

Fig. 114. (Top) Last-day fair postmark on front and back dated June 28, 1864, 10¢ blue. SF4

(Middle) The 20¢ green Sanitary Fair stamp canceled with a June 18, 1864 fair postmark. Judge Carpenter was a member of the Executive Committee from New Jersey, one of the three states making up the Great Central Fair. The two other states were Maryland and Pennsylvania. SF4

(Bottom) Postmarked the last day of the fair—June 28, 1864, 20¢ green. SF4

Fig. 115. (Top) The 20¢ green, "With Mrs. Gillespie's compliments"—June 28, 1864, last day of the fair, postmark. SF4

(Middle) A 30¢ black with June 11, 1864 fair postmark. Love letter enclosure. SF4

Fig. 116. (Top) A 30¢ black Great Central Fair stamp, double strike June 13, 1864 fair postmark. SF4

(Middle) June 18, 1864 fair postmark on 30¢ black, addressed to Charles H. Hart, Post Office, Sanitary Fair. When acquired in 1984 it brought to 14 the known covers with Sanitary Fair stamps and no more have been found since. SF4

(Bottom) The 30¢ black, double strike June 22, 1864 fair postmark. SF4

(Bottom) The 30¢ black with fair postmark dated June 11, 1864. Three-page May 28, 1864 letter included was probably one of the thousands of letters prepared in advance of the fair that waited for the special fair postmark and the purchase of the stamp at the fair. SF4

Fig. 117. Last-day fair postmark, double strike June 28, 1864, 30¢ black on legal size cover. SF4

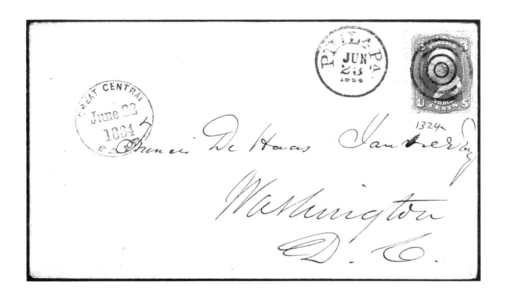

Fig. 118. On June 22, 1864 this letter was apparently dropped in the Fair Post Office mail box where it received a fair postmark dated June 22, 1864 and then was carried to the U.S. Post Office. The following day, June 23, the letter was postmarked Phila. and moved through the mails. SF3

Fig. 119. Counterfeit fair cover. The stamps are genuine.

ESSAYS AND PROOFS

Elliott Perry called the confusion regarding the Philadelphia Sanitary Fair proofs and essays a "world without end" and indeed they are. We are dealing with a period of over a century ago. The participants in the unraveling of the proofs and essays mystery are now long since dead. We have only the correspondence to rely on, many of those letters written some 10 or 12 years after the widespread appearance of this material. Whether it was Hiram Deats, Percy Mann, A. B. Slater, or Vincent Domanski, each had his own interpretation. Over the years the genuine proofs and essays have been entwined with the reprints, or "Schernikows", so that the confusion has been exacerbated. Collectors will run into the reprints (Schernikows) much more often than the originals and should attempt to make the distinction and be aware of what they are acquiring.

CONTEMPORARY PROOFS

True contemporary proofs for the Philadelphia Great Central Fair exist in the following modes and are not to be confused with the 1903 Schernikow reprints. Large die proofs, the scarcest of all, exist in these modes:

A. Se-tenant vertical pair of the 10¢ and 30¢ values (WV11TC-WV13TC) on glazed paper printed in greenish black. Two of these are known.

B. WV12TC 20¢ greenish black on glazed paper. These two examples represent the only two known to exist.

C. "No Value" greenish black on glazed paper. Only this one is known.

D. WV12TC 20¢ vermilion and 20¢ blue India on card. These are the only known.

Dimensions of originals are exact sizes of the copies known and are given for identification purposes. (Figs. 120, 120A, 121)

Just these four varieties (A, B, C, D) are genuine.

Fig. 120. (Left, right) Philadelphia Great Central Fair large die proofs. Se-tenant 10¢ and 30¢ greenish black on glazed paper. (WV11TC-WV13TC). 50 x 110mm; 53 x 100mm. SF4

Fig. 120A (Left, center) 20¢ greenish black (WV12TC) on glazed paper. 37 x 68mm; 49 x 49mm. SF3

(Right) "No-value" greenish black on glazed paper. 49 x 51mm. SF3

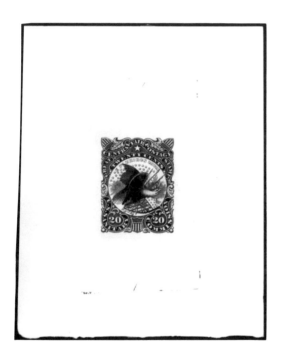

Fig. 121. 20¢ blue and 20¢ vermilion India on card (WV12TC). Blue 81 x 100mm; vermilion 60 x 90mm. SF3

Plate proofs imperforate on card exist for each of the issued stamps: 10¢ blue (WV11P), 20¢ green (WV12P), and the 30¢ black (WV13P). (Fig. 122)

The *perforated* trial colors are on wove paper perforated twelve. Only seven such are known and all are of about equal scarcity. They exist in carmine, vermilion, red brown, light green, bright blue, brown black, and gray black. (Fig. 123)

The *imperforate* trial colors are on wove paper and are known in 12 colors: vermilion, orange, brown orange (opaque paper), black brown, olive, yellow green, bright blue, light ultramarine, purple, claret, gray black (opaque paper), and black (experimental double paper). (Figs. 124, 125)

A variety or perhaps an error of color is a 20¢ blue although the blue is for the 10¢ issued color. The gum is intact so it does not appear to have been altered chemically. (Fig. 126)

Fig. 122. Blocks of four card proofs of actual stamps in blue 10¢ (WV11P), green 20¢ (WV12P) and black 30¢ (WV13P) with Butler and Carpenter imprint on 30¢ value. SF3

Fig. 123. Block of ten red brown perforated trial color proofs (WV12TC). SF3

Fig. 124. Block of nine brown imperforate trial color proofs (WV12TC). Double transfer on first stamp in the second row. SF3

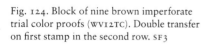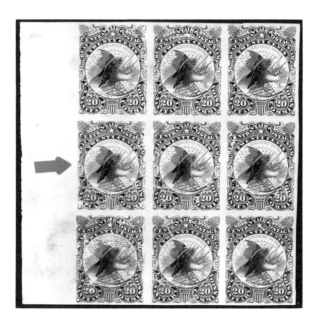

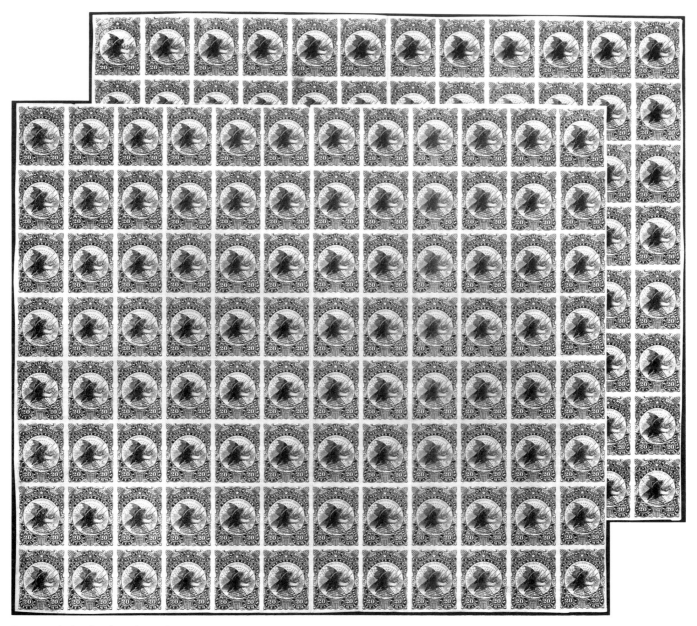

Fig. 125. Blocks of 96 from sheets of 126
(14 x 9) plate proofs (WV12TC), imperforate—20¢ *yellow green*, 20¢ *gray black*—
only known. SF5

Fig. 126. A 20¢ blue variety or an error of
color. Blue is the 10¢ issued color. SF3

EXPERIMENTAL PRINTINGS

On Aug. 1, 1914, Percy Mann, writing in the *Philadelphia Stamp News*, indicated that there may be some merit to the argument that while the Sanitary Fair stamps from Philadelphia were printed previously for one primary purpose, i.e., charity bazaars, there are so many different manipulations for experimental printings on unwatermarked paper in fugitive inks or on double fugitive paper that it is highly unlikely that all these trials would have been prepared for an issue with a projected life of three weeks. It was more likely that all the test material was manufactured for experimental purposes after the fairs had closed. Furthermore, it is improbable that anyone would take a charity stamp and attempt to clean it for fraudulent reuse and so there existed no real need for experimentation with the various patented devices designed to frustrate fraud.

All the experiments were carried out on the 20¢ stamp. There was no regular 20¢ postage issue until the early 20th century. Had the 10¢ or 30¢ stamps been used for experimental purposes they might very well have found their way into the postal system. The bank note companies showed singular good judgment in restricting their experiments to the 20¢ denomination.

One such effort to provide a means to eliminate the reuse of stamps was the experimental double paper patent. (Figs. 127, 127A) Were these double papers or scarified papers to have been used during the fair, they would have disintegrated in handling. Had the experimentals been used within the U.S. mails, the results would have been even more disastrous.

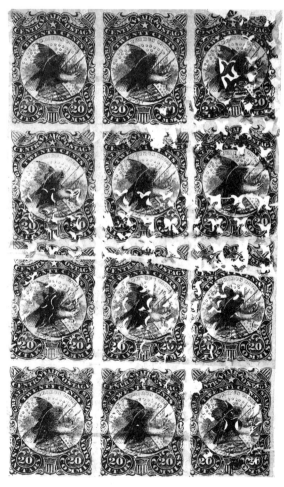

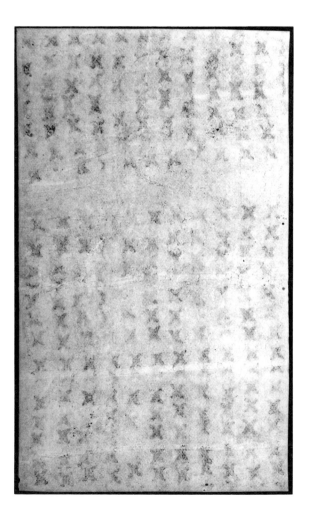

Fig. 127. Small design double experimental paper (scarified), black. Punched parchment on wove paper. Block of twelve (WV12TC). Front and reverse. SF3

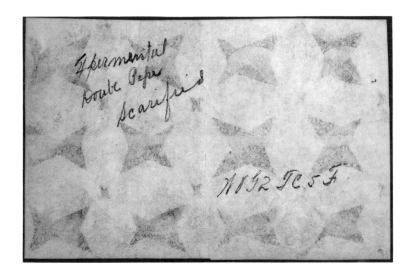

Fig. 127A. Large design double experimental paper (scarified), black. Block of eight (WV12TC). Front and reverse. SF3

During the Civil War, with so many men away from home, the volume of mail increased greatly. Families that had no previous occasion to write anyone were now confronted with the necessity of writing a letter to a loved one in service, so use of stamps, a custom only 14 years old in 1861, now became a significant item in the family budget. In terms of the 1863 dollar, a loaf of bread cost seven cents. Little wonder, then, that devious minds looked for every opportunity to send a letter either devoid of postage, hoping that the recipient would pay the fee, or with a reused postage stamp from which the cancellation had been removed by washing or bleaching. It was in this period that the various patents were issued to prevent the reuse of stamps. These patents covered fugitive inks, scarified paper, exploding stamps, grills, etc. The reader is directed to the Sol Altmann series in *The Essay-Proof Journal* for some of the more exotic methods of stamp cancellation.[21]

Altmann called attention to patent No. 89,213, dated April 20, 1869, secured by J.C. Gaston of Cincinnati, Ohio, to improve the cancellation of stamps so that they could not be used again. His idea was to scarify (to make scratches or cuts in the surface) the stamps to prevent their use a second time. He proposed that a blade be used with an adjustable guard so that the depth of the cut could be controlled just deep enough to break through the

21. *The Essay-Proof Journal*, No. 67, Summer 1960, Vol. 17, No. 3, p. 131. Additional information on the protection of postage stamps and patents for canceling may be found in the *Collectors Club Philatelist*, Vol. XXXV, No. V, p. 267 in an article by H.D.S. Haverbeck — "United States Various Patents for the Improvement and Protection of Postage and Revenue Stamps. 1862–79."

22. *The Essay-Proof Journal*, No. 68, Fall 1960, Vol. 17, No. 4, p. 177.

stamp without penetrating the envelope or its contents. According to Gaston, "It is obvious that the perforating points may be arranged to represent letters, as for instance, 'U.S.', when used for government purposes, or with the initials of the owner, if a private individual."[22]

A few years later on August 1, 1876, Louis H.G. Ehrhardt, of Philadelphia, secured patent No. 180,564. Ehrhardt assigned one-half of his patent rights to Joseph R. Carpenter of Butler and Carpenter, the security printers and printer of the Sanitary Fair stamps of Philadelphia. Ehrhardt's invention was also intended to discourage the reuse of postage stamps. Ehrhardt's invention provided that paper, stamp paper in this case, be soaked in a prepared sizing solution which would permeate the paper. The paper would then be printed in the ordinary way with ordinary ink and then gummed. Taking a clue from Gaston's patent, Ehrhardt, while not specifying in his patent, may have scarified the paper to the gum surface after gumming with the two design patterns shown on the 20¢ Philadelphia stamp. Once an attempt was made to soak the stamp off the envelope, the sizing agent would dissolve and the stamp disintegrate.

THE SCHERNIKOW REPRINTS

The term "Schernikows" refers to a group of posthumous or reprint essays and proofs made about 1903, for philatelic consumption, by Ernest R. Schernikow. He was an officer of the Hamilton Bank Note & Engraving Co. of New York, associated with his brother-in-law, N.F. Seebeck, of Latin-American reprinted stamp fame (or infamy). Like Seebeck, Schernikow was on the periphery of the stamp collecting business and saw a good opportunity for profit. When the dies, rolls, and plates of the defunct Philadelphia Bank Note Co., which included the Philadelphia Sanitary Fair material, were placed on public sale, according to philatelic lore among old time dealers (which may be apocryphal), Schernikow purchased them for $10,000. He had hoped to use the dies and rolls at the Hamilton Bank Note Company. When he found that most of his purchase was not suited to the then current banknote market he turned to making reprints of the 1851 issue, the 1861 contract essays, 1877 banknote contract essays and the Sanitary Fair stamps. His intent in making the reprints was to recoup his sour investment through the philatelic marketplace. He peddled them from a suitcase to dealers along Nassau Street prior to the first World War.

The Philadelphia Bank Note Co. was an outgrowth from the activities of Joseph R. Carpenter of Philadelphia, who earlier had printed U.S. internal revenue stamps under his own name and that of the firm name Butler & Carpenter. His own activities dated back to the firm of Toppan, Carpenter & Co. As mentioned previously, he served on the Post Office Committee of the Great Central Fair. It is the authors' belief that at the close of the fair Joseph Carpenter acquired the dies, etc. for the fair stamps and used them extensively to prepare examples of the type of work his firm was capable of producing. They were attractive and official looking, well suited to displaying various sorts of experimental safety devices. These fair designs were included in the sets of reprints made by Schernikow.

The best information on the Schernikow reprints has appeared in the writings of Clarence W. Brazer in his catalog, *Essays for U.S. Adhesive Postage Stamps* (1941) and in various ensuing issues of *The Essay-Proof Journal*. In summary, the facts are these: What are called Schernikows today, although they include the fair designs, are primarily reprints from the Toppan, Carpenter essay dies for the U.S. 1851 issue and the 1861 issue to which numerals had been added to all values except the 10¢ and 30¢. These latter dies were prepared for submission of essays with their proposal for the 1861 stamp printing contract, which they did not win. It was the distinctive custom of Toppan, Carpenter to keep a duplicate die of each engraver's work, such as the first state of the vignette alone, then with some lathe work added, and finally with the lettering added and the vignette completed. Only the completed dies of approved designs were given to the government, so these "progress" dies were available to Schernikow.

From all this metal Schernikow had 10 sets of prints made up in about 15 different colors on various types of paper and cards. Also included were some of the dies for the essays submitted with the Philadelphia Bank Note Co. abortive essays of 1876.

Brazer called all this material "privately made modern reprints, in no sense preparatory essays", but nevertheless late 20th century collectors prize these items highly. Unfortunately there is no definitive listing of all the Schernikow reprints of the Sanitary Fair stamps but the authors now attempt to compile one.

This attempt has been made more complicated by the existence of previous students' statements and correspondence which embodies incorrect information. For example, in 1978, in her 95th year, Elliott Perry's widow, Chrissie, in going through her husband's papers, forwarded to the authors Elliott's file of correspondence on Sanitary Fairs dating from 1912 when he began to collect these issues. Within the file was a letter written by A.B. Slater to Charles Severn. (Slater, one of the early collectors, did not at the time of writing have the necessary information to differentiate between contemporary proofs and the Schernikow reprints.)

Slocums R. I. December 7th, 1912

Mr. C. E. Severn Esq.

Dear Sir,

Having seen your article in the May 1912 number of the Collectors Journal on the stamps of the Great Central Fair of the U.S. Sanitary Commission I take the liberty of asking you for some further information concerning them. Is there any known check list of the plate and die proofs of them and if so where and how can I get a copy of it. I am somewhat interested in them as when I disposed of my U.S. collection some time ago I retained some of these stamps and their proofs and would like to get some idea as to how many varieties there are. I have some 80 different specimens representing the original stamps, perf. and imperf., also some plate proofs and proofs from the unfinished general die and the three finished dies on eleven kinds of paper and card and in fifteen entirely different colors. I also have been told by a very prominent dealer that there were quite a lot of proofs gotten out two or three years ago by the American Bank Note Co., I will greatly appreciate any information you may give me on any of these points…

Sincerely,
A. B. Slater

On Dec. 12, 1912, writing from Chicago, Severn replied that there was no check list of the die and plate proofs of the Great Central Fair which he too had been seeking. Mr. Slater then wrote back offering an explanation of the 10¢ and 30¢ die proofs, indicating that these two values were reprinted on extremely thin India paper and then pasted to the colored cards. The margins were too large to be plate proofs, and in Slater's opinion they were die proofs. The 20¢ value was printed directly onto the card. Slater disagreed with Severn's opinion that there was only one die, with the value changes made with the use of a slug change. Slater felt that one double die of the 10¢ and 30¢ was made and a single of the 20¢ and from these transfer dies the plates were then made. On Feb. 25, 1913, Severn wrote

23. Severn was referring to his 30-page pamphlet called *The Sanitary Fairs and Their Issues* printed in 1911 by Lindquist. Until the present time this was the only source of information on the fairs that had been written up.

*Refer to text of April 25, 1913 Deats letter to A. B. Slater on page 122.

24. SR refers to "Schernikow Reprints".

in a letter to Mr. Slater, "It is somewhat unfortunate that I could not have had the benefit of your study of the stamps before Mr. Lindquist, following an idea of his own, published my contributions to his paper, in pamphlet form"[23] and then in the postscript: "Let me add that your remarks about the scheme of dies and transfers are more logical than my theory, which was suggested to me by a gentleman who had given some attention to the question and which I advanced, I think I may say conscientiously, with some misgivings."

It was apparent to Slater that Severn did not have either the information that he needed to catalogue all the proofs nor the proofs themselves and so Slater wrote to Hiram Deats on April 17, 1913, requesting more information. Deats responded within a week* indicating that he could not take the time to make the study that Slater requested. He did advise that the proofs which Slater had sent for examination were of a recent make (Schernikows again). Deats wrote that Mr. Carpenter of Butler & Carpenter told him that the dies and plates of the Philadelphia Sanitary Fair stamps were sold as souvenirs at the fair. This statement based on evidence at hand is inaccurate. Deats went on to say, "I have a full proof sheet on card of *each* value." While the collection herein described has two sheets of the 20¢ value, one in the yellow green and the other in gray black, there is no evidence that a proof sheet was made of each value. It is more likely that Deats meant he had three proof sheets, two herein described; the third one's fate is unknown.

The distribution of the Schernikow sets is somewhat corroborated by a Perry letter of Oct. 23, 1967 that stated, "The reprints were made in a period 1900 to 1910. Percy Mann got the batch and Domanski got one of each color. Wray got an assortment many years later." And on a handwritten note at the bottom of the letter (Perry typed most of his letters) was the notation, "There seems to be a possibility that the 'Schernikows' were made for the Centennial in 1876." Generally speaking, Elliott Perry was accurate in what he wrote, but the present writers reject this last notation as incorrect.

Submitted here is the list of proofs and essays that neither Slater, Deats or Perry were ever able to compile because until now the material was in scattered hands and the true proofs and essays became entwined with the reprints of 1903 until the confusion was such that it took over 80 years until the puzzle was somewhat unraveled.

Reprints attributed to Schernikow appear in several different states. The 10¢ and 30¢ WVIISR[24] and WVI3SR exist se-tenant vertical (10/30) in the following colors. All are small die proofs on India mounted on laid paper except for three large die proofs on glazed card. Colors indicated are major colors and for simplicity slight changes in a shade have not been taken into account. Many of the 20¢ appear somewhat darker in shade. In describing "without value" light violet, the color could be called light brown violet.

COLORS OF THE SCHERNIKOW REPRINTS

	WVIISR & WVI3SR[25] Type I 10/30	Without Value[26] Type II	WVI2SR[27] Type III
Carmine		X	X	X
Red carmine		X	X	X
Vermilion		X	X	X
Orange		X	X	X
Brown		X	X	X
Yellow brown	X[28]	X	X	X
Olive		X	X	X
Yellow green		X	X	X
Blue green	X	X	X	X
Gray blue	X	X	X	X
Ultramarine		X	X	X
Light violet		X	X	X
Violet		X	X	X
Claret		X	X	X
Gray black		X	X	X

25. Small die (on India) mounted se-tenant vertically 10/30 on laid paper measuring approximately 59mm x 115mm.

26. Large die (on India) where the value would appear there is no value. On laid paper measuring approximately 65mm x 65mm.

27. Large die 20¢ value (on India) mounted on laid paper. These are somewhat more trimmed and the approximate sizes are at greater variance measuring 55–65mm x 62–65mm. There is an added line below the lower center shield. This is an important factor in identifying the 20¢ Schernikows.

28. Large die 10/30 on glazed card measuring approximately 51mm x 113mm; yellow brown on white glazed card, blue green on pink glazed card, gray blue on yellow glazed card.

Also attributed to Schernikow were colors on *green bond paper* without value, type II, and also with 20¢ value, type III.

Without value on green bond paper measuring approximately 66mm x 66mm were printed in the following colors:

Carmine

Brown

Blue green

Gray black

20¢ value on green bond paper measuring approximately 66mm x 66mm were printed in the following colors:[29]

Vermilion

Yellow green

Claret

29. There is an added line below the lower center shield on the 20¢ Schernikows.

In addition attributed to Schernikow were colors on *glazed paper* without value, type II, and also with 20¢ value, type III, measuring approximately 74mm x 74mm.

Without value in the following colors:

Carmine on yellow glazed card

Red carmine on dark pink glazed card

Orange on white glazed card

Olive on gray glazed card

Gray blue on light blue glazed card

Light violet on buff glazed card

20¢ value in the following colors:[29]

Vermilion on yellow glazed card

Brown on buff glazed card

Yellow brown on gray glazed card

Ultramarine on light blue glazed card

Violet on dark pink glazed card

Gray black on white glazed card

SCHERNIKOWS

Fig. 128. (Top left) Se-tenant 10¢ and 30¢ on India mounted on laid paper. Fifteen known colors. SF2

(Top right) Se-tenant 10¢ and 30¢ on large glazed card, three known color combinations. SF3

(Bottom left) Large die essay on India without value. SF2

(Bottom right) Large die essay on India with 20¢ value. Added line appears under shield. These large die essay reprints "without value" and with 20¢ value also appear on green bond paper and on glazed card. SF2

In July of 1963 William W. Steele offered the most rational explanation of the three different types. (Fig. 128) Type I proofs are those printed from the dies that were used to make the plates for the genuine stamps. All ¹⁰⁄₃₀ die proofs are type I and in Steele's opinion are the only type I proofs made by Schernikow.

Types II and III were made from two other dies, according to Steele, that were discarded for some reason by the printers in 1864 and were not used to make any genuine plates. These two types then are die essays rather than die proofs.

To summarize, you should be able to readily tell the difference between the genuine Philadelphia die proofs and the Schernikows by keeping the following in mind. They are the genuine die proofs IF:

A. On the se-tenant ¹⁰/₃₀ it is one of the two known on a large die greenish black in color on glazed paper.

B. On the 20¢ there is *no added line* below the lower center shield. Only two are known and are greenish black in color. There also exists a large die, vermilion, India on card and a large die in blue, India on card.

C. The "no value" is the only one known, greenish black on glazed paper.

In identifying the Schernikows these features will distinguish them:

A. They exist in fifteen different colors, small die on India mounted se-tenant vertically, ¹⁰/₃₀ mounted on laid paper; and of these fifteen colors three are also a large die mounted se-tenant vertically ¹⁰/₃₀ on glazed card.

B. On the 20¢ there is *an added line* below the lower center shield.

Of more than curious interest is the ultramarine Schernikow with a double impression that is not only unique but had its provenance in the Earl of Crawford Collection. (Fig. 129)

Fig. 129. On India, 54mm x 64mm, double impression. From the Earl of Crawford Collection. SF3

THE FAIR ILLUSTRATED ENVELOPES

Battlefield-scene envelopes were printed in eight different colors: black, violet, purple, brown, maroon, red, blue, and possibly green with a legend in the upper left corner "Great Central Fair for the Sanitary Commission". Most common are the cachets in black, violet, and purple, with the scarcest in blue and green. The green has been reported but never seen by the authors. The covers appear with a single or pair of the 1¢ blue (#63); a single of the 2¢ (#73); and a single, pair, or triple rate of the then current 3¢ (#65). Others were franked by Congressmen from the Philadelphia area. With the exception of four covers—two postmarked Wilmington, Delaware, one from South Windham, Connecticut, and another from Trenton, New Jersey—all others are postmarked from Philadelphia. Others, however, may exist from other cities. (Fig. 130, Plate 13) (Figs. 131, 132, 133, 134, 135, 136)

Fig. 130. (Top) Black imprint, postmarked Apr 4, '64, 1¢ circular rate. sf3

(Middle) Brown imprint (front only), postmarked Apr 5, '64. Covers to Mrs. James are usually fronts only. sf2

(Bottom) Maroon imprint (front only), postmarked May 13. sf2

Fig. 131. (Top) Oval Philadelphia postmark, purple imprint. The 1¢ prepaid unsealed circular letter rate for one ounce or less up to 500 miles. One-cent rated covers were sent prior to the opening of the fair and probably contained circulars soliciting participation. sf3

(Middle) Black imprint, postmarked Aug 9, after the close of the fair. sf3

(Bottom) Two 1¢ blues, violet imprint, postmarked July 5. Prepaid 2¢ circular rate. sf3

Fig. 132. (Top) Unique blue battlefield scene imprint, Wilmington, Del., April 19 postmark, 2¢ circular rate (front only). Manuscript notation denotes it originated within the Delaware Department. The Great Central Fair had the help and cooperation of the citizens of Delaware, New Jersey and Pennsylvania. Maryland also should have shared in this major event but Maryland was a border state and its loyalty was under some question. SF5

(Middle) Black imprint, Trenton (New Jersey), April 5, 1864 postmark. Only recorded New Jersey postmark on a Great Central Fair battlefield scene cover. SF4

(Bottom) Black imprint, postmarked March 11, approximately two months before the fair opened on June 7, 1864. SF4

Fig. 133. (Top) Patriotic purple Great Central Fair cachet, postmarked May 2. SF4

(Bottom) Reverse.

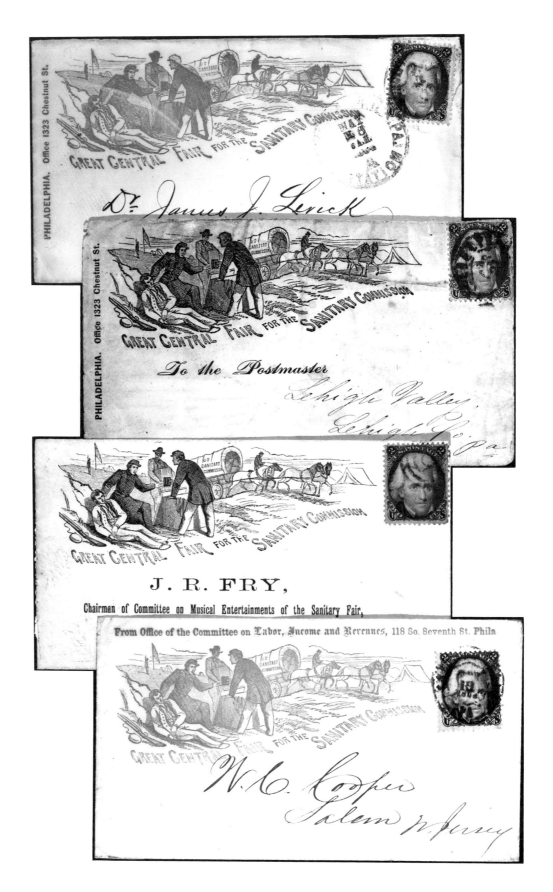

Fig. 134. (Top) Red imprint. SF4

(Upper middle) Black imprint, "To the Post-master". SF4

(Lower middle) Black corner card, pre-printed envelope addressed to J.R. Fry, Chairman of the Committee on Musical Entertainments of the Sanitary Fair. SF4

(Bottom) Red imprint, prepared for the "Committee on Labor, Income and Revenues". Everyone not in the military was asked to donate one day's labor (wages) in aid of the fair. SF4

Fig. 135. (Top) Brown imprint, 2¢ Jackson (#73). Handstamp at upper right of a local Philadelphia commission merchant. SF4

(Bottom) Brown corner card, postmarked July 11, 1864, after the fair had closed on June 28th. SF4

Fig. 136. Nearly one-fourth of the entire proceeds of the fair was raised by this committee—"One day's labor from the working classes from every branch of industry, one day's income from their employers and one day's revenue from all moneyed corporations." The postmaster in each city was requested to serve as chairman and to organize a local committee to raise funds. SF4

In conjunction with the fair and as an adjunct to fund-raising efforts, the Committee on Labor, Income and Revenue was formed. Their efforts were monumental. They called on industry and labor to donate the value of one day's labor, one day's income. Every district in Pennsylvania was contacted to assist in their gathering of funds for the fair in Philadelphia. Few refused the pleas of the committees set up throughout the state. Coal companies donated one day's income; so did the railroads, manufacturers, and others. Not mentioned, however, was the contribution of "The Ladies of the Night" who were most generous in donating their favors. Six of these "ladies" prepared this broadside: (Fig. 137)

Fig. 137. Six of General "Fighting Joe" Hooker's girls donate the proceeds of one day's labor in aid of the Great Central Fair. It was Brigadier General Joe Hooker who believed that by bringing strumpets into the camps under his command the soldiers would take more pride in their looks, cleanliness, personal sanitation, and be more temperate in their language. It just did not work out that way and the idea was soon dropped by General Hooker. The word "hooker", however, has remained in our language.

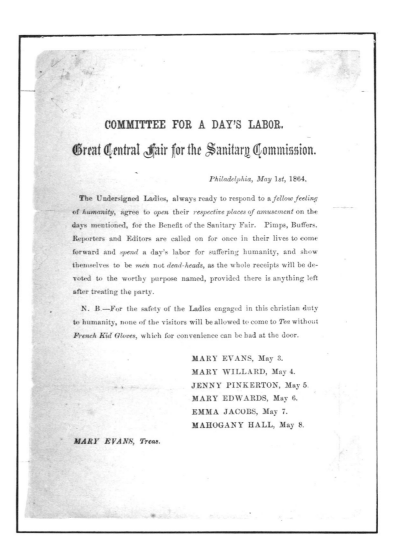

COMMITTEE FOR A DAY'S LABOR
Great Central Fair for the Sanitary Commission
Philadelphia, May 1st, 1864
The Undersigned Ladies, always ready to respond to a fellow feeling of humanity, agree to open their respective places of amusement on the days mentioned, for the Benefit of the Sanitary Fair. Pimps, Buffers, Reporters and Editors are called on for once in their lives to come forward and spend a day's labor for suffering humanity, and show themselves to be men not dead-heads, as the whole receipts will be devoted to the worthy purpose named, provided there is anything left after treating the party.

N.B.—For the safety of the Ladies engaged in this christian duty to humanity, none of the visitors will be allowed to come to Tea without French Kid Gloves, which for convenience can be had at the door.

Mary Evans, May 3
Mary Willard, May 4
Jenny Pinkerton, May 5
Mary Edwards, May 6
Emma Jacobs, May 7
Mahogany Hall, May 8

Mary Evans, Treas.

Great Central Fair envelopes were also issued with the 2¢ black embossed Andrew Jackson profile (U46) on buff-colored laid paper. Three such covers are known with the circular fair postmark dated June 23, 1864, (a Thursday). All the fair stamped envelopes are from die 1. This can best be described as the downstroke and tail of the numeral "2" uniting near the outer frame on the left even more than on the right side, where as on the other die varieties they do not merge. (Fig. 138)

Fig. 138. Black imprint on buff, 2¢ rate. These three Great Central Fair corner card entires (#U46) are all the known used fair entires, all with Phila., Pa. postmark and June 23, 1864 fair postmark. SF4

Fig. 139. A 2¢ (#U46) stamped envelope (or entire). SF3

Fig. 140. Purple corner card with shipping instructions on reverse. SF3

Stamped envelopes, or entires, were first issued 11 years before the fair, on July 1, 1853, and were always made by private contractors. They were then sold to the public for the postage plus a small fee for the manufacture of the envelopes. Between 1853 and 1870, George F. Nesbitt & Company manufactured them and was responsible for these envelopes as well. Like all other stamped envelopes and wrappers of the period, these, too, were watermarked. (Fig. 139)

In itself, the 2¢ Jackson or "Black Jack" has always been a much sought-after stamp, in adhesive or embossed form. Ever since the stamp was authorized by an Act of Congress on March 3, 1863, it has caught the eye of collectors. The engraving or image of Jackson with his sad and brooding look nearly fills the frame of the stamp. The 2¢ on a patriotic envelope is more desirable than the 3¢ on such a cover. The embossed 2¢ envelope (U46) with a Great Central Fair corner card is the only such envelope known with a patriotic design. There are, of course, 3¢ Nesbitt stamped envelopes imprinted with patriotic designs, which, while desirable, are more common than the 2¢ Black Jacks.

The same Congressional Act which authorized the 2¢ Jackson also set a uniform postage rate of 3¢ for first class intercity mail anywhere across the country effective July 1,

1863. So by that date the distance differential for postage rates was eliminated and while the majority of the Great Central Fair corner card mail was addressed to the Philadelphia locale, it is conceivable that a letter of less than half an ounce could have traveled all the way to California.

It may be assumed that most correspondence written from and sent under a corner card of the Great Central Fair was official business and usually solicited donations. The cover in Fig. 140 with a purple cachet was imprinted on the reverse with the admonition "DO NOT PREPAY ANY CHARGES FOR FREIGHT." (It was the practice for the freight companies to carry all goods to the fairs free of charge.)

Usages of three different color Great Central Fair corner cards within approximately one month are found in the following correspondence: On June 2, 1864, in a maroon cachet cover John B. Bachman of Lancaster County, Pa. was requested to quickly forward all funds collected in aid of the Sanitary Commission. Mr. Bachman had been written earlier on May 4 in a black imprinted cover and had perhaps ignored this request. He sent in his money, $766.70, and it was then acknowledged with a receipt and a letter written by James W. White. The receipt and letter were in a violet Great Central Fair battlefield scene cover. The last letter reads: (Figs. 141, 142)

Fig. 142. Violet corner card. With enclosed receipt and acknowledgment letter from the "Committee on Orations and Lectures of the Great Central Fair at Philadelphia for the Sanitary Commission". SF3

Phila June 6th/64

My Dear Sir,

I had the pleasure of receiving your very handsome Collection today. Enclosed please find receipt, and accept the very hearty thanks of the Committee.

I will acknowledge the amount rec'd in a few days, & send you copy of the Paper.

If duties well performed create happiness you ought to be a happy man.

Yours Truly
J.W. White

John B. Bachman Esq

(Figs. 143, 144, 145, 146, 147, 148, 149, 150)

Fig. 141. Maroon cachet. SF3

Fig. 143. Black imprint, postmarked April 21, So. Windham, Conn. This fair cover and three others are the only recorded ones that did not originate in Philadelphia. SF3

Fig. 144. Violet, May 23, 1864. Scratched out is the notation: "Please hand this to the President or Secretary of the Principal Literary Association of your Town." SF3

Fig. 145. Violet, Jun 9, 1864. SF3

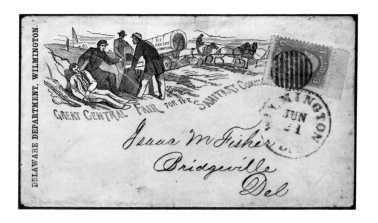

Fig. 146. Black imprint, Jun 21, Wilmington, Del. postmark, during the fair. Originated in the Delaware Department. SF3

Fig. 147. Triple rated. Black imprint, post-marked Philadelphia, Apr 5, 1864. SF3

Fig. 148. (Top) Brown imprint, oversized cover postmarked May 16, 1864, J.W. Forney frank and handstamped "FREE". SF3

(Bottom) Black corner card, May 30, 1864 postmark. SF3

Fig. 149. (Top) Brown imprint from the Labor, Income and Revenues Committee, May 20, 1864, Philadelphia postmark, "FREE", franked by J(ohn) W(ise) Forney, Secretary of the U.S. Senate. SF3

(Middle) Violet, franked by J.W. Forney, an active and loyal supporter of President Lincoln. Influential in Pennsylvania politics he stretched the use of the frank to unofficial business. Handstamped "FREE". SF3

(Bottom) Black imprint, J.W. Forney frank. Much fair mail was addressed to postmasters in towns around Philadelphia as they were expected to be the local leaders for contributions. SF3

Fig. 150. An imitation of the 30¢ black (WV13) exists, typographed in blue on thick paper.

IX

SOLDIERS' FAIR — STAMFORD

July 27 to July 29, 1864
WV15 — 15¢ Pale Brown

AND IN THE WAR... The siege of Petersburg continues. Confederate General Early burns the suburban Silver Springs home of Montgomery Blair, Postmaster General of the United States. Not pressing the incursion, Early retreats, much to the relief of Lincoln and the raw troops called up to defend Washington. On July 30th the gigantic mine explosion occurs at Petersburg with little effect on the eventual battle at Petersburg.

The three days' run of the Soldiers' Fair in Stamford, Connecticut was the shortest duration of any of the fairs, which is probably the reason for the scarcity of its stamps and information about them. In addition, the fair was held in an area of the country less populated than other centers. Only eight unused and five used stamps are known today.

The July 8, 1864 issue of the *Stamford Advocate*, the weekly newspaper of the time, contains some information about the fair in that city. It was to be held in Seely's Hall and was originally announced for opening on July 25 but did not actually open until July 27, 1864.

The July 29, 1864 issue of the weekly carried the following description:

> The room was decorated with evergreens, and the steps leading to the platform were surmounted by an arch wreathed with evergreens and flags. On a background of flags was a shield with an anchor and the name "Farragut" upon it. On the platform stood the "Post Office" completely draped in the Stars and Stripes. Anyone could see at a glance it was a Union post office where no rebel correspondence would be allowed to pass.

The same newspaper on August 5th summarized the events of the fair:

> The well known stage at the end of the hall was transformed almost beyond recognition. A flight of stairs covered with crimson carpet led up to it in the front, passing under an arch of evergreens and streamers; we reached the platform and found the Post Office in full operation under the guidance of Mr. James R. Walsh, the chairman of the P.O. Committee. Within a tasty tent of flags were grouped all the paraphernalia of the postal service, together with several extremely pretty young ladies, a commodity not usually included under Uncle Sam's management. But Stamford is a long way ahead of Uncle Sam, at least in postal matters. The Fair charged five times the government rates of postage and got it too. Each

letter bore a neat postage stamp printed in rose colored ink, bearing the design of a section of artillery in the background, while in the foreground stood a stalwart sentinel resting on his musket. The inscription ran "Stamford Soldiers Fair. Fifteen Cents." — the last two words serving to explain to the uninitiated the amount of the swindle. And yet the word swindle seems harsh; it was no swindle, for each dime and a half thus demanded will do far more good among our brave and suffering soldiers than it ever could if confined to Stamford pocket-books.

On January 8, 1969, Elliott Perry wrote the following letter to the authors about his recollections of the issue:

> In re Stamford:…I think I tried to find something about the fair in Stamford and failed. May not have had enough time, I bought the SF's John Luff had which included one cancelled Stamford. The other cancelled copy came from George Sloane, and the pair of 10¢ Young Ladies.
>
> As nearly as I can now recall Ackerman (one of the foremost collectors of the time) heard about a collection in Washington (D.C.) which was supposed to contain a Type I 1¢ of 1851, and suggested that I look at it. The "Type I" was a paint job, but the owner showed me an envelope containing 7 Stamfords and told me they had been a block which he cut shortly before I arrived. He kept one and sold me the others. At that time the only genuine copy I had seen was the copy I got from Luff.
>
> I don't recall the collector's name, but believe he was a nephew of Alvin A. Adee,[30] a well-known official in the State Department whose home had been in Stamford. Evidently Adee had gone to the Fair and bought about a dollar's worth of the stamps. Ackerman had been a State Senator and died in or about 1931, while he was Representative in Congress from this district. I was sort of philatelic secretary with him for about ten years and bought the U.S. part of his immense (600 volume) collection in 1927/1928.

The stamp was designed by an unknown local artist and printed by Mr. Campbell of Stamford.

The Scott WV15 measures approximately 21mm x 25mm and was issued imperforate. It was lithographed with a pale yellowish brown ink in panes of eight on white paper. (According to a notation made at the time of the fair, the color was described as "rose colored".) The used stamps are cancelled with the red July Stamford postmark. Visible on one is "JUL 2" and the top of a "7" which would clearly indicate that the stamp was canceled at the fair. None are known to exist on cover. (Figs. 151, 152)

A comparison of the Booth postmarked 3¢ 1861 cover with the clear Stamford cancellation on the used fair stamps seems to confirm the fact that the same U.S. post office postmarking device was used for both the cover and the Stamford Sanitary Fair stamps.

It was previously believed that the only known used copy existed in the John Luff Collection (marked with an asterisk in Fig. 151) and was probably the one first seen by Perry.

Counterfeits of this stamp are numerous but easy to detect. S. Allan Taylor seemed to be particularly delighted to reproduce it, as it is known in many colors including brown, green, blue, black, vermilion in various color combinations on white, yellow, pink, light green, dark green, light blue, dark blue and deep purple paper. Any collection of Sanitary Fair stamps should certainly include these "Cinderellas". They add interest to the pursuit of the elusive genuine Stamford Sanitary Fair stamp. (Fig. 153)

30. Alvey Augustus Adee (1842–1924) held various foreign and domestic posts in the State Department.

Fig. 151. (Left) These six Stamford Soldiers Fair stamps originally were arranged like this in a block of eight. SF3

(Top right) Two additional known unused copies. SF3

(Bottom right) Majority of known used copies. SF3

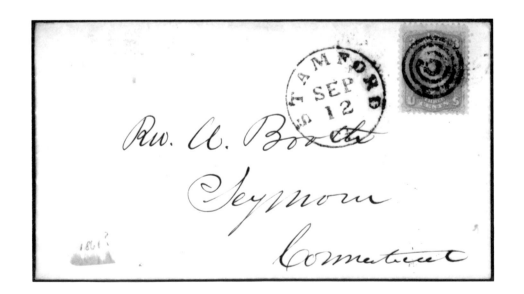

Fig. 152. Stamford circular cancel used at the time of the fair. SF1

There are several clues for ascertaining whether or not a Stamford is genuine or counterfeit. Imitations have a leaning "S" in the word "CENTS". Another determining feature is that the originals have the tassels at the ends of the ribbon inscribed "SOLDIERS FAIR" while the counterfeits lack the tassels at both ends of the ribbon. Still another way to tell the obvious Taylor-mades is by the fact that it is nearly impossible to duplicate the ink color of the original as over the years it appears to have faded somewhat to a more or less indistinct lilac.

Fig. 153. A sampling of the many counterfeits created by S. Allan Taylor.

X

NATIONAL SAILORS' FAIR — BOSTON

November 9 to November 22, 1864
WV3 – 10¢ Green

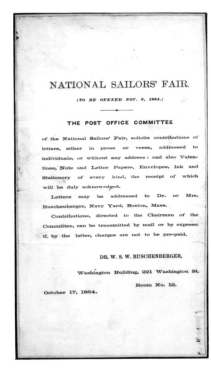

National Sailors' Fair Post Office Committee circular

AND IN THE WAR... *Lincoln has been re-elected on November 8, 1864, the day before this fair opens, with Andrew Johnson as his vice-president. Major George McClellan is defeated by nearly half a million votes. Two days later McClellan resigns from the Army. Sherman plunges deeper into Georgia. As the fair closes, Sherman departs devastated Atlanta on "his march to the sea."*

Proceeds from this fair were used for the establishment of a National Sailors' Home for disabled Union seamen. While the fair was held in Boston, it was generally supported by all of New England. It was the consensus of the organizers of this fair that Union seamen were a forgotten lot. While soldiers enjoyed canteens, rests, and military hospitals, the sailors were usually professional seamen who did not receive these benefits. Were they to be wounded, sick, or injured, they could turn to no one. Once the war came to an end, it was expected that these same sailors, if able, would return to the rigors of life at sea. During the early disheartening times of the land war, it was the navy that sealed off the southern ports and embargoed commerce to and from the Confederacy. The navy was one of the few bright lights in an otherwise dismal period. The war was already three and a half years old when the fair opened. Lincoln telegraphed the Fair Committee the day of his election, November 8, 1864, as follows:

Allow me to wish you a great success. With the old fame of the Navy, made brighter in the present war, you can not fail. I name none, lest I wrong others by omission. To all, from Rear Admiral, to honest Jack [ordinary seaman] I tender the Nation's admiration and gratitude.

A. Lincoln[31]

(Fig. 154)

The post office, supervised by Mrs. Hubbard W. Tilson, was table #6 at the fair. In the 14-day run, the fair netted $247,056.47. (Fig. 155)

31. The original copy of the telegram was purchased by one of the active managers at the fair and given to the Concord Free Public Library 12 years later.

Fig. 154. Lincoln telegram to the Sailor's Fair at Boston. (Library of Congress)

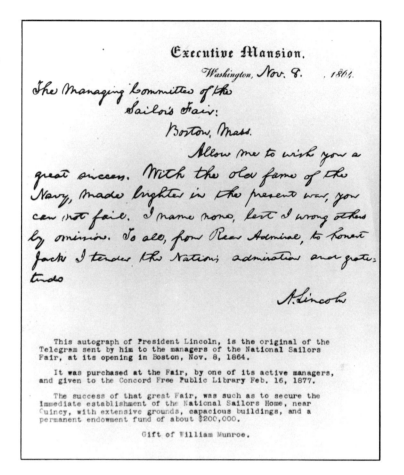

Fig. 155. Location of post office at the fair.

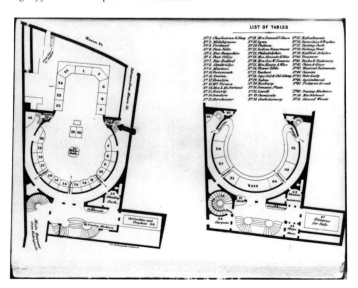

The Boston National Sailors' Fair stamp was lithographed, green in color, and bears a 10¢ denomination. It is oval-shaped, 23mm x 30mm, and the edges are serrated or scalloped. There are no known reprints or counterfeits. The irregular edging may have been provided to make counterfeiting more difficult or nearly impossible or merely for design purposes. (Fig. 156)

Fig. 156. Embossed stamped envelope (#u34), red Boston postmark dated Apr 14, black cork cancellation. sf3

While the Boston Sanitary Fair stamp on the cover shown is genuine, there is no evidence that the cover came together with the stamp at the fair. It may have been applied at a later date. The Boston postmark on the stamped envelope (#u34) was used from August 1861 until late 1864. There is no enclosure to verify that the letter was written at the fair. Fair literature does not reveal that the post office operated on the same basis as post offices at other fairs, i.e., as a semi-official carrier.

Elliott Perry, writing to Vincent Domanski on October 8, 1918, said that the first reference to Sanitary Fair stamps was in a listing in A.C. Kline's *The Stamp Collector's Manual*, Philadelphia, 1865. In the same letter Perry wrote that he had up to that date seen only six copies of the National Sailors' Fair stamp (wv3). We now know that at least 50 of these stamps exist, with six to eight of them appearing in various auction sales around 1975. After the stamps of Philadelphia, Albany, and the Metropolitan at New York, these are the most common. (Fig. 157)

Shown herein are the majority of known copies of the Boston stamp. While it may be possible to plate this stamp as has been the case with Albany, Brooklyn, Stamford, and Springfield, this feat has not been accomplished as yet. The slightly out-of-register die cutting gives some indication that there may have been several of these stamps lithographed on a sheet and then die cut, perhaps individually since all the cutting appears exactly the same.

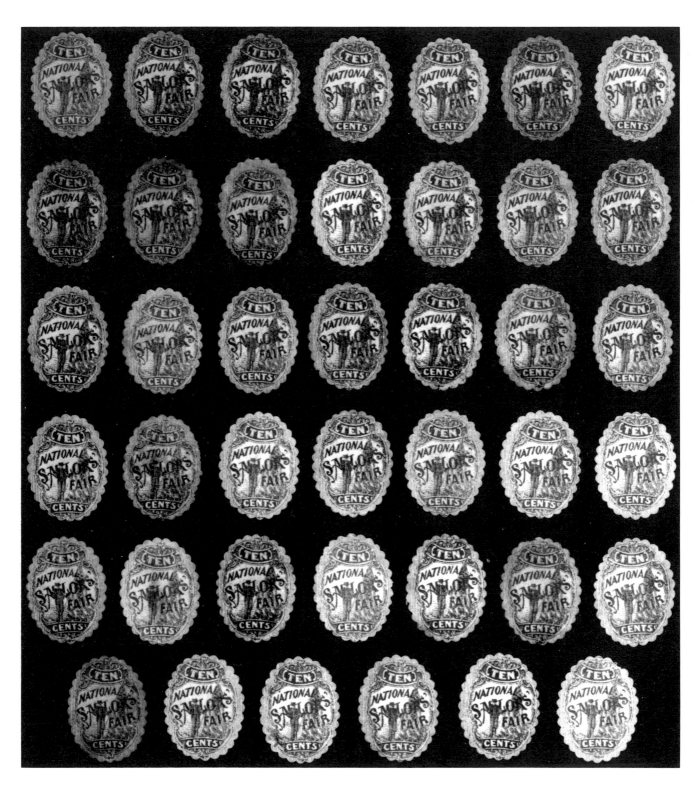

Fig. 157. Majority of known copies. SF2

XI

SOLDIERS' FAIR–SPRINGFIELD, MASSACHUSETTS

December 19 to December 24, 1864
WV14–10¢ Lilac

AND IN THE WAR…*Sherman is deep in Georgia heading for Savannah. Lincoln believes in a more conciliatory stance toward the readmittance of seceded states. The radicals, including Wade, are of a different opinion. The Confederates evacuate Savannah on December 20 and Sherman presents the city to the nation as a "Christmas gift…with 150 heavy guns and plenty of ammunition, and also about 25,000 bales of cotton."*

The Soldiers' Fair of Springfield, Massachusetts was held for five days, beginning on the evening of December 19, 1864 and ending on Christmas Eve, December 24, 1864. While the stamps issued for this fair are always considered Sanitary Fair stamps, the fair and the stamps were for funds for the Soldiers' Rest in Springfield rather than the United States Sanitary Commission. The Rest was located near the railroad route and provided a facility where soldiers en route home could secure a night's lodging, medical attention, a bathing area, and food. Like some of the other refreshment saloons of the period, this Rest and the others could be considered the forerunners of the United Service Organizations (USO), much welcome places away from home for World War II soldiers. One major difference prevailed, however. During the Civil War the Rests provided for the wounded in transit home or moving to another hospital or for those whose army pay had not followed them as they moved from hospital to hospital or from military unit to military unit. Generally speaking, the USOs during World War II were entertainment centers. Like so many other innovations during this Civil War period, the Sanitary Commission and other benevolent organizations were the forerunners of social and medical services now taken for granted as parts of our military establishment.

The fair in Springfield was held in the City Hall. Characteristic of other fairs, there was a "New England Kitchen" where dinners were served by the local townspeople. In addition, the other features included the post office. According to the fair newspaper *The Springfield Musket* of December 20th: "At the right of the stage is the Post Office, where any one can get a letter for the asking, which will amply pay in fun and wit, and be a pleasant memento afterwards." As at most fairs, the post office was tended by the younger girls who penned letters and then affixed stamps to them. The proceeds from the sale of the stamp contributed to the funds raised at these fairs. Again in the issue of December 21, 1864: "The post office at the Fair continues to dispense the mails daily to the perfect satisfaction of all who desire tenderly sentimental or comical letters from unknown friends." There is no report available about the funds raised in support of the Soldiers' Rest in Springfield.

The Sanitary Fair stamp (WV14) issued in conjunction with the Soldiers' Fair in Springfield, Massachusetts measures 24mm x 30mm and was issued imperforate. It was typographed from a woodblock by Thomas Chubbuck, the same craftsman who engraved the postmaster provisional stamp of Brattleboro, Vermont of 1846. The printing of the fair stamp was lilac ink on white paper. The value is for 10¢; the design depicts an officer doffing his hat to two ladies. The words "Soldiers Fair" and "Springfield Mass." are prominent. At the lower right appears Chubbuck's name.

At least 55 singles still exist. In addition, three strips of four stamps are known. All strips appear to be from a bottom right pane with the wide margin at the bottom and a somewhat smaller margin at the right. Unusual is the appearance of one stamp on two of the strips of four that is askew in relation to the others. (Figs. 158, 159, 160)

Figs. 158, 159. Majority of known copies.
SF2

Fig. 160. Strips of four. Top strip with left stamp askew. SF3

The special circular fair postmark in black measures 33mm across and bears the inscription "Soldiers Fair Springfield". All covers have the December 20, 1864 date, a Tuesday, in a bold, heavy strike. Known are at least eight small covers prepared for use but unaddressed and one large-sized envelope addressed to Wm. E. Ingersoll Esqr.

It would appear that the postmark acted as a cachet and all were applied on the one date at the one time. Some of the covers have a "DUE 10" while others do not. It is possible that the "DUE 10" represented the value of the stamp which had the 10¢ denomination. A more plausible theory is that in some instances the envelopes were prepared with the circular postmark and the "DUE 10"; when the purchaser bought the envelope and paid the 10¢, the stamp was then affixed. All the imprints are in black. (Fig. 161, Plate 14)

According to Bill Steele, the large Ingersoll Springfield cover was originally seen with a second stamp at the lower left which was subsequently removed. Examination under ultraviolet does not reveal this. (Figs. 162, 163)

Counterfeits of the Springfield stamp exist and are of two types. Type I lacks the designer Chubbuck's name in the lower right portion of the stamp and is printed in lilac on laid paper. Type II has the designer's name but is roughly typographed and is printed in lilac

Fig. 161. Majority of known Springfield stamps on cover with Dec. 20, 1864 fair postmark. "Due 10" on top cover. SF3

Fig. 162. Only known large cover with Dec. 20, 1864 fair postmark. "Due 10". SF3

Fig. 163. (Left) Counterfeit type I. Designer Chubbuck's name missing.

(Center) Counterfeit type II. With designer's name, roughly typographed in lilac on white wove paper.

(Right) Soldier overprint doffing his hat, on a 1¢ ultramarine (#212).

on white wove paper. The originals show five buttons on the soldier's uniform but this detail is missing in both counterfeits.

A counterfeit overprint of the Springfield stamp design is known on an 1887 1¢ Scott #212. It appears to be an aberration only without any special significance. It has been suggested that it may be a cancellation.

In the ephemera chapters is a listing of the fair medals and tokens, one of which was prepared for the Springfield Fair. In the December 23, 1864 issue of *The Springfield Musket* there is a reference to the presence of John A. Bolen, "one of the best die sinkers in New England", and to the fact that he had struck hundreds of medals during the week at his station at the fair. The obverse has the inscription "Soldiers' Fair Dec' 1864. Springfield, Mass." surrounded with a laurel wreath; on the reverse is the head of George Washington.

XII

MISSISSIPPI VALLEY SANITARY FAIR AT ST. LOUIS

May 17 to June 18, 1864

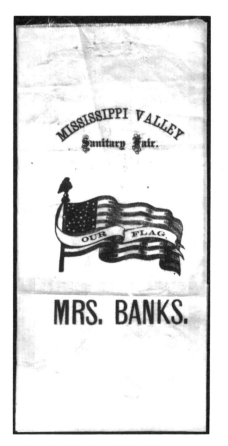

Badge of the Mississippi Valley Fair

AND IN THE WAR...*The news of the war is eclipsed with the announcement of the death on May 19th of Nathaniel Hawthorne. The last battle of Spotsylvania is fought. John C. Fremont is nominated by the Radical Republicans to run against Lincoln. June opens with the Battle of Cold Harbor—one of the costliest to Grant—and once again Lee saves Richmond. Lincoln is nominated at the National Union Convention. The attack on Petersburg begins.*

On September 5, 1861, General John C. Fremont signed the order creating the Western Sanitary Commission, totally separate from the United States Sanitary Commission. Its efforts and activities were confined mostly to the campaigns in the Western Department and the West. Fremont, ever true to form and of an impulsive nature, had ignored an order from the War Department stating that the United States Sanitary Commission was to be the official agency to aid and advise the Medical Bureau. The Western Sanitary Commission was really a duplicate service but for political reasons and for fear of losing Missouri, Lincoln gave the Commission his approval after succumbing to the argument of sectionalism. It was the longest-lived of the major relief agencies, operating for two decades after the war.

The first hospital railroad cars and river transports for the evacuation of the wounded were created by the Western Sanitary Commission. The best known of the river troop carriers was the *City of Louisiana*. It was later sold to the government and renamed the *R.C. Ward*. In addition to this vessel, other floating hospitals that plied the Mississippi and Ohio Rivers were the *City of Alton*, *Ruth*, *Glasgow*, and *Red Rover*. All these steamers proved their worth carrying many of the troops fighting along these two rivers, particularly the Mississippi.

While the efforts of this Commission were primarily directed at alleviating the suffering of the troops, approximately ten percent of its income was allocated to the cause of freedmen, the emancipated or freed former slaves.

By December 1861, 20,000 troops were encamped in Benton Barracks at St. Louis. With the skirmishes and battles of western Missouri, Arkansas, and Kansas, many more troops poured in. Only Tennessee and Virginia had been the scenes of more military encounters than Missouri. One out of every ten recruits came down with measles, typhoid, or diarrhea. These raw farm boys had never before been exposed to the confined conditions of many persons living together and they had never been subject to the risk of diseases. Their natural immunity systems had never come in contact with these infections. Small wonder, then, so many of them fell ill during the virulent, debilitating, and often fatal epidemics that would run rampant through a company or battalion.

To supplement the income of the Western Sanitary Commission the Mississippi Valley Sanitary Fair was opened in St. Louis by Major General W.S. Rosecrans, who served as its president. The building erected when fair plans were announced was placed on 12th Street from Olive to St. Charles. It was 500 feet long and 114 feet wide.

The fair lasted for nearly a month until June 18, when it closed. It was the longest running of any of the fairs. Total receipts were $618,782.28 of which $64,191.28 were expenses. The Western Sanitary Commission raised a total of $2,800,000 during its existence of which the fair contributed a net $554,591. The income of the post office amounted to $307.95. No stamps were issued for this fair.

In the second issue of *The Daily Countersign*, the fair newspaper, reference was made to the fact that post offices at other fairs had become mundane. It was the wish of the ladies that something new be tried. Instead of just one mail box at this fair, there were two, one for the men and one for the ladies. The ladies' delivery box would be waited upon by the men and the men's boxes by the ladies. The openings of the boxes were so placed as to encourage conversation between the giver and receiver of these letters. The undirected correspondence at other fairs would seem to indicate that the letters were written in advance and then "sent" as requested. At this fair the 50 members of the post office committee would also address letters to their friends. Further, this committee provided other letters with enclosures of copies of paintings, caricatures, and comic surprises. It was suggested that once read, the letter would be redeposited in the mail box and be used again. The post office at this fair appears to have been a message center as well but had none of the carrier features of the other fairs. All fair covers originated at the rooms of the Mississippi Valley Sanitary Fair on Lindell Street in St. Louis. (Figs. 164, 165, 166)

While several covers exist with the corner card "Rooms of the Mississippi Valley Sanitary Fair", it is unusual to find either a wrapper or a cover from the Western Sanitary Commission. An example of this distinction between the two agencies is a wrapper, #U47, Die I, with the 2¢ circular rate. The Commission occupied a different location from the fair headquarters.

The Soldiers' Home at Memphis had been the home of William R. Hunt, a southern sympathizer, now a colonel in the Confederate army. First used by General Grant as a headquarters, it was later turned over by him to the Western Sanitary Commission. Grant, then commanding in the western theater and from Galena, Illinois, would be likely to make this gesture because at this point in his career he considered himself a westerner. This home or "rest" was the financial responsibility of the Western Sanitary Commission. (Fig. 167)

The circular rated 1¢ is an open letter written by A.W. Plattenburg of the Western Sanitary Commission. It, perhaps better than any history or personal account, gives the day-to-day problems faced by this Commission and their agents in the field as well as similar problems faced by other Commissions. This sanitary agent with a personal pass from General Halleck served with General Curtis' army in Arkansas. (Curtis was later

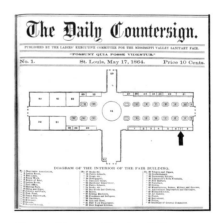

Fig. 164. Diagram of interior of fair building designating Booth #7 as the post office. *The Daily Countersign* was the fair newspaper.

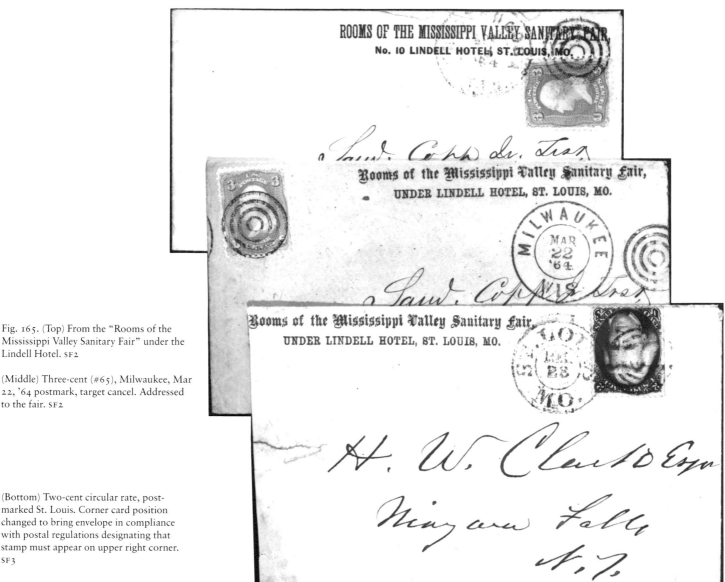

Fig. 165. (Top) From the "Rooms of the Mississippi Valley Sanitary Fair" under the Lindell Hotel. SF2

(Middle) Three-cent (#65), Milwaukee, Mar 22, '64 postmark, target cancel. Addressed to the fair. SF2

(Bottom) Two-cent circular rate, postmarked St. Louis. Corner card position changed to bring envelope in compliance with postal regulations designating that stamp must appear on upper right corner. SF3

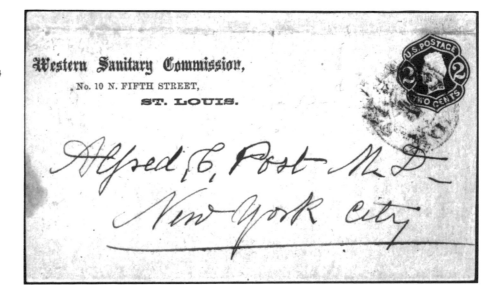

Fig. 166. Western Sanitary Commission corner card, scarce wrapper (#U47). SF4

Fig. 167. Soldiers' Home at Memphis operated under the auspices of the Western Sanitary Commission.

Fig. 168. One-cent circular rate, postmarked St. Louis, Mo. Integral circular dated April 2, 1862. Circular rate did not change to 2¢ until July 1863. SF2

relieved of his command of the Department of Missouri only to be reappointed commander of the Department of Kansas some months later.) Of special interest in the open letter is this comment: "I am fully convinced that no army was (so far as provision for the wounded was concerned) ever sent into the field in such destitute condition as ours, except the one that it fought and conquered. Our preparations were wholly inadequate; the enemy had, apparently, made none at all." (Figs. 168, 169)

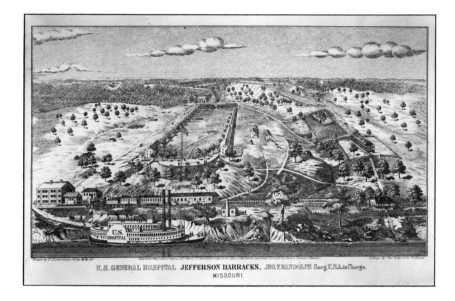

Fig. 169. U.S. General Hospital Jefferson Barracks at St. Louis, site of Mississippi Valley Sanitary Fair.

XIII

OTHER FAIRS AND BENEVOLENCES

CHILDREN'S SOLDIERS' FAIR.

While many Northern cities held fairs and bazaars, only a relative few left some philatelic record of the events. But the story of the Civil War benevolences touched nearly everyone. It was not unusual for a local populace, rural or urban, to participate either with goods or services or, if nothing else, a contribution of money while in attendance at these fairs.

FIRST CHICAGO FAIR—NORTHWESTERN SOLDIERS' FAIR

The first Sanitary Fair staged at Bryan Hall in Chicago (the second one was held two years later) was planned by Mary Livermore and Jane Hoge. While other fairs sought and received the help of men, the first Chicago fair was the result of the efforts of women only. The fair opened on October 27, 1863 and lasted two weeks. Close to one hundred thousand dollars was raised. No stamps or specially cacheted covers were issued.

One of the major gifts donated to raise funds for the fair was the original final draft or working copy of the Emancipation Proclamation written in his hand and then donated by President Lincoln. He wrote the following letter that accompanied the document.

Executive Mansion,
Washington, Oct. 26, 1863.

Ladies having in charge of the North-Western Fair
For the Sanitary Commission
Chicago, Illinois.

According to the request made in your behalf, the original draft of the Emancipation Proclamation is herewith enclosed. The formal words at the top, and the conclusion, except the signature, you perceive are not in my hand-writing. They were written at the State Department by whom I know not. The printed part was cut from a copy of the preliminary proc-

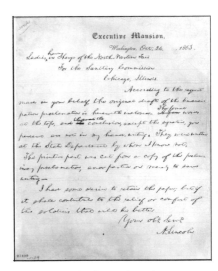

Fig. 170. Lincoln's letter of October 26, 1863 donating his copy of the Emancipation Proclamation to the first Sanitary Fair in Chicago. (Library of Congress)

lamation, and pasted on merely to save writing —

I had some desire to retain the paper; but if it shall contribute to the relief or comfort of the soldiers that will be better.

Your ob^t serv^t.,
A. Lincoln

The document was purchased for $3,000 by Thomas B. Bryan, who had previously donated the use of his building for the fair. Unhappily the document, purchased for the Chicago Soldiers' Home by Bryan, its president, and later given to the Chicago Historical Society, was lost in the Chicago fire of 1871. (Fig. 170)

Following the good fortune of the Chicago Fair, cities large and small in the North attempted to duplicate its success.

BUFFALO, NEW YORK—GREAT CENTRAL FAIR (Ladies' Christian Commission) (Fig. 171)

President Millard Fillmore delivered a major address at this fair on February 22, 1864. The speech branded Fillmore a "Copperhead". The former Whig President (1850–1853), who had assumed office upon the death of President Zachary Taylor, had been a local leader of the war effort as hostilities opened. However, as he saw the casualties mount and the financial burden grow and grow, he became obsessed with the thought that perhaps the war could have been avoided. His speech to the fair was his first public expression of disagreement with Lincoln and his war policies. He himself supported McClellan for the presidency against Lincoln. To loyal Republicans his utterances seemed to be proof of his disloyalty to the Union, which was not the case at all.

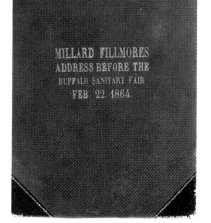

President Fillmore's bound copy of his "Copperhead Speech"

Fig. 171. The Great Central Fair at Buffalo, N.Y., Feb. 22 to March 2, 1864, under the auspices of the Ladies' Christian Commission raised $40,000. SF3

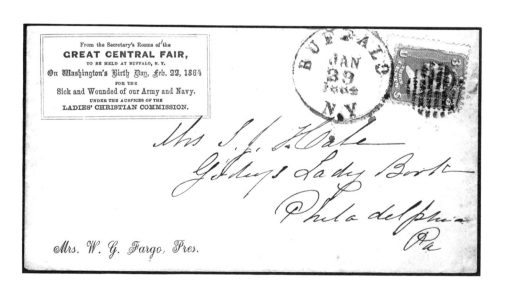

Fillmore wrote the organizers of the Christian Commission Fair at Buffalo the following letter that accompanied his handwritten, 26-page speech that day:

Buffalo, March 9, 1864

My dear Sir,

I have your favor of the 7th soliciting the manuscript of my recent address at the opening of the ladies Ch[r]istian Commission Fair in Buffalo, on the 22nd day of February last, and I cheerfully comply with your request by sending you the original address in my own hand writing as I wrote and delivered it. It is somewhat soiled because it has been in the hands of the printers. Though it has been attacked by the abolitionists, I adhere to it as it is without changing a word.

Respectfully yours
Millard Fillmore

H. P. McIntosh Esq.
Cleveland,

(Fig. 172)

CINCINNATI, OHIO–GREAT WESTERN SANITARY FAIR

December 21, 1863 saw the opening of the Great Western Sanitary Fair in Cincinnati. It closed January 9, 1864 after raising a total of $235,406.62. General Rosecrans, relieved of his command after his debacle at Chickamauga, served as president of this fair and also of the Mississippi Valley Sanitary Fair in St. Louis the following year. While no Sanitary Fair stamps were issued, a special cachet was prepared for use on what is referred to as the "Good Samaritan" cover.

The post office was considered one of the more attractive features in Greenwood Hall where it was located. "Ten cents is the postage charge, which paid, you receive a letter written by some fair hand in and of the cause."[32] The post office receipts for the 19 days of the fair came to $91.90 and if one can assume 10¢ for each letter that would be a total of 919 letters. (Fig. 173)

The notation on the cover reads, "Donations will be brought free by Express and by Railroad, to be sold for U.S. Sanitary Commission. Exhibition for two weeks, commencing on 21st December. Money or anything salable accepted. Excursion Trains daily at half

Fig. 172. President Fillmore letter to the Great Central Fair at Buffalo. SF5

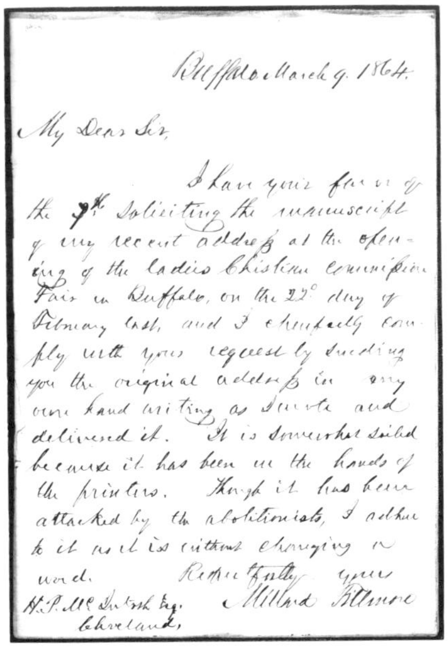

32. *History of the Great Western Sanitary Fair*, C. F. Vent & Co., publisher.

Fig. 173. (Top) "The Good Samaritan", the special cachet of the Great Western Sanitary Fair at Cincinnati, blue grid cancellation. SF4

(Bottom) Three-cent 1861 (#65), postmarked Cincinnati, blue grid cancellation; "The Good Samaritan". SF4

fare." Four of these covers are known; perhaps there are more. The cover addressed to Wiggon was originally in the George Wray collection. It was next in the Hon. J. William Middendorf's collection and it, along with another similar one addressed to Wm Idler of Philadelphia, is now in the authors' collection. The third cover is addressed to C.C. Chamberlain, president of the Soldiers' Aid Society of Delaware, Ohio. Still another, bearing a 2¢ 1863 stamp and addressed to Howard Chase Di Sallem, exists but it lacks a postmark. The grid cancellation is unlike the two shown. Postmarks are all of Cincinnati in blue with a grid cancellation.

In addition to these "Good Samaritan" covers that originated with the Great Western Sanitary Fair, there is an oversized envelope with three 3¢ stamps (#65) vertically placed and addressed to the Mayor of Milford, N.H. Triple-rated from Cincinnati, it lists among the fair officers and honorary officers "His Excellency Abraham Lincoln, President of the United States." Still a third type of cover prepared for the fair is also headed across the top "Head-Quarters Great Western Sanitary Fair", one addressed to Professor W. H. B. Thomas of Mt. Holley, N.J. (Figs. 174, 175)

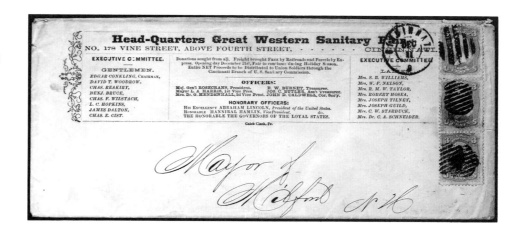

Fig. 174. Oversized cover bearing three 3¢ 1861 stamps, Cincinnati postmark, blue grid cancellation. Cincinnati did not enjoy the largess of free postage as did Cleveland. SF3

Fig. 175. (Top) Two-cent (#73) with blue grid cancellation, circular rate. SF3

(Bottom) Three-cent (#65), blue grid cancellation, postmarked Cincinnati, May 4. SF3

CLEVELAND, OHIO—NORTHERN OHIO SANITARY FAIR

Within days of the firing upon Fort Sumter by General Beauregard of the South, the Soldiers' Aid Society (of Cleveland) was organized and by April 20, 1861, it was a functioning group of ladies, with Mrs. B. Rouse as its president. As the area enlarged, encompassing more of the towns and villages around Cleveland, the name was changed on October 16, 1861 to the Soldiers' Aid Society of Northern Ohio.

Scene of the Northern Ohio Sanitary Fair at Cleveland

In the *Historical Sketch of the Cleveland Branch of the U.S. Sanitary Commission* appears a notation that all mail from the Cleveland Fair rooms went postage free by means of an informal arrangement with the post office through some friends of the Society. While the boast was made that all mail went free of postage, and most mail certainly did, in many cases postage was paid by the 3¢ 1861 stamp. The favor of free postage was "enjoyed" from March 1862 until April 1865 and enabled the Society to distribute its own documents and those of the United States Sanitary Commission more widely at great savings. Carrying the use of free postage to extremes, the Cleveland group even distributed thousands of pamphlets from the Union League and loyal publication houses in Boston, Philadelphia, and New York.

While no hint is furnished about the informal arrangements for proxy franking signatures, it appears from the myriad of franks of Ohio's Senator Benjamin Franklin Wade and Congressman Albert Gallatin Riddle that they might have been kept extremely busy night and day processing envelopes were it not for the many others who signed their names. Senator Wade was one of the real "fire eaters" of the Civil War and a power within the Senate. It is unlikely that the Post Office Department would have challenged the illegal use of his frank. The shield type, straight line corner card, and boxed type were supposedly franked by Wade who was continually harassing Lincoln. Nicknamed "Bluff Ben", his comment upon hearing of Lincoln's conciliatory stance toward the South was, "If we follow such leadership we will be in the wilderness longer than the children of Israel under Moses." As chairman of the powerful Joint Committee on the Conduct of the War 1861 to 1862, he and its other members continually tested Lincoln's authority as Commander in Chief of the Army. No doubt in illegally making use of his personal signature as required for a frank, he felt above criticism and was perhaps laying down a gauntlet for a confrontation between himself, the Post Office Department, and President Lincoln.

Soldiers' Home at Cleveland

In Bulletin #7 dated November 14, 1864 from the central office of the Soldiers' Aid Society of Northern Ohio at 95 Bank St. in Cleveland, C.P. Wickham, major of the 55th Ohio Voluntary Infantry, advises that every long-delayed letter held up at the post office for insufficient postage when sent to the soldier at the front and marked "Paid by the U.S. Sanitary Commission" is a morale booster that can only be accomplished by the generosity of those at home.

In the same bulletin an unnamed writer points out that every soldier who drops out of the ranks due to injury or sickness is thrown upon the Commission where he is clothed, and from sanitary stores lies on a sanitary bed and receives his eat and drink from the same source. Were it not for the Commission not one in ten would recover from hospitalization. (Figs. 176, 177)

Fig. 176. Albert G. Riddle, whose frank appears on this cover, served in the 37th Congress only. His term ended on March 3, 1863. Embossing on reverse, "U.S. San. Com. Soldiers Aid Society of Northern Ohio…", measures 35mm. Later Riddle, while on retainer for the State Department, aided in the prosecution of John H. Surratt, co-conspirator in the murder of President Lincoln. SF3

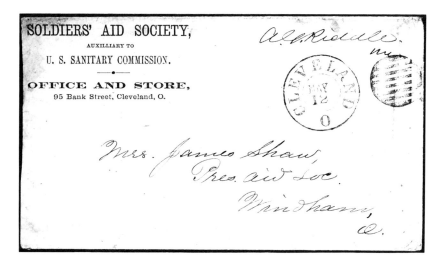

Fig. 177. Cleveland June 30, 1865 letter enclosure. Proceeds from the fair aided in the establishment of the Soldiers' Home at Cleveland, a halfway house for the wounded, furloughed, and discharged servicemen. SF2

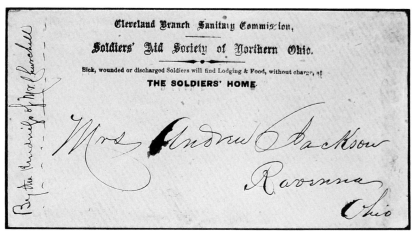

The Northern Ohio Sanitary Fair opened on Monday, February 22, 1864, and ran for 16 days. Promoted by the Soldiers' Aid Society of Northern Ohio, which at the time was the Northern Ohio Branch of the United States Sanitary Commission, it covered the area from Erie, Pennsylvania on the east to Jackson, Michigan on the west.

The fair was held in a special building constructed for that purpose. It covered over 64,000 square feet and was erected in the center of the Public Square, enclosing Commodore Perry's statue. After the fair closed, the building was sold to Pittsburgh for $8,500 to house that city's fair. The Cleveland Fair raised $78,000 for the Soldiers' Aid Society and the United States Sanitary Commission. (Fig. 178)

In Volume I, No. 1 of the *Sanitary Fair Gazette*, the Northern Ohio Sanitary Fair newspaper, there is a reference to the fact that "Post Offices were established for the sale of Sanitary Fair stamps to swell the fund [fair], and other cities copied the idea." A search was made as recently as February 4, 1978 by John Large and James B. Casey of the Western Reserve Historical Society Division of Archives and their investigations of the fair failed to reveal any stamps in that institution's collections. It is remotely possible that stamps may exist in the 41 boxes of fair records now in storage in the New York Public Library.

Fig. 178. (Top, middle) Amanuensis Senator Benjamin Franklin Wade franks. SF2

(Bottom) Fair cover franked by Senator B.F. Wade. SF3

The explanation of the multiple markings for the foreign usage of the Northern Ohio Sanitary Fair cover addressed to Rio de Janeiro is a detailed one. In a personal letter to the authors, George E. Hargest offered an explanation of this unusual and interesting cover: (Fig. 179, Plate 15)

> The cover originated in Cleveland, Ohio on February 8, 1863 (in advance of the fair's opening) addressed to the Hon. James Monroe, United States Consul, Rio de Janeiro, Brazil. The whole rate was 33¢ per ¼ ounce. On unpaid letters the United States would not participate in any part of the rate beyond France. Therefore, the Cleveland Office marked it with a *black* 15 in oval, obeying the regulations that required the rate be shown on unpaid letters. This was the international rate, i.e., the rate between the U.S. and France. The letter was forwarded to New York and sent aboard

an American packet boat that was going to England. Under the circumstances the U.S. was entitled to the sea postage as well as the inland postage. Sea postage was 6¢ and inland was 3¢, therefore, New York debited France with 9¢, as shown in the *New 9 York* (Feb 13) marking. The letter passed through Liverpool, London and Dover in closed mail which was opened on a day train, which arrived in Calais on February 25, 1864. The train crew (number 3) routed the cover to Bordeaux. At Bordeaux the cover received the balloon shaped F/23 mark. These were applied at the border offices in France, each office having a distinguishing number. The cover was transported by French packet to Rio de Janeiro, where France had one of its colonial agency offices. The red 540 is Brazilian and means 540 reis (33 cents) was to be collected. A rare and interesting cover. One reis equals .061 cents, at the time.

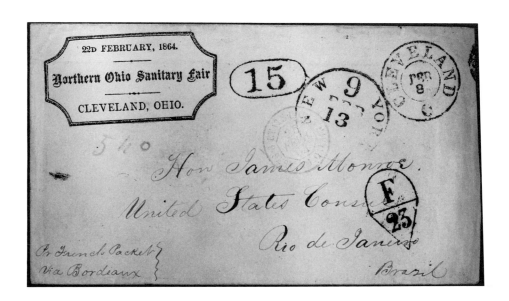

Fig. 179. Addressed to James Monroe, nephew of President Monroe, via New York, Calais, Bordeaux, and French packet to Rio de Janeiro, Brazil. SF4

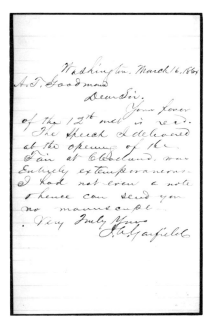

Fig. 180. Future President Garfield commented on his presence at the Cleveland Sanitary Fair. SF5

Future President James A. Garfield, wrote on March 16, 1864, some seven days after the fair closed, that his speech at the Cleveland Fair was entirely extemporaneous and that he was unable to furnish any notes for his remarks. At the time the letter was written Garfield was serving in the House of Representatives. He had resigned his commission as a major general in the Union Army the previous December. He continued to serve eight more terms in Congress before assuming office as president. (Fig. 180)(Fig. 181)

COLUMBUS, OHIO—THE SOLDIERS' AID SOCIETY

On October 21, 1861, a Soldiers' Aid Society was formed under the leadership of Mrs. W.I. Kuhns, its president. The Columbus branch raised about $7,000 a year toward the efforts of the United States Sanitary Commission which recognized it as an auxiliary in 1861; Columbus stood in the same relationship to that body as did the Woman's Central Relief Association of New York. Throughout the war a large part of the work of the Soldiers' Aid Society was directed to the relief of soldiers and their families. (Fig. 182)

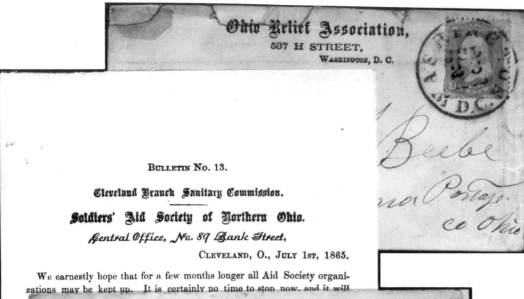

Fig. 181. (Top) The Ohio Relief Association with offices in Washington, D.C. was typical of state relief offices in Washington where soldiers from Ohio received care. SF1

(Middle, bottom) By July 1, 1865, the date of the enclosure, funds were slow in coming to the Soldiers' Aid Society and the admonition was for the people of Cleveland to continue with their generosity. SF2

Fig. 182. Bureau of Soldiers' Claims in Columbus, Ohio, Columbus postmark. SF1

HARTFORD, CONNECTICUT (Fig. 183)

The Hartford Soldiers' Aid Association was organized in May 1861 immediately after the fall of Fort Sumter on April 14, 1861. It claimed the privilege of being the first to minister to the needs of Connecticut soldiers. Its avowed purpose, in the true tradition of "states' rights" at the time, was "the supplying of Connecticut soldiers with articles of necessity and comfort not provided by government". States' rights was one of the major causes of the Civil War and was echoed by the Confederacy time and time again as a major reason for their secession.

Fig. 183. Hartford Soldiers' Aid Association. Nov 24, 1864 and Apr 17, 1865 postmarks. SFI

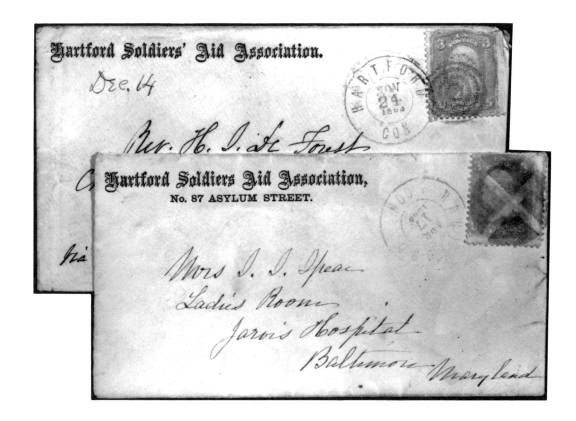

INDIANA SANITARY COMMISSION

Organized February 1862 at Indianapolis, the Indiana Sanitary Commission, in spite of its name, endeavored "to carry relief to suffering soldiers, wherever from and wherever found; and its aim was to contribute to every general hospital within its reach as large a supply, in proportion to the number of Indiana soldiers in those hospitals, as any other state. When this was done, any thing that remained was devoted to the use of Indiana soldiers in preference to any others".[33] The Indiana Commission remained independent of the United States Sanitary Commission to the end of the war. (Fig. 184)

33. *The Tribute Book*, by Frank B. Goodrich, p. 319.

Five good examples of Indiana Sanitary Commission covers are shown. The first three, picturing Governor Oliver P. Morton, the founder of the Indiana Sanitary Commission, illustrate corner cards with different printed type styles. The cover addressed to a Mr. Woody was sent with postage due of 3¢ and does not reflect a further 3¢ penalty for the deficit as the letter originated with a soldier. Bearing no endorsement as having originated at a hospital, the letter enclosed, curiously written on stationery furnished by the Northwestern Sanitary Commission (Chicago), reveals that the writer had been sick for six weeks. The endorsement required by the chaplain or officer indicating soldiers' mail was no longer being enforced. (Fig. 185)

Fig. 184. Indiana Sanitary Commission. Oliver P. Morton, war-time governor of Indiana, was head of the Indiana Sanitary Commission. Largely through his efforts and determination Indiana remained within the Union despite a hostile legislature. SF3

Fig. 185. (Top) Indiana Sanitary Commission, postmarked Indianapolis, Ind., Jun 9, '64. SF1

(Bottom) Three-cent (#65), postmarked Springfield, Ind., buff colored. On reverse, Columbus, Ind., Aug. 31 postmark and manuscript "not called for". SF3

NORTHERN IOWA SANITARY FAIR

By June 1, 1863, it became apparent to the Iowa Sanitary Commission that their soldiers were spread far and wide across all battlefield fronts. Originally, like Indiana, Iowa planned on aid only to Iowa servicemen. Giving a soldier from Iowa necessary medical stores while denying these same stores to the soldier in the next bed somehow did not seem the right thing to do. Accordingly and eventually the largess was distributed where needed.

The Northern Iowa Sanitary Fair opened at Dubuque on June 21, 1864 at the City Hall. It raised a total of $60,725, of which $48,348 was sent to the Chicago Branch of the Sanitary Commission. Iowa contributed more than its proportionate share to this branch. The Iowa group also occupied a desk at the Northwestern Sanitary Fair in Chicago in May 1865. (Fig. 186)

Fig. 186. Cover dated Jun 7, 1864, post-marked Buffalo, N.Y., just 14 days before the opening of the Northern Iowa Sanitary Fair. Addressed by President Millard Fillmore who could have franked the envelope but instead affixed a 3¢ 1861 stamp. The autograph was submitted for sale at the Dubuque Fair that opened on June 21, 1864 at City Hall. SF5

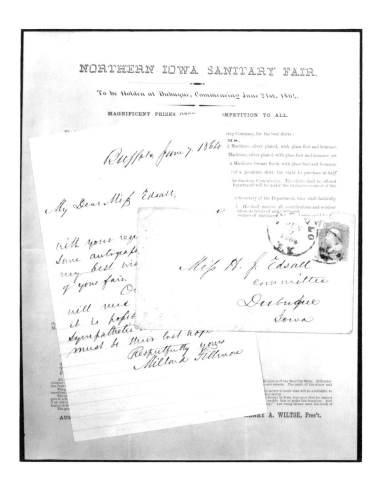

As noted previously, in February 1864 President Fillmore had delivered an address at the Great Central Fair in aid of the Christian Commission in Buffalo. Now he submitted more autographs for sale at the Dubuque fair; his covering letter reads:

Buffalo, June 7, 1864

My Dear Miss Edsall,

In compliance with your request I send you some autographs, and you have my best wishes for the success of your fair.

Our brave soldiers will need all the relief that it is possible to give, and the sympathetic heart of woman must be their last hope.

Respectfully yours
Millard Fillmore

MAINE AGENCY

The Maine Agency, the Ladies' Aid Society, was organized in April 1862. As similar groups in many states did, it provided aid for indigent veterans, not relying on the federal government to provide for their needs. (Fig. 187) Following is a transcript of a cover enclosure on the letterhead of the "Maine Agency for Sick and Wounded Soldiers—No. 53 Exchange Street" answering an inquiry about the return of the remains of a soldier:

Portland, June 26, 1865

John P. Wellman, Esq.
Dear Sir,

As I wrote you this morning in regard to the Body of John H. Thompson that the great expense attending in the obtaining the Body would enhance the cost greatly. In order to make the Agency whole you will please remit me $25—more which with the money you sent makes $150.

Upon no consideration could we get another Body until after the 1st of Oct, [few soldiers were embalmed and refrigeration was not yet known] double expenses had to be paid on every transaction made as they take all advantage on account of no prices being established by the Dept. The desire of the sisters to get the Body was the only inducement of my pursuing the thing at this time.

L.G. Davis—State Agent

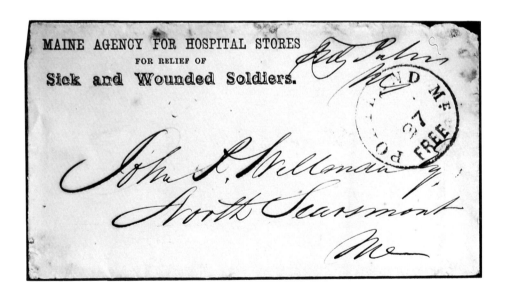

Fig. 187. Postmarked Portland, Me., (June) 27 (1865), Free, franked by Sidney G. Perham, Member of Congress from Maine. Not relying on the federal government for aid to the wounded or sick, many northern states took it upon themselves to provide for the needs of the indigent veteran or his family. Enclosed was an inquiry for the return of the remains of a soldier. SF2

MASSACHUSETTS SOLDIERS' RELIEF ASSOCIATION

Little information can be gathered on the Massachusetts Soldiers' Relief Association located in Washington, D.C. Evidence of its existence is the corner card of the cover shown. Like other state organizations, this association was probably for purposes of succoring Massachusetts soldiers as they passed through Washington. Following the First Battle of Bull Run, retreating troops had no place to find shelter. Many slept in streets; even the Capitol, not quite finished, was used as a place of retreat from the elements. The need to shelter troops came out of this lack of providing for the needs of transient soldiers. (Fig. 188)

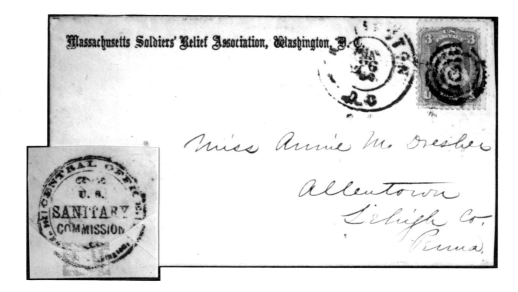

Fig. 188. Washington, D.C. postmark, May 26, '64, target cancel. Central Office U.S. Sanitary Commission handstamp on reverse. SF2

MASSACHUSETTS UNIVERSALIST CONVENTION—SOLDIERS' MISSION

The exact date of the establishment of the Soldiers' Mission of the Massachusetts Universalist Convention cannot be determined from the two covers shown. The Soldiers' Mission must take its place among the many tract societies that operated in and about the hospitals and camps. While the Sanitary Commission was primarily concerned with physical needs, there were other groups besides the Christian Commission who tended to spiritual needs and were concerned with the saving of souls. It was not unusual for simple requests for water and other needs to be denied until the hapless patient would assert his acceptance of the "word of God". (Fig. 189)

Fig. 189. (Top) Postmarked Washington, D.C., the word "Universalist" scratched out and in its place is written "Baptist". SF1

(Bottom) Cover of the Massachusetts Universalist Convention, postmarked Washington, D.C., Apr 10, '65 with a "Due 3", docketed "A Soldier's letter". Passed through the mails without an additional 3¢ penalty for non-prepayment. SF1

NEW ENGLAND SOLDIERS' RELIEF ASSOCIATION

The New England Soldiers' Relief Association was organized in April 1862 to aid and care for all soldiers from New England passing through New York, and later a care facility was established in Philadelphia. The soldiers' rests were located near steamboat landings and railroad stations. Prior to the war this organization was known as the New England Society and had functioned for charitable and social purposes.

The New England Soldiers' Relief Association's influence spread not only to New York, where it had originally been formed, but to Philadelphia as well, where on February 26, 1863, the group opened facilities. One of its covers with a 3¢ 1861 stamp advises that its rooms in Philadelphia were at Thirteenth and Chestnut Streets. Of the two New York covers from the group, one has the 1¢ 1861 plus the 1¢ New York carrier handstamp, while the other bears a 3¢ 1861 stamp postmarked New York. (Figs. 190, 191)

Fig. 190. (Top) A 1¢ blue (#63) and a New York City Paid 1 ct. carrier handstamp. SF2

(Middle) Three-cent dull red (#65), post-marked New York, Jun 30, 1863. SF1

(Bottom) Three-cent pink (#64), Philadelphia, Feb 25, 1863 postmark. SF3

Fig. 191. One-cent (#63) circular rate, post-marked Boston to Durham, N.H. The women's auxiliary of the New England Soldiers' Relief Association (New England Women's Auxiliary Association — N.E.W.A.A.) furnished the nurses and aids for the soldiers' rest. They attended to 68 beds in New York. SF2

NEW YORK SURGICAL AID ASSOCIATION

The New York Surgical Aid Association recruited many of the surgeons who served in the Union military, and the New York State Soldiers' Home in Albany was no doubt one of the hospitals for discharged soldiers. The New York Surgical Aid Association cover shown here has the 3¢ 1861 stamp incorrectly placed; as a result it was canceled by the postmark instead of the target cancel. The New York State Soldiers' Home cover has a Dec 9 postmark. (Fig. 192)

Fig. 192. Both covers with 3¢ stamp (#65), one with New York, Aug 6, 1862 postmark and target cancel; the other with an Albany postmark. SF2

Interior of the fair at Pittsburgh (Carnegie Library of Pittsburgh)

PITTSBURGH SANITARY FAIR

Pittsburgh planned its fair not knowing that the dates, June 1 to June 18, 1864, would conflict with the Great Central Fair in Philadelphia. Buildings were erected for the fair in the Alleghany Diamond Square. Almost $320,000 was raised for presentation to the United States Sanitary Commission. (Figs. 193, 194)

The cover for the benefit of the Mercy Hospital was probably hand-delivered at the fair since it has no postal markings. It is of special interest because of the heading "U.S. Post Office Department", although there was no official connection between the fair and the Post Office Department. It is even possible that this fair was held sometime after the war ended. The "10" within the fleuron was typical of the fee charged for composing a poem for some willing "dandy". These two verses of the four enclosed are good examples of what one could expect to find within these fair envelopes:

I told her you were handsome
That you had a splendid air;

And you'd like to call upon her,
She said, she "didn't care."

I added you were well-known
For the valiant deeds you'd dare.
Still in monotone she answered
"Indeed she didn't care."

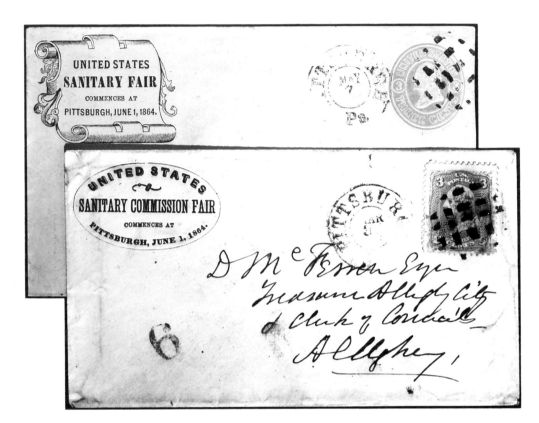

Fig. 193. (Top) (#U35) pink on buff entire, May 7, Pittsburgh postmark. SF3

(Bottom) Oval corner card, Pittsburgh postmark, 6¢ postage due, 3¢ for the overweight (booklet enclosure) and 3¢ penalty. SF3

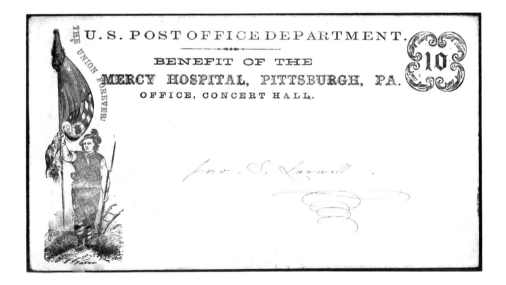

Fig. 194. Fair cover for benefit of Mercy Hospital at Pittsburgh. SF3

POUGHKEEPSIE, NEW YORK—DUTCHESS COUNTY AND POUGHKEEPSIE SANITARY FAIR

On March 15, 1864, the Dutchess County and Poughkeepsie Sanitary Fair opened at the Vassar Emporium of Sanitary Relief. As at other fairs there were booths where merchandise was sold and a hall of trophies which always seemed to include a token, perhaps even a canceled check, of Jefferson Davis. The post office contributed $113.91 to the income of the fair. No stamps were issued. A total of $16,282.72 was raised at this fair for the Commission and all proceeds went to the central treasury. (Fig. 195)

Fig. 195. Two-cent (#73), manuscript cancel, drop letter rate, Poughkeepsie postmark. Addressed to Mrs. Benson J. Lossing, vice-president of the Women's Relief Association of Poughkeepsie, New York, an organizer of the fair and wife of the prominent historian, Benson J. Lossing. SF3

THE WISCONSIN AID SOCIETY

The Wisconsin Soldiers' Aid Society was formed on April 19, 1861. Later the name was changed to the Wisconsin Aid Society. It was allied with the United States Sanitary Commission, and most of the supplies accumulated for soldiers were sent through Chicago. Locally it was concerned with assisting the families of Wisconsin soldiers, securing work for wives and mothers, and providing for widows and orphans. (Fig. 196)

Fig. 196. Wisconsin Soldiers' Aid Society, auxiliary to U.S. Sanitary Commission with label "In UNION is strength.", 3¢ (#65), Milwaukee Mar 21, '64 postmark. SF1

SECOND CHICAGO FAIR–NORTHWESTERN SANITARY FAIR

Fig. 197. Soldiers' Home at Chicago with Stephen A. Douglas monument at the right.

THE WAR IS OVER... *Lee has surrendered the month before at Appomattox Courthouse. Lincoln has been assassinated. On May 10th President Johnson proclaims that armed resistance has ended. What of the returning soldier? With limited opportunity, there is always the West...but what about the freed black? The trial is in progress for the Lincoln conspirators. Later, on June 30th, the eight, including one woman, are all found guilty.*

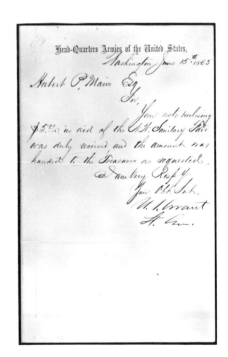

Lt. Gen. Grant's contribution to the Second Chicago Fair

Plans for opening this fair on February 22, 1865, could not be met, so it was then postponed until May 30. By the time the fair closed on June 24, 1865, the unhappy event of April 14, Lincoln's assassination, had occurred and a pall was placed over the fair and all its activities. The fair, in addition to its intended purpose of soldiers' relief and help for the Sanitary Commission and Christian Commission, became, in a sense, a memorial to Lincoln.

The buildings were constructed in the area roughly covered by the present-day City of Chicago Cultural Center, the former main library, on Michigan Avenue and Washington Street on the then-shore of Lake Michigan. The principal building was called Union Hall.

By 1864, both a soldiers' home and a soldiers' rest had been built in Chicago, the latter for temporary confinements and the former for permanently disabled soldiers. (Fig. 197) (The soldiers' home can still be seen at 35th Street and the lake across the street from the tomb and statue of Stephen A. Douglas.) The second Chicago Sanitary Fair was planned to cover the expenditures for the homes at Chicago and Cairo, Illinois plus all the other activities of the Northwestern Sanitary Commission that had drained the treasury. (Figs. 198, 199, 200, 201)

By June 2, 1865, the character and purposes of the Sanitary Commission had begun to change. Reacting to a crisis as it had at the beginning of the war, it now found in 1865 a need for veteran's assistance. At this time there were large numbers of discharged servicemen who needed help on filing claims for disability, back pay, and subsistence allowances.

The "Union Rose" East and West originating from the Northwestern Fair in Chicago is among the scarcest of Civil War patriotic stationery. And used, there is but one known, the one sent to Eben Townsend, Esq. and pictured here. It was printed by Charles Magnus.[34] Originally it was thought that only he produced the "Rose" designs but there were others— G. Heerbrandt of New York and Hunckel & Son of Baltimore. The inside of the "Rose" shows panoramic views of different cities. There are seven other "Rose" designs. The name "Rose" is derived from the pictorial views of cities, die cut, then folded into eight segments with the rose only showing; when opened, the piece takes the form of an open rose.[35] (Fig. 202, Plate 16)

Additional fairs had been held in other cities. Covers or stamps are unknown from the following fairs: Lowell, Massachusetts, February 24, 1863; Bramhall Fair, Portland, Maine, October 28, 1863; Boston Fair, December 14, 1863; Rochester, New York, December 14, 1863; Wheeling Fair, Wheeling, West Virginia, June 28, 1864; Nantucket Fair, Nantucket, Massachusetts, August 3, 1864; Westfield Fair, Westfield, Massachusetts, December 28, 1864; Soldiers' Fair at St. Paul, January 8, 1865; Wapakoneta Sanitary Fair, Wapakoneta, Ohio; Maryland State Fair in Baltimore (Christian Commission Fair), April 18, 1864; and many others from cities, towns, and hamlets across the country that left no recorded evidence in the history of the period. With Lincoln's death and the second Chicago Sanitary Fair closing on June 24, 1865, the era of Sanitary Fairs came to an end. Although the Sanitary Commission had already begun to close out its operation, the concept of fairs and bazaars persisted for some years, with fairs for orphans and widows, disabled veterans, etc.

34. For a more comprehensive biography of Charles Magnus refer to: "Some Characteristics of Charles Magnus and His Products", by Raymond Marsh, *The American Philatelist*, Vol. 62, No. 12, Sept. 1949.

35. For more information on the "Roses" refer to: "Rose and Panorama Envelopes of the Civil War", by George N. Malpass, *The American Philatelist*, Vol. 65, No. 4, January 1952.

Fig. 198. Two-cent (#73), cork cancel. The Northwestern Fair at Chicago to aid the Sanitary Commission and Soldiers' Home. As plans for the fair progressed, it was decided that funds raised were to be shared with the Christian Commission. SF3

America was tired of the war. The return to peacetime became the next large-scale effort. There were not only wounds to be healed but there was a country divided to be healed. The race issue was yet to be settled. Families that were fortunate were once again reunited. The period of reconstruction was about to begin in earnest.

NORTHWESTERN

Sanitary Commission Rooms,

66 Madison Street.

Chicago, Feb. 17th, 1865.

CIRCULAR OF THE

Special Committee on Floral Decorations,

Appointed by the Executive Committee of the Great Northwestern Sanitary
Commission and Soldiers' Home Fair, to be held in
Chicago, Ill., May 30th, 1865.

The undersigned, a special Committee on Floral Decorations, would most
respectfully solicit your co-operation by contribution to our Fair of TREES, PLANTS,
VINES and other ornamental articles, that may add beauty to this department.

We feel that in making this (we trust our last call) for the benefit of our brave
soldiers who have been disabled from wounds or disease, and are now lying in
hospitals or on the field, that we have a claim alike on the friends of the soldier in

Fig. 199. Three-cent (#65), Chicago, Ill.
postmark. May 23, 1865 letter on page 3 of
enclosure. SF3

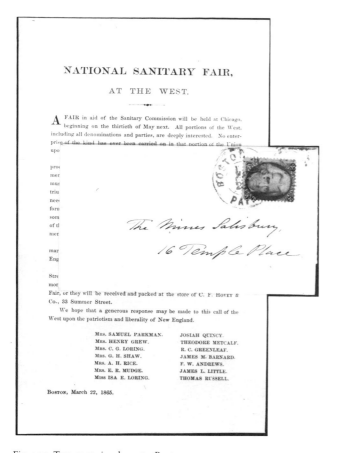

Fig. 200. Two-cent circular rate, Boston, Mar. 25 (1865), Paid postmark. Requests for funds for the National Fair at the West (Chicago) were solicited from as far distant as Boston. SF3

Fig. 201. (Upper right) An appeal to the people of Philadelphia for aid to the Chicago Fair. Use of the eagle Philadelphia Great Central Fair stamp design from 15 months previously on letterhead.

Fig. 202. (Top) "The Union Rose–East and West" patriotic envelope (the only known used) by Magnus, in bronze with Northwestern Sanitary Fair building on cover, city views in folded rose enclosed. Three-cent 1857 (#26), Feb 8, New York postmark. SF5

(Bottom) Reverse of cover.

XIV

MILITARY MAIL AND
THE SANITARY COMMISSION

SOLDIERS' LETTERS

On July 22, 1861, Congress enacted legislation permitting soldiers to send letters through the mails of the United States without prepaying postage; on January 21, 1862, this same privilege was extended to sailors and marines within the service. The postage was paid by the recipients of the mail. It was not until April 1862 that the necessary endorsement indicating the piece of mail was a "Soldier's Letter" had to be applied. Further, a major, acting major, or any other field or staff officer of the regiment had to confirm that it was a soldier's letter. The number of the regiment and the state to which the regiment belonged also had to appear on the endorsement.

(It may be assumed that a large number of the covers shown herein with a Sanitary Commission or Christian Commission corner card were indeed written by soldiers but for purposes of definition this chapter deals with a specialized type of soldiers' mail, i.e., that with the manuscript endorsement or printed designation "Soldier's Letter" on which postage may have been paid, not paid, incorrectly paid, or short paid. While these soldiers' letters could have appeared in other chapters, it was a choice as to whether the covers best served as examples in this chapter or in another area.)

A letter from a sailor or marine had to bear the certification "Naval Letter" and had to be signed by a commander or lieutenant on board the vessel, giving the name of the vessel. This ruling was to apply only to enlisted personnel. Commissioned officers, both of the army and navy, were required to prepay postage. Prepaid letters *to* soldiers and sailors could be forwarded from point to point as the location of the regiments changed without the payment of additional fees.

Mail regulations previously granted to soldiers were extended to sailors. The *U.S. Mail and Post Office Assistant*, a contemporary periodical for postal workers, furnished postmasters with instructions how soldiers' mail was to be handled. For example, the March 1862 issue, Vol. II, No. 6, carried the following:

> AN ACT in relation to the letters of sailors and marines in the service of the United States.
>
> *Be it enacted by the Senate and House of Representatives of the United States of America in Congress assembled*, That the provisions of the Act of July twenty-second, eighteen hundred and sixty-one, authorizing soldiers to send letters through the mails of the United States without prepayment of postage, is hereby extended to the sailors and marines in the actual service of the United States, under such regulations as the Post Office Department shall provide, the postage thereon to be paid by the recipients.
>
> Approved, January 21, 1862.

In the next month's issue of this publication appeared a clarification of the regulation, applying this time to both soldiers and sailors:

> Letters *from* Soldiers, Sailors and Marines may be mailed without prepayment, if so endorsed and certified on their face—the postage to be collected at the office of delivery. A letter from a Soldier must bear the certificate, "*Soldier's Letter,*" signed by the Major, acting Major, or any other field or staff officer of his regiment, who must give the number of the regiment and State to which it belongs. A letter from a Sailor or Marine must bear the certificate, "*Naval Letter,*" signed by a Commander or Lieutenant on board the vessel, giving the name of the vessel.
>
> All letters addressed to soldiers, sailors, or marines must be prepaid; and commissioned officers, both of the army and navy, are required to prepay the postage on their letters as heretofore.

In June of 1862 the regulation was extended to cover patients in military hospitals detached from their fighting units. A chaplain or surgeon, as well as any field officer, could endorse the letter and this, too, would be equally recognized by postmasters, the postage to be collected on delivery.

On the other hand, letters written *to* soldiers had to be prepaid in the full amount, single weight rate if single weight, double if double, and so on. On page 554 of the *Sanitary Commission Bulletin*, Vol. 1, No. 18, July 15, 1864, appears an admonition that postage must be prepaid, pointing out that the postmaster has no discretionary power. "The law in this respect is absolute". A slightly overweight letter on which only the single rate of postage had been applied might not only be delayed in the post office for many months but would be assessed a three-cent penalty plus the three-cent charge for the overweight portion. The soldier in the field, instead of receiving the letter promptly, would first need to be notified by the post office that a letter with fees due awaited him. Then he would have to respond to the notification, make the trip to the post office, pay the requisite postage, and hope that the letter would catch up with him should his unit move to another battlefield.

Incredible as it may seem, officers writing on official matters were required to prepay postage on letters to soldiers and their families irrespective of the contents. Discharge papers, descriptive rolls, notification of next of kin—all could have remained in a post office for lack of the required postage.

On May 20, 1864, William L. Kelly, the Special Agent of the Post Office Department of the Military Department in Louisville, wrote J.S. Newberry, Special Agent of the Sanitary Commission, advising that he, Kelly, had just returned from a tour of Chattanooga and Nashville and found quite "an accumulation of mail for the soldiers under Gen. Sherman, detained for unpaid postage." Both offices, according to Kelly, had sent out notices to the front but there had been few responses. He then appealed to "that great Charity" (the United States Sanitary Commission) to add one more claim upon the gratitude of the army and the people by prepaying the postage. "It is needless for me to tell you what joy, what faith, what courage, you will thus be the means of imparting to many a war-worn soldier, by sending promptly forward the letter from wife or child, which, otherwise would be left to await the tardy process of notification."

The United States Sanitary Commission, acting on Kelly's letter, met on July 13th, a Wednesday, at 1:00 P.M. at their offices at 223 Broadway in New York. It was noted in the Minutes of the Commission that it had come to the attention of the Commission that thousands of letters, addressed to officers and soldiers presently on active duty or sick in hospitals, were accumulating as a result of imperfect direction of the letters.

The United States Sanitary Commission had previous experience in assisting in the movement of mail and letters. This new service for prepayment of postage and forwarding mail was an augmentation of the resolution of an earlier directive, that of August 1, 1861, in which the Commission recommended that each hospital have the steward, ward master, or intelligent convalescents made agents of the Commission. They would then be responsible for a store of stationery, imprinted with the name of the Commission and "either franked or furnished with postage stamps, if the use of the congressional [soldier's letter] privilege is not preferred by the soldier", or in some cases where the endorsement of a field or service officer at or above the rank of major was not available.

To further emphasize its commitment to the speedy movement of mail, the Commission resolved that its officers at various post offices should pay the necessary postage on letters to soldiers in the field and in hospitals which due to regulations may be needlessly delayed... "each letter thus forwarded to bear the stamp of the commission."

Encompassed within the sphere of collecting Sanitary Fair and Sanitary Commission postal memorabilia, the serious hobbyist finds an opportunity to make an interesting collection of soldiers' letters, hospital covers, and naval covers from a period that saw the proliferation of the mail service. The movement of mail during the Civil War was hampered at times by a myriad of regulations, a lack of adequate distribution of stamps, troops on the move, a lack of sufficient coinage, hardships encountered by troops in the field, disorganized mail service unable to keep up with troop movements, and an uninformed home front not altogether familiar with postal regulations. Then the collector of today, over a century later, attempts to unravel the puzzles that these covers present!

In *Hardtack and Coffee* John D. Billings observed that soldiers' letters were usually written on the lap using the side or end strip of a hardtack box. With the shortage of silver money early in the war, soldiers just about to leave for the war carried large quantities of stamps with them to act as small change. They were passed around in little envelopes containing 25¢ and 50¢ in value. From the constant handling, the condition of most stamps quickly deteriorated.

Many a soldier found his pack of stamps in a compact mess from rain, perspiration, or compression when he attempted, after a hot march, to get a stamp for a letter. If he could split off one from the mass, he considered himself lucky. At that, he might have to soak them apart and dry them on a griddle.

In this day of rapid and full communication we tend to forget that computers and their word processing capabilities are of recent origin or that ball point pens began with Reynolds Pens following World War II. Before that, after the quill pens of the colonial period,

Hospital Steward, a pharmacist (Smithsonian Institution)

and between the discovery of the vulcanization of rubber by Charles Goodyear (1844) and the invention of the first practical fountain pen by Lewis Edson Waterman (1884), came steel pens of the mid-19th century. The Civil War soldier in the field either had to use a pencil, first mass produced in America in 1856, or had to carry a steel-pointed pen and use an inkwell that he carried with him wherever he went, along with rations, tenting, ammunition, and other military gear. A small number of these "traveling inkwells" still exist, a chapter in the history of communication.

It must have been a great inconvenience for a soldier to carry this liquid ink wherever he went. It seems safe to assume that the majority of letters written in ink and preserved were written at a permanent base camp or at a hospital where they were written by either a ward steward or one of the many women who called on the wards to succor the wounded. Penciled letters more likely were written in the field. While many pencil-written letters have survived, most are smudged and illegible. A pen-written letter is more easily read and thus more likely to be saved. The majority of soldiers' letters that have survived are written with ink. (Fig. 203)

Fig. 203. Traveling inkwells.

Typical of other field post offices, the one at the Headquarters of the Army of the Potomac was well described by Alexander Gardner, the renowned Civil War photographer. While not as well known as Mathew Brady, he produced photographs with a more interesting quality because of his colorful descriptions and objective observations that accompanied each one. Gardner wrote that many thousands of letters passed through the post offices each day. In the movement of the army, the presence of a post office in any theatre was as important as that of any other department. Each regiment had a post boy who carried the letters of his command to brigade headquarters where the mails from all the regiments were placed in one pouch and sent to division headquarters and then on to corps headquarters. There they were received by agents and delivered to the principal depot of the army and then on to the agent at General Headquarters. Mail would move out either by rail or steamer. Large numbers of men were used for the handling of mail and most of them were privates.

One of the easier Civil War army duties, and out of line of combat, was that of postmaster for a division or regiment. Selection of that person could be on the basis of many things but in *Private Smith's Journal—Recollections of the Late War*, published by the Lakeside Press in 1963, he indicated that as a reward for securing eight recruits he was appointed assistant postmaster of his company.

The photographs taken at the Brandy Station general post office and at the Falmouth, Virginia post office show the tents used by these facilities for the Army of the Potomac. These or similar installations would have been duplicated at the other army headquarters. The cases for the letters were described as being made from rough boards, which on a march would be packed away and then set up at a new location. The entire assemblage of tents, cases, and furniture would fit within one wagon.

During the Grant campaigns at Fort Henry and Fort Donelson in January 1862, the mail service for the Army of the Tennessee was launched under Colonel A.H. Markland (later General Markland). The post office for the Army of the Potomac was under the supervision of Postmaster William B. Haslett. It operated so well that a letter leaving Boston on the first of the month would reach Washington on the second day and would usually be delivered by the fourth day. At times however, the mail would accumulate at Washington where it would be placed in several army pouches assigned for each corps and then dispatched when an opportunity arose or the troops settled in a semi-permanent encampment or bivouac. On July 22, 1866 it was reported by S.J. Bowen, the postmaster of Washington, that on the average 250,000 letters were received and sent each day during the war. (Fig. 204)

(Left) Post-office Headquarters of the Army of the Potomac

(Right) General Post Office, Army of the Potomac, Brandy Station

The activities of sutlers were under some control, especially as to what they could sell, the quality, and the value. Early in the war the entire sutler system was established. Many amenities that are furnished soldiers today on a regular basis were not provided during the Civil War, so the sutlers performed a function somewhat similar to the army post exchanges of today. From them a soldier could buy his tobacco and the cast iron frying pan along with the grease that contributed so much to the soldiers' stomach disorders.

Fig. 204. Army Mail Leaving Headquarters — Post Office — Army of the Potomac. (Library of Congress)

One sutler was allowed per regiment. They were all civilians whose prices were set by the military authorities. Most soldiers believed that sutlers should not be allowed to operate but there was nothing or no one else to take their places. (The Post Exchange (PX) system came later, being established by the Secretary of War's Post Exchange Regulation, General Order #46 dated July 25, 1895.) Few sutlers charged reasonable prices despite the sup-

Fig. 205. Sutlers' Headquarters near Petersburg, Va., 1865. (Library of Congress)

posed price controls. Within a day as much as five thousand dollars in stock could be sold. The federal government guaranteed the sutler's payment for goods. In general, soldiers despised the sutlers and threw up all kinds of hindrances to their operation, including the burning of their stores. (Fig. 205)

Usually located behind the lines, sutlers followed the army along with a host of army followers. Billboards on sutlers' buildings advertised their wares. In addition to the basics, condensed milk was available, as were oysters and even stamps for a time until General Order #97 from E.D. Townsend, Assistant Adjutant General ended the sale of stamps, at least for a profit. It would be unlikely afterwards that any sutler would sell stamps as there could be no gain.

General Order #97   War Department
                                             Adjutant General's Office
                                             Washington, D.C.

Sec III: The attention of Sutlers, and all others concerned, is directed to the second section of the act of March 3, 1855, which provides that it shall be unlawful for any postmaster or other person to sell any postage stamps or stamped envelopes for any larger sum than that indicated upon the face of such postage stamps, or for any larger sum than that charged therefor by the Post Office Department; and that any person who shall violate this provision shall be deemed guilty of a misdemeanor, and, on conviction thereof, shall be fined in any sum not less than ten nor more than five hundred dollars.

By Order of the Secretary of War

                                             E.D. Townsend
                                             Assistant Adjutant General

There is little doubt that the issuance of this general order effectively put sutlers out of the business of selling stamps.

Two interesting foreign uses of Sanitary Commission and Christian Commission envelopes are shown, both sent to Germany. This was not unusual since 35% of the half million foreign-born who served in the Civil War, attracted by the desire to serve their new homeland and by the enlistment bounty, came from Germany. Foreign-born Germans, of which there were 175,000, represented nearly 9% of the over two million who served on the Northern side.

The United States Sanitary Commission cover with a soldier's letter imprint is addressed to Lamspringe in Germany. The proper 15¢ postage and a New York Paid 15 postal marking in red was applied. On the back is a transit marking in oval from Hamburg with the date 27 10 (18) 65 (October 27, 1865) and a receiving mark of Lamspringe of 10 28 (October 28). (Figs. 206, 207)

The Christian Commission cover is lacking any United States marking and could have found its way into the German mails via two routes. One explanation is that someone carried this envelope to Germany as an unused extra piece of stationery and used it there. The more logical explanation is that the letter was carried outside the mail and was placed in the German mails in Hamburg, a major seaport. It was addressed to Falkenberg; because it lacked postage a manuscript "3" in blue was applied. The destination was more than 10 geographical miles distant but less than 20. (The German or geographical mile equals 7.42 kilometers.) For this distance the uniform German Austrian Postal Union postage was two silber groschen. Because the letter was unpaid, a one silber groschen penalty was applied,

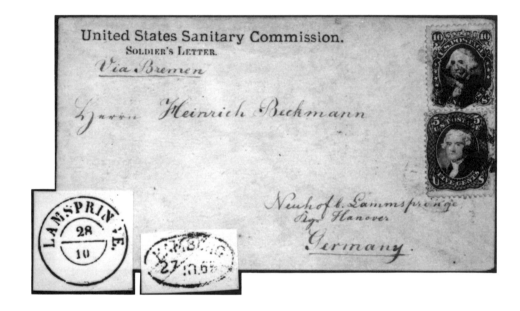

Fig. 206. Foreign usage of Sanitary Commission cover. Paid 15¢ at New York with red postmark. SF5

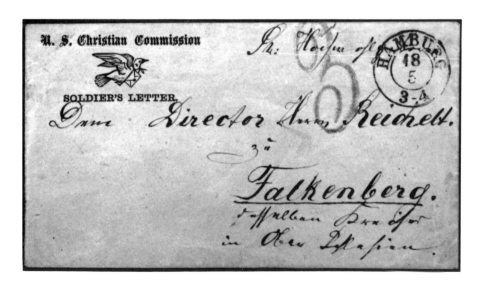

Fig. 207. Christian Commission cover used outside the U.S. mail. Script "3" is for 2 silber groschen plus one silber groschen fine for unpaid or penalty, for a total of three. SF3

Fig. 208. (Top) Shield-type Sanitary Commission corner card, properly endorsed. "Due 3". SF1

(Middle) Cover originated in Louisville. Postage prepaid. "Due 3" in script for forwarding. Had there been a chaplain's endorsement, there would have been no extra charge. SF1

(Bottom) Attractive magenta-colored cover. Lacking proper endorsement, stamped "Due 6" — 3¢ for postage and 3¢ penalty. The Sanitary Commission applied the 3¢ stamp and handstamped oval "Paid by U.S. Sanitary Com.". SF3

making the total three silber groschen. For this explanation we have Allan Radin, a postal historian, to thank.

(Fig. 208, Plate 17)

(Figs. 209, 210, 211)

Another missive, this one written on the stationery of the U.S. Sanitary Commission at Murfreesboro, Tennessee on April 28, 1865, after the end of the war, illustrates the unpleasant task of chaplains to inform parents of a soldier of their son's death.

Murfreesboro, Tenn
April 28th 1865

Mr. R.J. Caddington
Dear Sir

It becomes my painful duty to inform you of the death of Alfred P. Caddington, Co. D, 1st Mich Arttiery [sic], which painful event took place at the U.S. General Hospital at this place on the 15th inst. Permit me to sympathise with you in your sorrow, and assure you your friend died in the most glorious cause that ever called for the efforts of man. He was buried in the *Battle Field Cemetery*. His end was peaceful. Should you desire to remove his remains you can readily do so as his grave is marked. Please inform me what you wish done with his effects. If you wish them sent home send me *Power of Attorney* and I will gladly attend to it for you no charge will be made. Any further information you may desire I will gladly furnish. May God bless you.

Sincerely yours
William Earnshaw
Chaplain U.S.A.

(Fig. 212)

Fig. 209. (Top) Blue oval handstamp "U.S. Sanitary Commission 18 Carondelet St. N.O. (New Orleans)". Endorsed by Chaplain Williams, letter was charged the 3¢ due without penalty for non-prepayment. Postmarked New Orleans, Mar 18, '64. Enclosed letter written to soldier's widow. SF2

(Bottom) Postmarked Cincinnati, Jan 23 (1865). Eight-page letter written by the soldier details army life. The cannoneering that took place at Murfreesboro is described where Confederate General Forrest mounted an attack on that date… "As good luck would have it I am detailed to guard the cattle yard at night and am out of all danger." SF2

Fig. 210. (Top) 3¢ 1861 with plate No. 14, postmarked New York, Feb 17. SF3

(Bottom) Lack of correct soldier's endorsement, stamped "Due 6" — 3¢ postage and 3¢ penalty. Four-page enclosure: "I thought it very uncivil for after they took us Prisoners...told us to pull out our pockets ...they took every thing from me...pocket book with some two or three Postage stamps and about fifty cents in Postage currency..." SF2

Fig. 211. (Top) A homemade Christian Commission mourning cover with proper endorsement. Miamiville, O., Camp Dennison, O(hio) double circle postmark, "Due 3". SF1

(Middle) Required endorsement permitting mail to move without prepayment of postage. "Due 3" handstamp applied, Alexandria, Va. postmark, May 27, '64. SF1

(Bottom) Misuse of soldier's letter endorsement. Note similarity of handwriting of endorsement and address. Both were prepared by the chaplain. The chaplains as officers "whether on official business or not must prepay their mail". The chaplain endorsed the letter and the recipient paid the portion due. The letter was written by the chaplain informing King D. Winans that his son had been "wounded in the thigh...brought in the hospital in a low condition...he gave me his name and post office...He was not in a condition to talk *much*...his thoughts were of the Lord and God...he died about 6 o'clock this morning". SF1

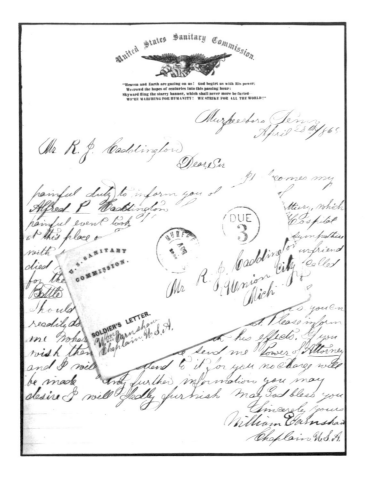
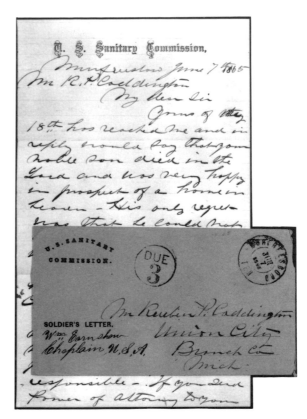

The good Reverend Earnshaw, misusing the endorsement of a soldier's letter, sent the letter unpaid. The recipient paid the 3¢. Apparently the letter did not sit well with the father of Alfred Caddington, as the chaplain in all his feigned sincerity did not even bother to note that the surnames were the same and rather than a friend it was Mr. Caddington's son who was killed. The father replied on May 18 and again on June 7, 1865. Reverend Earnshaw responded—again abusing the postal privilege. Minister Earnshaw or someone else (note the difference in the handwriting and Mr. Caddington's initials) wrote:

Fig. 212. (Left) Endorsed with marking "Due 3" as there was no prepayment by the soldier who was dead. The letter was written by an officer (chaplain) and should have been prepaid. SF2

Fig. 213. (Right) Reverend Earnshaw's second letter to the father of the deceased soldier. SF2

Murfreesboro June 7th, 1865

Mr. R.P. Caddington
My dear Sir

Yours of May 18th has reached me and in reply should say that your noble son died in the Lord and was very happy in prospect of a home in heaven—His only regret was that he could not see you and the rest of the family before he died. His effects are in the hands of the Surgeon in Charge of hospital—and you can get them by writing to him. I have no control over that part—the surgeon is alone responsible—. If you send Power of Attorney to your Nephew he can get them at once and that would be decidedly the best plan. May God bless you—and may you meet your noble son in heaven.

Yours sincerely
William Earnshaw
Chaplain U.S.A.

(Fig. 213)

Despite efforts to deliver each piece of mail, address deficiencies caused thousands of letters to end up at the Dead Letter Office in Washington, D.C. Here each was carefully opened and the contents reviewed. Anything of value was removed, with no mention made in the records as to the disposition of the valuables. Those letters without valuables were returned to the post office from which they were originally mailed if it was possible to ascertain the identity by the postmark or the contents of the letter. Special care was given to letters from parents, siblings, or wives. The local post office would then post a list of the letters that it had on hand from the Dead Letter Office and keep the list on public view for a month. After that period, the letters would be returned to the Dead Letter Office for the second time where they would be destroyed. The letter to Mrs. Olcott follows and is such an example.

The Post Office Department letter, while not strictly a soldier's letter within our definition as stated at the outset of this chapter, fits in nowhere else within this volume. It tells a story of lack of sensitivity in charging postage due, yet good judgment on the part of the Post Office Department in not using the name "Dead Letter Office" in the case of a deceased soldier. The letter returned to Mrs. Olcott addressed to her husband is a tender one and especially a sad one since her husband had died. The instructions to the postmaster appear on the face:

NOTICE TO THE POSTMASTER

The enclosed letter is sent to the writer, under an Act of Congress approved, January 21, 1862. The date of receipt at the Post Office must be marked on the letter, and an entry made in the account of mails received …If not delivered and the postage collected within one month, the reason for non-delivery must be endorsed on it, and it must be returned to the Dead Letter Office, at the time and in the manner prescribed for Return Letters, in Instruction No. 8 published with Act of March 3, 1863. If returned, the letter must be post marked on the sealed side.

It should not be advertised. (Figs. 214, 214A, 215)

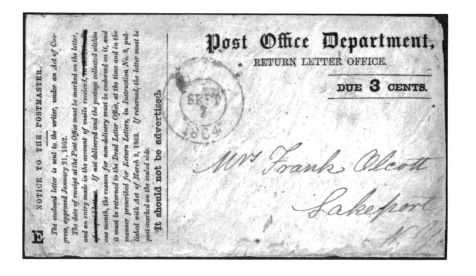

Fig. 214. Printed "Due 3 Cents" —charging the family of the deceased soldier. SF3

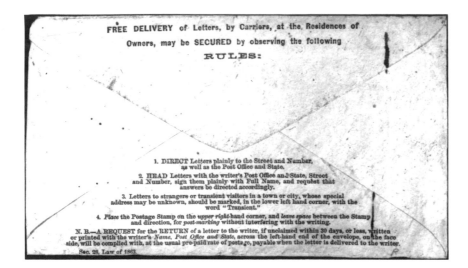

Fig. 214A. (Reverse) Return Letter Office (Dead Letter Office) — giving instructions for free delivery.

Fig. 215. "Unclaimed" letter returned to writer (Mrs. Olcott) per Post Office regulations printed on "Return Letter Office" envelope. SF3

The letter was originally written to Frank Olcott at Fort Haggarty. It was the custom to address all noncommissioned officers and privates as "Mr." during the Civil War. Apparently Mr. Olcott, to whom the letter is addressed, was not with his regiment and the letter was then sent to the General Hospital where it was stamped "UNCLAIMED". Across the left side of the envelope appears a manuscript postmarking of Lakeport, June 15, N.Y., which would be one day after the letter had been written. After the letter went unclaimed, it was sent to the Dead Letter Office where it was opened and read. Since the letter was from a member of the immediate family, it was returned to the family in the Post Office Department envelope. Directly under "Post Office Department" are the words "Return Letter Office". On the third line appears "Due 3 Cents". One can only assume that Mrs. Olcott, after waiting months for the return letter, since the postmark is September 7, 1864, had to pay the non-prepayment due fee of 3¢.

SAILORS' LETTERS

Richard B. Graham wrote a detailed study of Civil War sailors' letters in his article in *The Chronicle of the U.S. Classic Postal Issues*, #58, of May 1968, so the letter to John Yort can shed only a little light on the subject. Like most others, it does not give the point of origin (ship name) as required by postal regulations in order to move without prepayment of postage. What we do know about this cover is that the circular "U.S. Ship 3 cts." provided a means for northern sailors blockading the South to send letters unpaid in accordance with regulations and without the double rate penalty. Mr. Graham makes the point that there are very few covers bearing endorsements or containing letters which indicate their naval origin. We do know that there were many ships guarding the ports along the coast, most of these ports falling early in the war. Even more ships were on blockade duty to stop contraband from going into the South. According to the *Civil War Naval Chronology*, some ships of the navy were specifically designated as mail steamers, such as *Gladiator*, *Electric Spark*, *Fawn*, and *Morning Star*. The "Due 3", as on any soldier's letter unpaid, indicated payment by the recipient but without penalty when endorsed. Note that in accordance with that part of the regulation requiring endorsement this letter was properly endorsed by a chaplain. That fact, however, raises yet another point. (Fig. 216)

Fig. 216. (Top) Due 3¢ naval letter addressed to John Yort. U.S. Ship 3 cts. Circular handstamp "Due 3", addressed to Lowell, Kent County in Michigan. Like most ship covers, there is no indication of ship origin but it probably originated from a U.S. Navy ship on blockade duty. SF3

(Bottom) "U.S. Ship 3 cts." in lieu of 3¢ prepaid postage. New York Branch of U.S. Christian Commission corner card. Savannah, March 29, 1865 four-page letter enclosure. The ship was a federal vessel, otherwise the fee for a private carrier would have been 2¢ plus a penalty, or 4¢ due. SF3

Following the signature of Chaplain Porter on the Yort cover is the designation "U.S.A." (United States Army). This would lead one to believe that ship mail was first carried to an army post where it was then stamped "Ship Mail". Naval chaplains would not ordinarily make up the complement on a ship. It does not appear that any stamping was done aboard ship. As for stamps, it is unlikely that any sailors would attempt to carry a gummed stamp aboard a ship with its high humidity. Military men who served in Pacific areas during World War II recall that in order to preserve the gum on stamps they would first coat them with talcum powder to prevent their sticking together. But if the stamps did stick together, they would bury them in the ground for a time until the moisture would permeate the paper and release them from their neighbors, a procedure that obviously could not be attempted aboard a ship.

Fraudulent embossed covers with the legend "U.S. Sanitary Commission" and "U.S. Christian Commission Soldier's Mail" exist but they were never used during the war and are of a recent vintage. The embossing is sharp and goes through the back portion of the envelope. They are easily detected. (Fig. 217)

Fig. 217. A counterfeit U.S. Sanitary Commission Soldiers Mail cover; determined by bold embossing.

Aboard a ship: "Mail from the North"

Aboard ship: "Pleasures of Letter Writing: Mercury 98°F"

XV

HOSPITAL AND HOSPITAL TRANSPORT MAIL

The Naval Hospital "Red Rover."

The opening gun shots of the Civil War fired near a stream little known at the time ushered in the human miseries of the next four years. Here at Bull Run near Manassas, Virginia on July 21, 1861 General Irwin McDowell of the North faced General Pierre Beauregard of the South. The resultant carnage left the wounded and dead strewn on the battlefield with the Medical Department of the United States Army under W.S. King ill-equipped, ill-advised, and incapable of dealing with the wounded. Most of them were either left to die on the battlefield or, by their own sheer determination, walked the 30 miles back to Washington to be met by unprepared and inexperienced medical department personnel. Medical practitioners in 1861 still had not heard of Louis Pasteur, whose germ theory of disease was not known until 1862, and Lister's work on infection was not accepted until 1867. Fortunately, ether and chloroform were known and in general use where available. Bleeding and purgation were accepted practices and "laudable pus" was encouraged.

The North started with 114 officers and three clerks in the Medical Department. One general hospital with only 40 beds existed in Fort Leavenworth, Kansas. Up to this point in time the army had been concerned primarily with encounters with the Indians of the West.

At the top of the chain of command of the Medical Department of the United States Army was the Surgeon General. On April 25, 1862, over the opposition of regular army surgeons and Secretary of War Stanton, William Alexander Hammond, with Lincoln's approval, was appointed Surgeon General of the United States Army. Stanton, in August of 1864, succeeded in bringing court martial proceedings against Hammond over Hammond's order to ban the use of mercury and calomel as medicines for internal use and charges (which were later unfounded) of diverting government funds. Before his release from the army, Hammond was credited with many advances in military medicine, including care of the sick and wounded, lowering the death rate, lowering the medical department expenses, and establishing government laboratories to test medical supplies.

In 1879 President Rutherford B. Hayes reversed the court martial and restored Hammond to the rolls as Surgeon General. (Fig. 218, Plate 18)

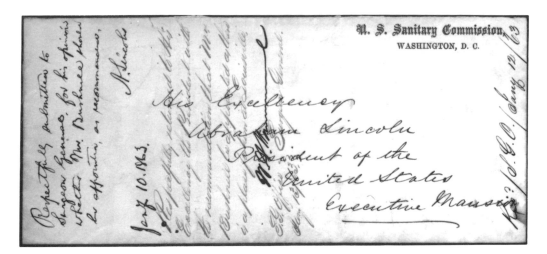

Fig. 218. Lincoln endorsement and Surgeon General Hammond endorsement. SF5

Respectfully submitted to Surgeon General, for his opinion whether Mr. Bushnell should be appointed, as recommended.

A. Lincoln

Jany 10. 1863.

Respectfully returned to His Excellency the President with the recommendation that Mr. Bushnell be appointed as there is a place for him at Louisville,

W. A. Hammond
Surgeon General

S. G. Office
Jany 13/63.

The Confederate Medical Department was organized only two months before the bombardment of Ft. Sumter and was made up of Surgeon General Samuel Preston Moore, four surgeons, and six assistant surgeons.

Prior to the era of improved medical arts that were to evolve out of the Civil War, relatively few battlefield casualties survived. Northern regulations provided that hospital accommodations be allotted in proportion to the number of men on the regimental rolls. The wounded's first encounter with the military medical services was a small tent that had little in common with the large civilian hospitals that existed then. Through later experience and largely through the efforts of the United States Sanitary Commission, it was demonstrated that pavilion-type hospitals which provided adequate ventilation to minimize airborne infection, sufficient nurses and doctors, and proper food preparation and surgical facilities could best serve the wounded and sick and consequently aid in their recovery.

As the regimental tents filled up to their capacity with the sick and wounded, other cover was sought or commandeered. A regulation canvas shelter, a neighboring house, train depot, school, church, factory or any other large building could be turned into a brigade or general hospital. As a result, the numbers of these hospitals proliferated until at the end of the war more than twenty-five hundred army-commandeered hospitals and facilities existed.

Early in the war the hospitals were opened in the home states of the soldiers on the theory that a man who required hospitalization would be better taken care of by his own home folks. This was a good thing for the soldier and he did secure care better than he might have in the field, but the practice opened up more abuses than it cured. Once a soldier left the army and returned to his state, he was no longer under the control of the national government. Control then often rested with a powerful state politician who at that time might be more interested in garnering hometown votes than in trying to return a soldier to duty. As a result, that soldier could either be lost to the service by confinement for a longer period than otherwise might be the case, or he could leave the service altogether, or, if he had a skill needed around the hospital, he could be detailed there indefinitely.

The first Union military hospitals were opened in Washington at the E Street Infirmary and the Union Hotel, both receiving patients in May 1861. The Infirmary was destroyed by fire accidentally in November and the Union Hotel was abandoned a year later, with

President Lincoln

patients being directed to the recently established Cliffburne Hospital. Where the army could not build hospitals fast enough or did not have sufficient casualties in an area to warrant its own facilities, contracts were made with local civilian hospitals at the rate of 50¢ to 75¢ daily per bed. The Mason Hospital in Boston was a private residence given rent-free by its owner; it was the only general hospital established in Boston during the war and for the greater part of the war the only government hospital in Massachusetts. Later on Readsville and Dale General Hospitals were established. The Hygeia Hotel, Fort Monroe, Virginia near Old Point Comfort, was for a time the only hospital south of the Department of Washington. Later on the Chesapeake Female Seminary was converted to the Chesapeake Hospital.

As needs increased more hospitals came into being. At Lexington, Kentucky, for example, the University buildings were pressed into service; at Quincy, Illinois a furniture factory became a hospital; at Louisville a machine shop and a plow factory became hospitals; at Helena, Arkansas the residence of Confederate General Hindman became a hospital; at Little Rock, St. John's College, a former Confederate hospital, became a Union institution, and so down the line hospitals were established where none had existed before. While all these preparations were for white troops, the black troops' hospitals were established in sheds that had been cotton presses or warehouses. Even barns and stables where tetanus was endemic were used for black troops. When walled in and ventilated by louvered turrets, it was said that "they made excellent wards".

The Judiciary Square and Mount Pleasant Hospitals in Washington, D.C., built in early winter of 1861–1862, were the first two institutions that followed plans and suggestions of the Sanitary Commission for the construction of hospitals. They were placed on high ground and were of the pavilion type, that is, elongated so that each bed was close to a window with adequate ventilation rather than the box construction older hospitals offered. Each hospital had five pavilion wards that measured 84 feet by 28 feet. While these two hospitals served as a prototype for future institutions, there were serious construction and sanitation errors that were corrected in future buildings.

The Surgeon in Charge had full and complete military command or authority over a hospital. While officers of a higher rank may have been detailed to a hospital, as in the case when it became necessary to guard military prisoners, it was always the Surgeon in Charge who had the final authority concerning hospital matters. Next to the Surgeon in Charge was the Executive Officer. Among his other duties was the responsibility for the movement of mail within the hospital, both in and out. At the bottom of the chain of command were the chaplains[36] who were attached to most of the large hospitals. In addition to furnishing the spiritual needs of the wounded and sick, the chaplain maintained a list of the names and addresses of the nearest of kin of the soldiers. Further, he was expected to see that letters were written to family members if the soldier could not write or read letters that were received. The chaplain was in charge of mail services at the larger hospitals as well as the reading rooms, library, and cemetery.

As the numbers of troops increased and as more illiterates were pressed into service either as volunteers or through bounties, it was soon apparent that the chaplain could no longer minister to the spiritual needs as well as the temporal needs. It should be noted that as time went on some of the letter writing and reading became the function of women in these hospitals. With more women in hospital attendance, leaving the home in larger and larger numbers where they once had been confined, they now were liberated, so to speak. They not only performed valuable ward services in the form of nursing and record keeping but it was they who accounted for many of the letters that moved in and out of the hospitals. At the same time women no longer were satisfied with the more menial tasks and began to assert themselves. Most women had already indicated a willingness to share in the work of the home front through civilian paramilitary works or through fair fund raising.

A hospital ward

36. Under the terms of the Volunteer Act of 1861 each chaplain had to be a "regular ordained minister of some Christian denomination". The restrictive language excluded rabbis but provided the first recognition of Roman Catholic priests to serve as chaplains. It was not until Rabbi Arnold Fischel, representing the Board of Delegates of American Israelites, won the approval of President Lincoln that rabbis could serve as chaplains. A year later, in 1862, the law was amended to read "a regularly ordained minister of some religious denomination".

A lay delegate in the hospital

Now they wanted a more active voice in matters. It can be said that the presence of women within the wards listening to wounded and spiritless soldiers whose morale had been sorely tried gave rise in some ways to the now-acknowledged benefits of sharing one's inner thoughts and emotions with another human being; their service could be called a forerunner of the field of psychotherapy. Soldiers away from home, and many of them very young, received encouragement if not treatment from the women who were called into the wards by the chaplains.

While some soldiers' letters were written in pencil, spelled and punctuated poorly and generally illegible, many letters in a neat and orderly handwriting survive. One can assume that many soldiers unable to write for various reasons often called upon visitors to the hospitals to write their letters. Off-duty musicians from marching bands had as one of their duties the added task of working in hospitals and assisting in letter writing. It can also be assumed that a hospital letter could have been written by someone from either the Sanitary Commission or Christian Commission or a lay person.

Writing paper, the library, and postage were provided at many of the larger hospitals out of the "slush" fund which was built up from the sale of bones, fat, stale bread, slops, straw, and old newspapers to farmers for their livestock. A tax on sutlers further contributed to this fund. At McClellan Hospital and Harewood Hospital this averaged as much as $250 a month. Libraries were established and newspapers provided for the patients; some of the larger hospitals even had printing presses. Off these presses came the hospital newspaper and probably the hospital envelopes much sought after today. In the list of stores purchased by the Medical Department of the Army there is no listing of envelopes ever being purchased for soldiers' use.

Opium was regarded as one of the useful medications in the Civil War. It was prescribed in the treatment of post-surgery pain, wounds, and dysentery. Quinine was used for fevers, including "miasma fever" (a disease that can best be described as a fever resulting from mist, dew or fog—a disease that defies present-day medical terminology). Few soldiers escaped the use of opium and this accounted for much addiction following the war. This addiction gave rise to the popularization of patent medicines, many of which used a narcotic as a base and served to satisfy the craving for this habit-forming drug. The widespread use of these patent medicines brought on the taxing of them and out of this evolved the "match and medicine" stamps; this in turn gave rise to yet another field of stamp collecting. Despite the Harrison Narcotic Act of 1914 limiting the use of drugs, their abuse is still with us. While opium and morphine were being used, they were always in relatively short supply and where the drugs could not be obtained, whiskey was used as a substitute. Whiskey had the added advantage of its alcohol content being used for a disinfectant; what was left was quickly disposed of in other fashions.[37]

Medical officers captured on a battlefield at first were treated as prisoners of war. It was not uncommon for a medical officer to abandon his patients when it appeared that he might be captured and faced imprisonment. In 1862, both sides agreed to treat medical officers as non-combatants and to release all medical prisoners. This agreement was suspended for a time but in 1863 the plan was resumed and maintained until the end of the war.

A list of the regimental and battalion hospitals would be almost impossible to assemble. It is estimated that while the number of general hospitals totaled close to 110 facilities there were approximately 2,400 additional places where the injured were housed. A roster of general hospitals giving their location and capacity as of December 17, 1864 follows in Appendix II.

Postal covers originating from northern hospitals must be considered scarce. Covers originating out of southern hospitals are even scarcer. Northern hospitals, because of slush funds, sometimes used special "corner cards" or cachets, but this is not true of southern hospitals. With some northern hospital covers, it is possible to encounter a printed corner

37. "Drug Addiction: 'The Army Disease'", by Byron Stinson, *American History Illustrated*, December 1971.

card, but it is more likely that the collector will have to rely on either a handstamp or a manuscript indication of origin within a hospital. Not to be overlooked are the contents of a Civil War letter that may contain information that a soldier was confined to a hospital. Some of the hospitals even prepared letterheads that would identify them and their location. The more elaborate designs were sold by sutlers or to the general public through retail channels.

Usually general hospitals were located near a waterway, a railroad, a theater of operation or a city that could furnish personnel for a hospital. Covers are known from some of these hospitals. The U.S.A. General Hospital, Div. No. I at Annapolis was located on Chesapeake Bay close to operations on the Rappahannock and James Rivers thereby permitting the evacuation of the wounded via hospital steamers. Two covers shown here were

Fig. 219. (Top) U.S.A. General Hospital, Div. No. I (753 beds) in Annapolis, Annapolis postmark. SF2

(Middle) U.S. Army General Hospital on Holliday Street identified by enclosure as the former Continental Hotel. Postmarked Baltimore, Feb 17 (1863). SF2

(Bottom) U.S. Army General Hospital on Holliday Street in Baltimore, May 21 (1863), Baltimore postmark. Both covers addressed to James Evson but in different hands. The letter enclosed is in yet another hand. SF2

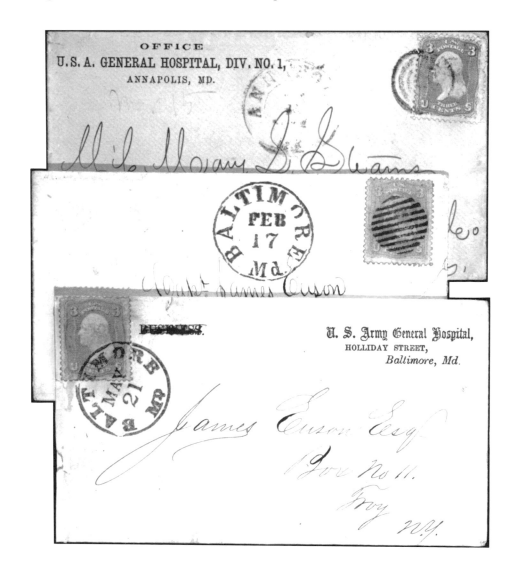

postmarked Baltimore and were from the General Hospital on Holliday Street. The Patterson Park Hospital at Baltimore cover has been postmarked at Alexandria, Va. The Knight Hospital in New Haven envelope bears a clear New Haven postmark. The U.S.A. General Hospital at Fort Schuyler, N.Y. corner card confirms the location of the hospital known as McDougall General Hospital. The DeCamp General Hospital was situated at Pelham, New York. New Albany in Indiana just across the Ohio River from Louisville housed one of the major hospitals. Other examples of hospital covers to and from other cities confirm the existence of strategically placed medical facilities. (Fig. 219) (Fig. 220, Plate 19) (Figs. 221, 222, 223)

Fig. 220. Patterson Park General Hospital (1,350 beds) in Baltimore. Postmarked Alexandria, Va., Nov 2, '64. A Charles Magnus cover. SF5

Fig. 221. (Top) Knight General Hospital (607 beds), New Haven, Conn. with New Haven postmark and Star of David cancel. SF2

(Middle) McDougall General Hospital (1,184 beds) at Fort Schuyler, N.Y., May 1863, Ft. Schuyler postmark. SF2

(Bottom) De Camp General Hospital (1,700 beds) at David's Island, New York Harbor with Pelham, N.Y. postmark. SF2

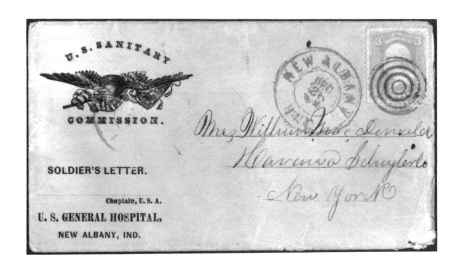

Fig. 222. U.S. General Hospital at New Albany, Ind. (860 beds), New Albany, Indiana postmark, Dec 26, 1864. SF2

Fig. 223. (Top, middle) Jefferson General Hospital at Jeffersonville, Indiana was one of the larger general hospitals, which may account for the several different types of corner cards. With 2,399 beds the hospital presumably had its own printing press. Two varieties of covers from the Jefferson General Hospital at Jeffersonville, Indiana. Postmarked Louisville, Jun 19, (18)63. Postmarked Jeffersonville, Indiana, Aug 12. SF2

(Bottom) By 1864, Jefferson General Hospital had its name changed to Joe Holt Hospital in honor of Judge Joseph Holt who sat on the court-martial trial of Lincoln's assassins. SF2

The Jefferson General Hospital at Jeffersonville, Indiana, across the river from Louis-ville, was one of the larger general hospitals, which may account for the existence of several different types of corner cards. With 2,399 beds the hospital probably had its own printing press. This hospital was so placed in Indiana because of its proximity to the western theater and because both Governor Oliver Perry Morton of Indiana and Judge Joseph Holt had largely been responsible for keeping Indiana out of the Confederacy.

Another style corner card of Jefferson General Hospital is shown, with the postmark of that town. A hospital this size would probably have had a resident agent of the United States Sanitary Commission who may have applied the postage stamp to the letter. In accordance with regulations, had it not been stamped it would have been necessary for the chaplain to apply his endorsement certifying that the letter was a soldier's letter; it then could have been forwarded without the prepayment of postage. The soldier's message is enclosed.

The Clay General Hospital No. 2 was located in Louisville, Kentucky, and while a small hospital with only 178 beds, its corner card is a distinctive one and is similar to Walcott #2236.[38] The Louisville postmark dated Mar 3 1863 is in the upper right corner where ordinarily the three-cent stamp might be expected. Rather, there is a proper soldier's en-

38. *The George Walcott Collection of Used Civil War Patriotic Covers*, compiled by Robert Laurence, 1934. The Walcott Catalogue lists and pictures many of these scarce and colorful corner cards.

Fig. 224. Clay General Hospital No. 2 in Louisville. Bold "DUE 3", design similar to Walcott #2236. SF3

Fig. 225. Letter mailed to a soldier and then forwarded to Hospital No. 19 at Nashville where he was confined. Three one-cent blues (#63). SF2

dorsement; the postmaster, instead of applying a "Due 6" which would have been the original postage and a penalty, has only indicated a "Due 3". (Figs. 224, 225)

An interesting example of forwarding soldiers' mail is the cover addressed to a soldier in the hospital at Nashville, Tennessee. The Union forces had occupied Nashville since February 25, 1862. The cover has three 1¢ blues (#63) that have been pen canceled. On the back appears the notation in the soldier's hand, "Received Monday August 24th, 1863, from Sister Rachel. This letter went to the front and was sent back to me. Answered". Had this letter been sent to a civilian and then forwarded, another 3¢ would have been due. Prepaid letters to soldiers could be "forwarded" from point to point, as the location of their regiments changed, without extra charge.

(Fig. 226, Plate 20)

Fig. 226. (Top) Originating at Potomac Creek Hospital (993 beds), canceled with bold "PAID", addressed to the Sanitary Commission in Washington. SF2

(Middle) Webster General Hospital (475 beds) at Manchester, N.H., 2¢ (#73) drop letter rate. SF3

(Bottom) Chester General Hospital (878 beds) at Chester, Pa., addressed to Paris with 30¢ orange (#71) tied by grid and red Philadelphia "24" transit. Red French Calais, Dec. 1, '62 transit marking and Paris (on reverse), Dec. 2 transit. SF5

There were 12 general hospitals of note in Philadelphia, including Germantown. All were well-organized and efficient when judged by the standards of the time. Satterlee General Hospital, also known as West Philadelphia General Hospital, with a total of 3,519 beds was the largest of any of the Union institutions. Since there were so many patients, it was necessary that more than one chaplain certify the unpaid soldiers' mail. The hospital had its own postmaster, William Alexander Bulkley, who also served as the hospital steward. (Fig. 227)

The advertised cover from Satterlee General Hospital is postmarked Mar 5, 1864 from Philadelphia. Addressed to Mr. David E. Downey at St. Lawrence County in New York, it was then stamped "Advertised Mar 14", some nine days later. It was a post office practice to advertise in a local newspaper that undeliverable mail was being held to be picked up. A fee of 1¢ was added for mail so advertised for pick-up. (Figs. 228, 229, 230, 231, 232, 233, 233A, 234, 235)

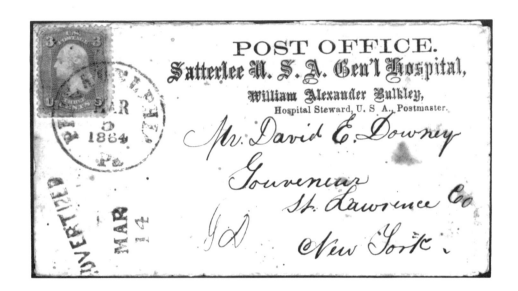

Fig. 227. "Advertised" cover originating at the Post Office in Satterlee General Hospital (3,519 beds) in Philadelphia. SF3

Fig. 228. (Top) Chaplain V. West endorsement, from Satterlee Hospital, "Due 3¢", letter enclosed. SF2

(Middle) Satterlee Hospital chaplain hand-stamp on Sanitary Commission shield corner card, Philadelphia postmark. SF2

(Bottom) Satterlee Hospital patriotic cover in purple, 3¢ 1861, postmarked Philadelphia. SF3

Fig. 229. (Top) Summit House General Hospital (1,204 beds) in Philadelphia. Endorsed "Soldier's letter". SF2

(Middle) Broad Street General Hospital (525 beds) in Philadelphia. SF2

(Bottom) Cuyler General Hospital (646 beds) located in Germantown, now a suburb of Philadelphia. Philadelphia, Sep 14 postmark used as cancellation. Germantown Sep 14 postmark on reverse. SF2

Fig. 230. (Top) McClellan General Hospital (1,089 beds) in Philadelphia. U.S. Sanitary Commission shield. Script lower left "in hast(e)". Chaplain endorsement. One of the larger hospitals, it owned a printing press and used it for imprinting the endorsement. The envelope was furnished by the Commission. SF2

(Bottom) Rubber-stamped oval Sanitary Commission corner card includes Philadelphia under "U.S.". Chaplain's endorsement is on affixed label. SF3

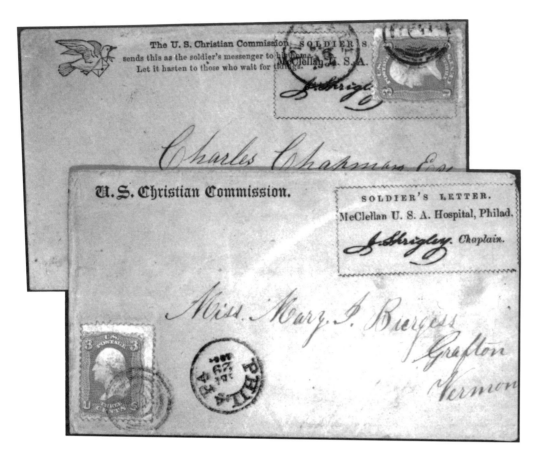

Fig. 231. (Top) Three-cent (#65) over chaplain's endorsement. These two covers originating from McClellan General Hospital show that although the chaplain's label was available the Christian Commission applied the postage. SF2

(Bottom) The Christian Commission corner card from McClellan U.S.A. Hospital, Philadelphia postmark. SF2

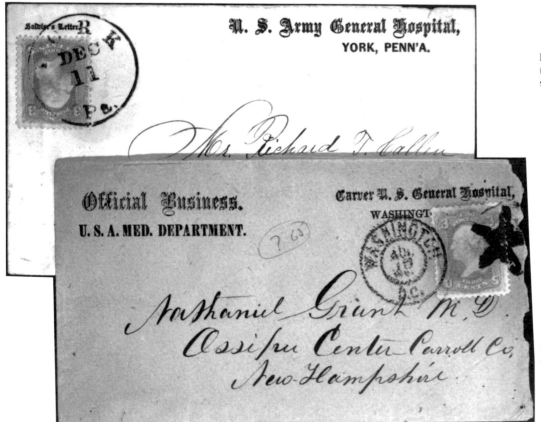

Fig. 232. (Top) York (Pa.) General Hospital (1,600 beds), York, Pa., Dec 11 postmark. SF2

(Bottom) Carver General Hospital (1,300 beds) in Washington, D.C., star cancellation. SF2

Fig. 233. Mount Pleasant General Hospital (1,618 beds) in Washington, D.C. Washington with 16 hospitals had the distinction of having the largest number of hospital beds. It also had the distinction of being one of the unhealthiest cities.

Fig. 233A. (Reverse) Sangerfield, N.Y. postmark. While other examples of overall hospital views exist in color, this is one of the few used covers. SF5

Fig. 234. (Top) Lovell General Hospital (1,464 beds) in Portsmouth Grove, R.I., Portsmouth Grove, Jan 10 postmark. Upper right oval embossed design. SF2

(Middle) Lovell General Hospital corner card, Baldwin City, Kan(sas) postmark. SF3

(Bottom) Originating in Portsmouth Grove, R.I. From an army surgeon to a navy surgeon, showing prepayment of official mail between two commands was necessary. SF3

In the *Sanitary Reporter* of July 1, 1864, Louisville, regulations clearly state that even official mail going from one command to another must be prepaid:

> Surgeons in charge of hospitals, and officers of Posts and Barracks, having occasion to address official communications to officers and others in the field, will be careful *to prepay in full* postage when intended to be sent by mail.
>
> Failure to do so subjects such matters to double charges and causes its detention at the Post Office until the persons addressed shall pay the amount due and in many cases results in its total failure to reach its destination.

Wm. L. Kelly
Special Agent P.O. Dept.
In charge of mails,
Military Division of the
Miss.

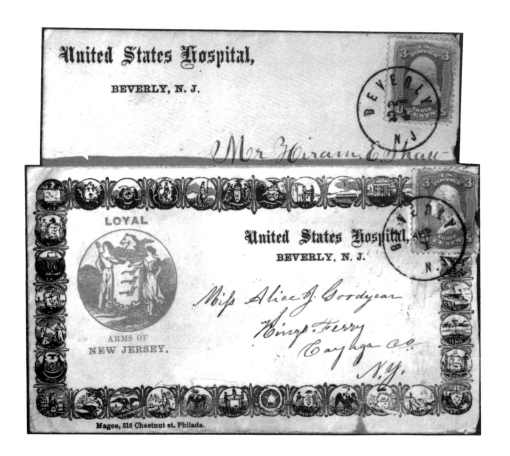

Fig. 235. (Top) Beverly General Hospital in Beverly, N.J. (1,000 beds). SF2

(Bottom) Beverly General Hospital added to the total of 136,894 beds for all Army General Hospitals in all cities during the Civil War. By the end of the war, as much as possible, hospitals were established away from Washington, D.C. and Philadelphia. SF3

The three Giffin covers tell the whole story of the misery and suffering of the Civil War. Lt. Dan S. Giffin on July 31, 1863, while stationed in Washington with the 142nd Regiment of the New York Volunteers, received the first letter. Apparently all was well with him. By the time he was to receive the second letter postmarked at Malone, New York on April 18, 1864, his regiment had moved to Kiowak Island in South Carolina and now Captain Giffin, either wounded or ill, had been moved to Chesapeake Hospital at Fort Monroe in Ward 4. Once again, on May 21, 1864, a letter was sent to Captain Giffin at the Chesapeake

Hospital but this time the forwarding address has been crossed out and there appears the dreaded handstamp "DEAD RETURN TO SENDER". To the left appears a half-circle handstamp "MISSENT" and "FORWARDED", and in the lower right is a postmark Hamilton, N.Y., Jun 6 '64. Along the left side appears a manuscript postmark or marking of Hamilton St. Law(rence) Co. N.Y. (Fig. 236)

Fig. 236. The three Giffin covers. SF4

Included within the James Enson cover from the Third Division General Hospital is a letter written by A.D. Teachout, M.D., a private doctor, to the Surgeon in Charge of that institution. (Fig. 237) The letter reads as follows:

> Private James Henry Enson of Battery K 7th Regiment N.Y. Heavy Artillery having applied for a certificate on which to ground an application for an extension of furlough I hereby certify that I have had him under my care since his return home for a severe wound in the thigh received at the battle of cold harbour and that he will not be able to report at the King Street Hospital at Alexandria for several weeks to come and further that he is unfit for duty and will not be able to report in thirty days and therefore ask to have his furlough extended that length of time.

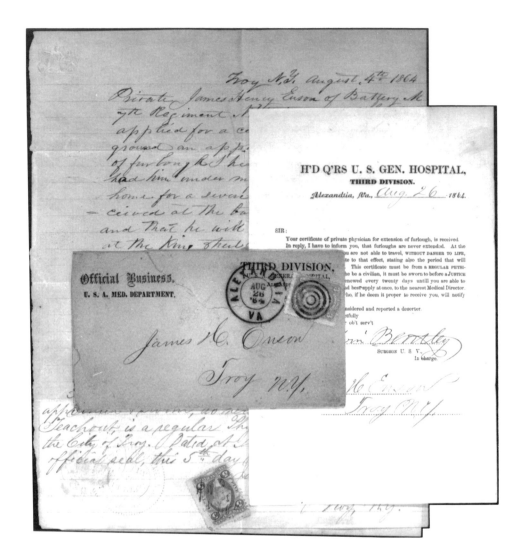

Fig. 237. Official Business U.S.A. Med. Department corner card. To James H. Enson from the Third Division General Hospital (1,350 beds) in Alexandria, Virginia with interesting enclosures. SF3

The letter was then signed by the doctor. Appearing directly below the doctor's affidavit is a sworn statement of a notary public, and to this the notary affixed his seal and a 5¢ Inland Internal Revenue stamp (#R27) and dated the document August 5, 1864. To further verify the truth of the doctor's statement, Edwin Brownell, the Clerk of the Rensselaer County, added his notary seal and affixed another 5¢ Inland Internal Revenue stamp similar to the previous one.

The letter was then dispatched to the Third Division Hospital where on August 26, 1864, Edwin Bently, Surgeon U.S.V. (United States Volunteers) in charge, sent James Enson a form letter acknowledging receipt of the certificate from his private physician for an extension. Obviously, as the surgeon's reply was on a form, there must have been many such requests. The military surgeon writes in the form letter that furloughs are never extended and that unless a set procedure is followed the recipient must report or be considered a deserter. Along with the form from the Surgeon in Charge, the doctor's letter and the two notary statements were returned to the soldier in the same envelope.

A postmark and killer cancel appear on the cover addressed to Reverend Jeremiah Porter, Chaplain United States Volunteers at McPherson General Hospital at Vicksburg. (Killer cancels were used to prevent the reuse of stamps. Had the stamp been placed on the right rather than the left, the cancel would have obliterated the stamp as intended.) Vicksburg had fallen to the Union, under General Grant, on July 4, 1863. General McPherson, after whom this hospital was named, was killed at the Battle of Atlanta on July 22, 1864, therefore dating this cover sometime after this date. (Fig. 238)

On September 4, 1864 Atlanta fell and was occupied by four army corps commanded by General William T. Sherman including the XIV Corps, which was the final destination of the registered letter to Mr. Louwis Fritz at the 7th Ward Hospital. On June 30, 1863, the registration fee of 20¢ had been put into effect and was to be paid in cash. The 3¢ 1861 stamp was canceled with a "Registered" handstamp. A clear Cincinnati, O. postmark dated Nov 4 appears in the lower left and the U.S.D.L.O. (U.S. Dead Letter Office) marking on the right. (Fig. 239)

Fig. 238. To the chaplain at McPherson General Hospital in Vicksburg, Miss., post-marked Memphis, Tenn., Oct 28. SF1

Fig. 239. Registered hospital letter with U.S. Dead Letter Office marking. SF3

As the war wound down there was less and less need for hospitals and medical installations. A hospital, never a comfortable or healthy place to be confined in the Civil War, was always rife with opportunists and many do-gooders. It was not uncommon for agents of the Christian Commission and Tract Societies to make their way through the wards beseeching a wounded soldier to accept Christ before he died. In some instances the agents would offer an orange to a scurvy-ridden soldier in exchange for his commitment to accept "the ways of the Lord". All through the war the lack of ascorbics was a serious concern and resulted in the ravages of scurvy. The soldier pictured is being offered an orange which was rich in Vitamin C and a valuable source of ascorbic acid.

While general hospitals occupied the major concern and efforts of the Medical Department of the Army, there were many hundreds of hastily converted shelters including homes that had been pressed into service. By the end of the war many owners of these homes and shelters had come to depend on the income from the billeting of troops on their premises.

Barely three weeks after the assassination of President Lincoln, Adele Douglas, owner of one of these private shelters, wrote President Johnson asking that he not close her hospital that she refers to as Douglas Place. Note that Mrs. Douglas' letter is written on mourning stationery. It reads:

"THAT'S WORTH A HUNDRED DOLLARS." Page 310.

Fruits and vegetables helped eliminate scurvy

> To the President.
>
> I learn that it is the purpose of the government soon to give up the buildings rented from private citizens, for army hospitals and as such a step would if taken at this time seriously affect my interests as I am wholly dependent upon the rent for the support of myself and my children of the Douglas Hospital I beg leave to call your attention to the subject and to request that it may be retained by the government so long as it can consistently be used for the public interest.
>
> The building has been adapted for Hospital purposes and much money has been already expended upon it for those men. At this season I could not rent it for a private residence and its occupation as a hospital will of course prejudice it for some time. Hoping that my petition will meet with a favorable hearing I am, with great respects
>
> Adele Douglas
>
> Douglas Place, May 4 1865.

President Johnson on May 5, 1865, only one day later, referred her letter to the Surgeon General and indicated that her request was a reasonable one, and sought to have Douglas Hospital, as he now called it, kept on the rolls. His signed endorsement with "President U.S." only 20 days after his being sworn in, makes this association of the President and hospitals even more interesting. The endorsement written by a clerk but signed by President Johnson is as follows:

> Executive Office
> Washington City
> May 5. 1865.
>
> Respectfully referred to the Surgeon General U.S. Army. It is my desire that Mrs. Douglas should be gratified in the very reasonable request expressed within, and I therefore respectfully ask that the Surgeon General direct the retention of the Douglas Hospital so long as it can be consistently held and used for hospital purposes.
>
> Andrew Johnson
> President U.S.
>
> Inform Mrs. Douglas of the President's decision.

(Fig. 240)

Hospital train

Interior of a hospital railroad car

Advertisement for use of hospital railroad cars

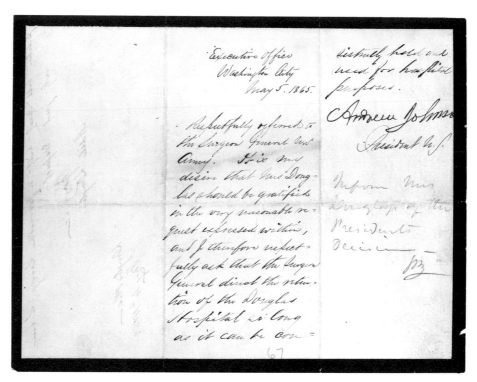

Fig. 240. President Andrew Johnson letter, May 5, 1865, concerning the closing of a Washington hospital following the end of hostilities the previous month. SF5

HOSPITAL TRANSPORTS

RAILROADS

The railroads, so heavily relied upon to supply and to move troops, were also used to evacuate the wounded from the battles. Once the injured were removed from the battlefield by the ambulance corps, they were then sent north either by modified railroad cars or boats. The railroad cars and their design were largely the result of the Sanitary Commission's studies of how best to handle the injured. It was mainly through the United States Sanitary Commission that a plan was evolved for the removal of the wounded through the ambulance corps. The Commission was instrumental in seeking the change from the two-wheel ambulance with its rough ride to the four-wheel "Tripler" or "Coolidge" wagon and its smoother ride.

A contemporary broadside advised that a special Soldiers' Railway Ambulance Car would be provided with stretchers on elastic springs and easy hospital chairs for the wounded... "fare at government rates." Each car was under the supervision of the Sanitary Commission, which designed many of the appliances and devices that aided in the comfort and treatment of the wounded. The *Documents of the Sanitary Commission* and *The Sanitary Commission Bulletin* were a source of knowledge and information used by the surgeons and their own field people.

As of this writing, no special marking or cancellation for hospital railroad covers is known. This is understandable because of the physical condition of the newly wounded, the physical limitations of the railroad cars, and the short distance usually traveled.

WATER TRANSPORTS

The river system, particularly in the Western Department, lent itself readily to the evacuation of the wounded aboard a hospital transport. In order to evacuate a soldier, however, it was necessary for the quartermaster to shunt aside what he considered first priority, namely war materiel, for the ever-expendable soldier, and it could be days before a quartermaster ship lifted anchor and moved in the direction of a hospital. Because of these delays and the need for troop carriers, the first hospital ship, the *City of Memphis*, was commissioned in September 1863. With the cooperation of James E. Yeatman, president of the Western Sanitary Commission, the steamer *D.A. January*, later the *U.S. Hospital Steamer Charles McDougall*, was purchased and placed on active duty. When it became apparent that these two transports alone could not take care of the wounded, two of the largest steamers on the Mississippi, the *Empress* and the *Imperial*, were added to the fleet.

"The Sister(s)" of the Order of the Holy Cross, the first navy nurses

Over the years of attempting to form a hospital cover collection, the authors found that while hospital covers are scarce, covers from hospital ships are very scarce, and the example shown herein is the only one that has been acquired. Confinement on a hospital ship was usually for no more than a few days. The soldiers evacuated in this manner were the more seriously wounded. The supplies of pencils and paper were almost nonexistent and in most cases the would-be writers of the letters were incapable of writing as a result of their injuries. These vessels were not general hospitals and did not have a chaplain assigned to their complement, and it was the chaplains' department that would have been in charge of the mail. At best, accommodations were spartan and mail was not given a high priority.

At the beginning of the war the ships were under the control of the Quartermaster Department, but later on as the number of hospital ships increased, they were placed under the direction of the Medical Department of the Army. Regulations provided that in the transporting of troops an agent of administration for the Sanitary Commission had to be appointed for each vessel "who will be regarded by those on board as responsible for the ship's fittings and supplies." Further regulations provided:

> Each vessel will be divided into hospital wards, designed each for the accommodation of from fifty to one hundred and fifty patients. In case of convalescents, a larger number will be properly included in a ward.
>
> Surgeons, assistant surgeons and two or more nurses per ward on duty. Before patients are taken on board, the vessel should be properly moored or placed, gangways or other means of entrance arranged and performance of other duties completed.

The Western Sanitary Commission, always separate from the United States Sanitary Commission, ran a fleet of its own on the waterways of the western campaign area. These ships included some of the following:

> *R.C. Wood*, originally called the *City of Louisiana*, ran from Pittsburg Landing, Tennessee (Shiloh) to northern points; in charge of Surgeon Thomas F. Azpell, U.S.V.
> *D.A. January* ran from Tennessee and the lower Mississippi to northern hospitals; in charge of Surgeon A.H. Huff, U.S.V.
> *Red Rover*, captured from the Confederacy at Island #10 and purchased by the Western Sanitary Commission for $3,500; in charge of Assistant Surgeon G.H. Bixby, U.S.N. This sidewheeler was the Navy's first hospital vessel. The nursing staff was headed by the Sisters of the Order of the Holy Cross, the forerunner of the Navy Nurse Corps. They were the first women on any naval ship in service.
> *City of Memphis* ran between the lower Mississippi and hospitals of Mem-

phis; in charge of Surgeon W.D. Tunner, U.S.A. and later, Surgeon S.A. Sprague, U.S.A.

City of Nashville, permanently located near Milliken's Bend, Louisiana; in charge of Surgeon L. D. Strawbridge, U.S.A.

Temporary steamers were:

Empress, which made six trips between Tennessee and the Mississippi River.

Imperial, in charge of Surgeon J.H. Grove, U.S.V.; in service only two months. It and the *Empress* were the first two large steamers pressed into hospital service.

City of Alton.

Ruth evacuated the wounded from Vicksburg and Arkansas posts.

Ships operated by the United States Sanitary Commission on the East Coast used in the evacuation of wounded soldiers included:

Sea steamers, fitted for long passages outside coastal waters:

S.R. Spaulding	*Daniel Webster No. 1*

Coast steamers which had to make harbor on the approach of a storm and could not be sent beyond Philadelphia, unless the necessity was urgent:

Elm City	*Commodore*
State of Maine	*Kennebec*
John Brooks	*Daniel Webster No. 2*

Coast steamers which could not be run outside a safe anchorage at all:

Vanderbilt	*Louisiana*
William Whilden	*Knickerbocker*

Sailing vessels adapted to be used as stationary hospitals or for towing outside a harbor:

St. Mark	*Enterpe*

Other ships designated as temporary evacuation ships or hospital ships were: *Lancaster #4, Ocean Queen, Wilson Small, Alida, Connecticut, West Metropolis, Elizabeth, Bay State, De Molay, Baltic, Atlantic, Cosmopolitan,* and *Wissahickon.*
(Figs. 241, 242)

Hospital Ship *Nashville*

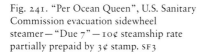

Fig. 241. "Per Ocean Queen", U.S. Sanitary Commission evacuation sidewheel steamer — "Due 7" — 10¢ steamship rate partially prepaid by 3¢ stamp. SF3

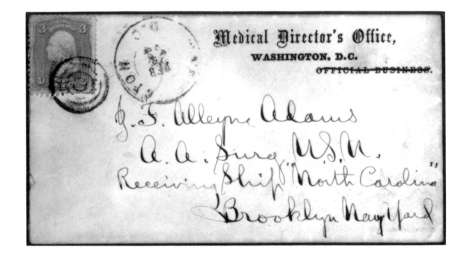

Fig. 242. To a surgeon aboard the Receiving Ship *North Carolina* stationed in Brooklyn. From the Medical Director's Office in Washington. A receiving ship was a ship permanently stationed in a harbor for purposes of receiving seamen and holding them in readiness for a cruiser. SF2

The Cincinnati Branch of the Sanitary Commission outfitted the *Tycoon* and the *Monarch*.

The aggregate capacity of these vessels was about 4,000 patients or when necessary, 5,000. In most cases the embarkation point for the injured was at White House Landing, Virginia. Runs varied from as much as seven days to New York or two days to Old Point Comfort.

The letter written from the hospital steamer *Kennebec* was penned as McClellan evacuated White House Landing on the Pamunkey River in Virginia. The city had been left burning by the withdrawing Federals to prevent any stores from falling into the hands of the Confederates. The letter is an interesting and informative one and is partially quoted. The *Kennebec* was one of the vessels converted by the United States Sanitary Commission for use as a hospital ship and ran between White House Landing and Philadelphia, a journey that took six days. (Fig. 243)

Fig. 243. Postmarked Old Point Comfort. June 30, (18)62 enclosure written aboard *Kennebec*, hospital ship of the Sanitary Commission, details evacuation of the wounded at White House Landing, Va. SF2

> Hospital Steamer Kennebec
> June 30th/62
>
> Dr. Vermilye
> Dear Pastor,
>
> Since I last wrote to you I have gone, as I told you I would, on the hospital steamer Kennebec.
>
> Before this reaches you, you will have learned all about our abandoning White House.
>
> The Kennebec was lying there at the time & was ordered to take a load of sick to the hospital at Portsmouth. This done we were ordered back to White House. As we entered the Pamunk(e)y river we met great numbers of transports laden with all kinds of hospital & military stores going down the river to claim the protection of our big guns at Yorktown. All the night before we had seen the fires at White House burning the commissary stores that could not be removed. The house itself was also burned. We went on up the river agreeable to orders until within about ten miles of the place where White House stood. We then received orders to turn round & help some of the transports down the river…We then proceeded to Yorktown then to Fortress Monroe where we are now awaiting orders.

My address at present is Steamer Kennebec Fortress Monroe.

We do not know what has caused all this movement. Rumor says that the rebel General Jackson has broken thro' the right wing of our army and was intending to seize the military stores at White House & then make a descent upon Yorktown. I only know there are about three hundred transports under the guns at Yorktown and all the Hospital steamers are here F.M. (Fortress Monroe) expecting orders to go up James River to bring back the wounded.

We are now having excessively warm weather here. I shall be glad if we are ordered North, with the next patients.

Hoping that God may spare you long to minister to his people I remain
very respectfully &
affectionately
yours
Fanny Campbell

July 1st

P.S. We have received orders to go to City Point up James river. We have several companies of the 17th N.Y. on board & they were of the right wing that were cut off by Jackson. They had a fight at White House no one killed.

The Confederate General mentioned is, of course, "Stonewall" Jackson. It was as a result of this retreat that General McClellan wrote Lincoln blaming him for his defeat because "you [Lincoln] have done your best to sacrifice this army."

Spanning nearly four decades between publication in 1942 of the Eugene Klein *U.S. Waterway Packetmarks 1832–1899 Supplement* and the more recent October 26–27, 1977 Sotheby Parke Bernet stamp auction there appeared no covers with markings of hospital ships except for the *Hero of Jersey* cover in the latter sale. To emphasize the scarcity of ship hospital covers in general, this particular cover was the only one bearing a 2¢ Jackson stamp (#73) in that entire sale. (Fig. 244, Plate 21)

Fig. 244. Hospital Steamer, *Hero of Jersey*, 2¢ Jackson (#73). SF5

Two explanations of the marking of the *Hero of Jersey* cover are possible:

One is that the proper postage should have been 3¢ rather than 2¢ since communications by officers from one military post to another were required to be prepaid at the full domestic rate of 3¢. Accordingly, the circular "Due 2" was applied, one cent for the required postage to bring it up to 3¢ and the other cent for a 1¢ penalty. In the upper right printed in black is "Hospital Steamer" and below that "Hero of Jersey," "Bermuda Hundred, Va."; in the upper left, also printed in black, is "Official Business." and below that "U.S.A. Med. Department." The cover is addressed to Fort Monroe, only a short distance away. Note that the stamp is canceled with a fancy cross (Skinner/Eno type CR-X19[39]) and the "Due 2" with another killer type cancellation. The cover carries a Philatelic Foundation certificate as genuine.

The other explanation is that this letter was in reality a drop letter requiring only 2¢ postage. The "Due 2" was not applicable and accordingly was canceled or obliterated out.

The ship *Hero of Jersey* was named after Major General Lord Sterling (William Alexander), the hero of Jersey, a senior colonial officer from the state of New Jersey during the Revolutionary War. Bermuda Hundred was on the Appomattox River near the junction with the James River. When the combined forces besieged Petersburg, the Army of the James under General Butler was encamped nearby. This would date the cover late 1864 or early 1865. The recipient, Dr. Litch, is mentioned several times in the *Medical and Surgical History of the War of the Rebellion*. Curiously, of the four cases mentioned involving Dr. Litch, three of the patients died.

On January 23, 1865, a military dispatch was sent to Brig. General D.H. Rucker, the Chief Quartermaster, from Brigadier General R. Ingallis. In that correspondence Ingallis stated that the Army of the James had only three hospital ships—the *George Washington*, the *Hero of Jersey* and the *Thomas Pownall*. He informed the quartermaster department that it could use the ships any time it wanted to but that they were not seaworthy. In the same letter Ingallis noted that the mail boats due the day before from Washington and Baltimore had not arrived as yet. He asked that the Potomac (River) be watched. "It is reported that the *Express* is sunk forty miles below Washington."

39. A list of cancellation types is given in *United States Cancellations 1845–1865*, by Hubert Skinner and Amos Eno, 1980.

TO THE SURGEON.
Ho! ho! old saw bones, here you come,
Yes, when the rebels whack us.
You are always ready with your traps,
To mangle, saw, and hack us.

Civil War comic valentine

XVI

CIVIL WAR PRISON CORRESPONDENCE

"Distributing the Mail"

Early in the conflict the Sanitary Commission attempted to formulate a policy for supplying Union prisoners in the Confederacy with essentials that were known to be unobtainable there. They sought to avoid sending food and clothing parcels to prisoners as this would overwhelm and burden the Confederates and would ultimately lead to a closing down of the program altogether. The distribution of supplies was usually done by southern officers. On December 11, 1863, the South stopped the supplying of goods that originated from the North. The ban continued until the summer of 1864, or for about six months. All goods passed through the exchange point—City Point, Virginia.

It was southern policy that goods originating with the federal government or northern civilian organizations including the United States Sanitary Commission were not permitted to move through the lines. The exchange of goods and letters from individuals was permitted. The United States Sanitary Commission, taking full advantage of this loophole, was able to secure letters and lists of prisoners from Libby Prison. Packages were then sent to these prisoners provided each package appeared to have been packed by an individual, with no two boxes looking alike.

Neither side was prepared for the large number of prisoners that each captured. The North used penitentiaries and military prisons and built stockades to house the 462,634 southerners who were seized. The South had more meager facilities and took over factories and warehouses and eventually fell back on open stockades and compounds similar to Andersonville to hold the 211,411 northern soldiers that it captured. The mortality rate was high in these prisons, 12 per cent in the North and 15 ½ per cent in the South. The prison figures represent the total held during the war, many of the men, of course, escaping, dying or paroled during the four years. The Andersonville type of stockade was not confined only to the South, and many prisoners succumbed in northern compounds such as Elmyra,

Johnson's Island, and Camp Douglas. All were equally harsh, unsanitary, raging with disease, and all with sparse food rations.

At first all Confederates captured were treated as rebels and traitors and could expect little but bitter treatment. Threatened reprisals against Northern prisoners of war ameliorated this problem and treatment settled back from harsh to only slightly less than harsh. All prisons were overcrowded; had the exchange of prisoners and their parole been honored as agreed upon at the cartel of 1862, the situation would not have been as bad as it was. General Grant suspended the exchange because it was found that the South was impressing soldiers once paroled. Because the population of the South was much less than the North, Grant felt that by manpower attrition alone the day would be won as the South ran out of new troops to replace those captured or killed.

On April 20, 1864, a circular was issued by the Office of the Commissary General of Prisoners of the Union Army that superseded the regulation issued by the same office on July 7, 1861. Article XVII provided that southern prisoners held in northern confinement would be permitted to write and to receive letters, not exceeding one page of common letter paper, and the contents were to be of a strictly private nature. The letters were to be examined or censored by a competent non-commissioned officer before being delivered or forwarded.

On March 3, 1864, Secretary Stanton in a letter to Commanding Officers of Federal Prisons ordered that sutlers could sell to prisoners, in addition to necessities, steel pens, lead pencils, paper, envelopes, and postage stamps. By August 10, 1864, as conditions hardened for northern troops in southern prisons, most of the permission to sell these necessities was rescinded but writing materials and stamps were high on the list of permissibles. There is no evidence that northern prisoners in southern prisons enjoyed any kind of reciprocity.

It was expected that all letters to southern internees be prepaid and that their letters be dispatched prepaid. Prisoners' funds were limited and stamps often non-available. While it is unlikely that the practice was a widespread one, Robert Lowry, Chaplain U.S.A. at David's Island reported: "I was supervisor of the post office, and officially appointed to examine the contents of letters, which were mailed and forwarded on my approval. Paper and envelopes were furnished (to Confederate prisoners) gratuitously, and post stamps when needed, were supplied to the extent of one hundred and fifty dollars to my knowledge, gratuitously. From three hundred to five hundred letters were forwarded daily after the first arrival of prisoners."

Northern soldiers confined in southern prisons apparently did not fare as well with their mail if we are to judge by the testimony of Prescott Tracy of the 82nd Regiment, N.Y.V. In a sworn statement about the handling of mail at Andersonville Prison at Camp Sumter in Georgia, he said:

> Letters from home seldom reached us, and few had any means of writing.
> In the early summer, a large batch of letters — five thousand we are told —
> arrived, having been accumulating somewhere for many months. These
> were brought into camp by an officer, under orders to collect ten cents
> on each — of course most were returned, and we heard no more of
> them...According to the rules of transmission of letters over the lines,
> these letters must have already paid ten cents each to the rebel govern-
> ment.

Letters to northern prisoners of war in the South had to conform to the following regulations:

> 1. The letter must not exceed one letter page of matter, purely domestic,
> signed by the writer's name, with P.O. address in full.

2. The letter must be inclosed in an *unsealed* envelope, on which the address of the prisoner is plainly written.

3. The letter thus *unsealed* must be inclosed in a *sealed envelope*, and addressed

To the Commanding General
of the Department of Va. and N.C.,
Fortress Monroe,[40] Va.

For Flag of Truce.

4. Five cents must be inclosed to pay rebel postage to Richmond—ten for points beyond.

It is well to inclose an envelope with a blank sheet of paper and a U.S. postage stamp, to furnish means to the prisoner to reply. Money may be inclosed at the risk of the sender. Letters forwarded strictly in accordance with these rules, will be sent through the rebel lines, and, in some cases at least, will reach those to whom they are addressed.[41]

All letters sent to Fortress Monroe without strict compliance with the rules were transmitted to the dead letter office.

On May 30, 1864, aboard the *Mail Steamer* on the James River, Edward Everett Hale, author of *The Man Without a Country*, wrote to Frederick N. Knapp, Executive Secretary of the United States Sanitary Commission, concerning the needs of and information about prisoners in the South. He also attached a list of unwounded officers in Libby Prison. This list is especially important as the largest and most dramatic escape from Libby Prison had occurred on February 9, 1864. The list may have consisted of those that remained behind. Hale wrote as follows:

Mail Steamer on James River
May 30, 1864

Rev. Fred N. Knapp
Secretary of the Sanitary Commission

1. I have the pleasure of furnishing you a complete list of the unwounded officers left in the Libby Prison by Dr. Ferguson and Capt. Brittan on Saturday last. Dr. Ferguson is the Surgeon of the 8, N.Y. Cavalry and Capt. Brittan Capt. of the 1st N.Y. Diagnosis:—the first commissioned officer captured by the rebels this summer. Both of them are most intelligent gentlemen. Capt. Brittan is paroled against Capt. McLean.

2. These gentlemen make to me the most urgent request that the Sanitary Commission shall furnish supplies to our prisoners in a manner which they indicate. They assure me that Major Turner the officer in charge at the Libby and Commissioner field agent for exchange will see that boxes addressed to individual officers by name in the Libby will reach them unmolested.

3. It will be essential that these boxes shall not appear to come from any common source, least of all from the Sanitary Commission, against which the Rebels express the most unholy animosity. "They are malignant toward it" Dr. Ferguson says. They should be packed as if by private friends, in various shaped boxes of different construction. Not more than fifteen or twenty boxes should be sent by one boat. They should be addressed to the care of Colonel Ould, Commissioner of Exchange, and Major Mulford at Fort Monroe. Major Mulford undertakes all care of them. He is a

40. Fortress or Fort Monroe—Fort Monroe is the correct designation. The fort was originally designed by Brigadier General Simon Bernard, noted French military engineer, in 1819 and completed in 1834. At first it was called Fortress Monroe; then on February 1, 1832, an order was issued that "the work at Old Point Comfort be called Fort Monroe, and not Fortress Monroe." During the Civil War even the military were sometimes confused as to its correct name. The *New York Herald*, a leading newspaper of the period, had a column headed "News from Fortress Monroe" and this served to popularize the misnomer. To compound this the Post Office Department in 1880 changed the name of Old Point Comfort to Fortress Monroe. Finally on November 15, 1941, the Post Office Department ended the confusion by changing the official designation to Fort Monroe. There is a difference between a fort and a fortress. A fort is a fortification containing a garrison of troops, while a fortress is a fortification that encloses a town within its walls.

41. *The Connecticut War Record.* Vol. II, No. V, New Haven, December 1864, p. 324.

most intelligent and humane officer. I would suggest however that even he need not know the sources whence your boxes come.

4. Dr. Ferguson & Capt Brittan tell me that the officers pledge themselves to distribute whatever is received, not only among each other but among the privates in Richmond, where they have a means of reaching. Of these there are now about eight hundred; about twenty four hundred having been lately sent to Danville.

5. Even the stores to be sent had best not have the appearance of coming from one depot if it can be avoided. You may regard them as making a common stock after they arrive there. Dr. Ferguson says that they need shirts, and a very few pair of pants:—but especially that they need food. He begs you to send pork packed in cans or small kegs;—a little beef-stock, with coffee and sugar. The present ration is a ration of worm eaten beans which they boil, one quarter ration of corn bread and one quarter ration of corn meal. They get salt though it is not allowed—but a little pepper would be desirable. Dr. Ferguson is very correct in saying that food is more necessary than anything else which can be sent.—and that pork is better than anything beside.

6. Dr. Ferguson also assures me that if Hospital stores can be sent in the same way, as from a private source to Dr. Sample in charge of Hospital No. 21 they will be used for our wounded and will be of inexpressible value. He says they need terribly food as beef stock, sugar, coffee, boxes crackers, stimulants, chloroform, adhesive, plasters, & dressings & bandages...Dr. Ferguson sends his compliments to Dr. Sample and begs him to use these stores as far as possible for the wounded under his charge. He says our wounded men almost all die for want of proper nutrition.

News in Libby Prison

If Dr. Ferguson does not wait upon you himself, and I suppose he may not now, in his haste to pass home, it is because he has stated the whole case to me, and has promised to attend to it *officially*. Please notify me at once therefore, if any difficulty occurs to you in carrying out this suggestion, addressing me at Boston—

Believe me Very truly Yours
Edward E. Hale
Associate Member
& Acting relief Agent
U.S. Sanitary Commission

Nothing should be said in public of this till the war is done.
Food, Medical Stores rather
than clothing

(The list of unwounded officers in Libby Prison is in the authors' collection and has not been included within this text for reasons of conserving space.)

Camp Douglas began accepting Confederate prisoners after February 1862. The prisoner of war cover with the corner card of the U.S. Christian Commission, Young Men's Christian Association Rooms, Chicago–Illinois originated there and was postmarked Chicago, April 9. The "CAMP DOUGLAS EXAMINED. Prisoners' Letter" marking is classified as Type I Camp Douglas, Chicago in the Earl Antrim study of POW correspondence. A letter enclosed would have had to conform to the following regulations as outlined by D.B. Tiffany, Prison Postmaster:

1st. One page Medium size Letter Paper (not inter-lined) is allowed, not more.—

2nd. The writer's name in full must be signed to each letter, or communication.—

3rd. The No. of the prison and mess must be stated, with a request that your letters be directed accordingly.—

4th. Postage must be pre-paid.—

5th. If prisoners wish to speak of kind treatment they can do so in general terms, but not of particular persons.—

6th. All letters must be put in the Post Office or Letter Box.

(Fig. 245)

Fig. 245. (Top) Camp Douglas in Chicago. Type I (Antrim) federal prison censor marking adopted in 1865. SF3

(Bottom) Point Lookout, Md., Type Ia censor handstamp "Prisoner's Letter Examined", postmarked Jan 14, '65. SF3

Type I

Type Ia

42. August Dietz, author of the *Dietz Confederate States Catalog and Handbook*.

An example of a prisoner of war handstamp with a United States Sanitary Commission corner card contains a letter to Henry Bear, Mainesborouh P.O., in Franklin Co., Pa. It has a 3¢ 1861 stamp, postmarked Point Lookout, Md., Jan 14, '65. The enclosed letter was written two days previously by the prisoner, F.B. Bear, a relative of the recipient from whom he requests money. Note the marking "Prisoner's Letter EXAMINED", which is Antrim's Type Ia of the Point Lookout, Maryland markings. On the back of the cover is a notation by August Dietz[42] referring to the fact that it is unusual to find a prisoner of war cover in as good condition as this one. It is not quite clear if the letter is addressed to Bear's father, uncle, or brother, but it is obvious that it is a very formal request for money. While Bear asks the recipient to oblige him and send the money, it is more likely that the prisoner had been intimidated to make this request to avoid punishment by the prison authorities. It was a common practice that when a prisoner arrived at a prison compound he was searched and anything of value was then taken from him. The letter appears to be so contrived, even to the extent of good writing equipment and paper, that it is more than a simple request for money. The letter is as follows:

> Prison Camp
> Point Lookout M.d.
> Jany 12th 1865

Mr. Henry Bear
Dear Sir

    I have been in prison for some time, and I am very much in need of sum money and would be under many obligations to you if you would be so kind as to send me a small amount of money.

    And I will certainly pay you when ever I am released from prison Please write to me soon direct your letter to F.B. Bear Co. H, 5th Division Prison Camp Pt Lookout M.d. and oblige your friend

> F. B. Bear

PRISONER OF WAR — NORTH TO SOUTH

The Martin cover shown here is an interesting one in that Rawley White Martin, the writer, was himself an interesting person. He was born in 1835, which would have made him 28 at the time of the writing. Colonel Martin of the Confederate States of America led Pickett's Division at Gettysburg and was the first man over the wall. For his valor at Gettysburg he received a serious wound while attacking the Federal lines. He was then transferred to a field hospital for three months before being sent to Fort McHenry in Baltimore and finally to Point Lookout in May of 1864, when he was exchanged.

    This cover is one of the best examples of a prisoner of war cover, involving a southerner in a northern prison hospital, which is a far rarer circumstance than a northern prisoner in a southern compound. It is a good example of a hospital cover as well, but is placed within this section because its significance as a prisoner of war cover is greater than its interest as a hospital cover.

    It carries the 3¢ rose stamp (#65) over a U.S. Army Medical Department corner card. The blue Baltimore, Md. postmark of Jul 11 (1863) was applied just seven days after the Battle of Gettysburg. The black Richmond, Va., August 5, 1863, postmark was applied 25 days after Baltimore, indicating that mail moved rather quickly across the lines. The letter is addressed to Pittsylvania C.H. (Court House) and has been stamped "Due 10", the postage necessary to move the letter from Richmond to Pittsylvania. Note that the Virginia designation is followed by C.S.A. (Confederate States of America). In the upper right corner is a soldier's letter endorsement. Had this letter gone to the North from a Union enlisted man confined in a Confederate prison, the due would have been only a "Due 3" as soldiers' mail in the Union Army moved without a penalty. (An officer's letter would have been "Due 6" — 3¢ postage plus 3¢ penalty.) The rates in the North were less than in the South. It should be remembered that in the South the only persons having the free franking privilege were C.S.A. Postmaster General John H. Reagan and certain other post office officials. All others paid postage, including Jefferson Davis.[43] Martin has endorsed the cover "R.W. Martin, Lieut Col, 53 Va Vols".

    Included is a poignant letter headed "Genl Hospital 2d Army Corps Near Gettysburg Pa". He described his wounds in detail and made arrangements for his body to be buried at home, and generally was in a depressed state, as could well be expected. However, he lived another 49 years. (Fig. 246)

43. The franking privilege was abolished by the Confederate States of America with the Postage Act of March 15, 1861 (a month before Fort Sumter was fired upon) except for the postmaster general and various other Post Office Department Officials when corresponding on official post office matters. Such mail was to be endorsed "Official Mail" over the signature of the correspondent.

Fig. 246. Written at Gettysburg. 3¢ rose (#65) over U.S. Army Medical Department corner card, blue Baltimore, Md., Jul 11 and black Richmond, Va., Aug 5, 1863 postmarks. "Due 10" to Pittsylvania C.H., Virginia, C.S.A., with enclosure. sf5

Two examples of covers addressed to a southern prisoner of war hospital are those to Richard Dunne and to John T. Halsted.

The Dunne Cover is an "inside" cover. Regulations required that an "outer" envelope, unsealed, with the proper postage, be addressed to the prisoner of war. In the same envelope was to be included the "inner" envelope with the proper postage to assure delivery to the prisoner from the exchange point onward. The authors of the New Dietz Catalog indicate that as a result of this cumbersome handling of the mail few such letters ever reached their destination. As a result there is a small number of such "outer" and "inner" covers.

The "inside" cover addressed to Richard Dunne of the 69th New York State Militia (Irish Brigade) is marked in care of General Winder. Covers addressed to Gen. Winder after April 1862 refer to General Winder Hospital which opened after that date and are usually prisoner of war covers that have been sent to Union soldiers confined to a southern prison hospital. General Winder was in charge first of Richmond prison hospitals and later on of all southern prison hospitals. All operated under Samuel Preston Moore, Surgeon General of the Confederate Medical Corps.

Dunne had been wounded at Bull Run (the first Bull Run was fought between July 16 and July 22, 1861) while working with a Union Army surgeon. Two facts substantiate the encounter as the first Bull Run rather than the second Bull Run. The first Manassas Battle was in 1861 and the postmark is November of that year. Second, early in the war before ratification of agreements between the North and the South concerning the exchange of mail, Norfolk was used as a southern exchange point. Later on Petersburg was used for a short time. As the need arose, other exchange points were activated. Later in the war the main exchange points were City Point, Virginia and Fort Monroe. Southbound letters entered the mails through City Point and entered the Confederate mail through Richmond. Northbound letters went through Fort Monroe and then through Old Point Comfort.

The cover is clearly marked "Prisoner of War" by the sender, and is postmarked at Norfolk with a distinct "5" marking in blue indicating that the Confederate postage was paid either with a coin enclosed in the "outer" envelope or with a Confederate stamp. The address of Mr. Richard Dunne is 69th Regt Co. J, N.Y.S. (State) M. (Militia) Hospital Richmond. Under the postmark is a handwritten annotation "Encl C."—perhaps standing for coin enclosed to pay the Confederate postage. At the lower left appears the notation "Care of Genl Winder". (Fig. 247, Plate 22)

Fig. 247. (Top) Hospital prisoner of war "inside" cover, postmarked Norfolk, an early usage (1861). 5¢ Confederate postage paid. Marked care of Gen'l. Winder. SF3

(Bottom) Addressed to a Minnesota soldier at a prisoner of war hospital in Richmond. 3¢ rose tied by blue "Cincinnati O. Nov 30" duplex postmark. Examined by censor, "Exd. D.W.C.", then went through the lines via Fortress Monroe. Blue "Norfolk Va. Dec 9 1861" postmark records its receipt in that city. Handstamped "5" for southern postage due. SF3

Very early in the war John T. Halsted of the 1st Minnesota Regiment was wounded, captured, and moved to Richmond in the South. While confined in a prisoner of war hospital he received his letter after it had gone through the exchange point at Fort Monroe. In Richmond the letter received the marking "5" for the postage fee to Richmond. It was not until April of 1862 that the Confederate rate was increased to 10¢. United States postage of 3¢ was paid from Cincinnati to the exchange point.

PRISONER OF WAR—SOUTH TO NORTH (Fig. 248)

This cover with its contents in every way is a classic prisoner of war cover. Within the space of the six lines allotted for writing, its contents tell a whole story. The letter is addressed to Captain Thayer's mother in Franklin, Massachusetts. As an officer he would have been confined to Libby Prison in Richmond. In the upper left is a Sanitary Commission imprint corner card. In the upper right is the manuscript marking "Ex" (examined) followed by the examining officer's initials. Below that appears a handstamp "Due 6 cts" that represents 3¢ postage due and 3¢ penalty for not prepaying the postage. This officer did not qualify for exemption from the 3¢ penalty portion as this privilege was given only to privates and non-commissioned officers. In accordance with the rules on mail from prisoners of war, any

Fig. 248. Libby Prison at Richmond.

letter not conforming to regulations was sent to the Dead Letter Office. This letter, despite its origin and the importance of its contents, was directed to that office. As was the custom, letters designated for the Dead Letter Office were opened, read, and forwarded if possible. Mrs. Thayer did receive the letter from her son and it reads:

Libby Prison—
Sanitary Commission

Dear Mother—

Richmond Apr 2d–63. I arrived this 6P.M. from Gordonsville (Va.) Wounded through fleshy part of right thigh—doing well 10 Privates of my reg't are with me. A Flag of truce boat is here & will take them off tomorrow—No chance for Officers to be Paroled or exchanged. 2 from my reg't are here before me. I can write only 6 lines—write soon all of you—goodbye love to all.

Chas. H. Thayer
Capt 1st R.I. Cavalry

Twenty days later Captain Thayer wrote a second letter which appears to be from the same sheet of Sanitary Commission stationery:

Libby Prison Richmond Va
April 22d 1863—

My dear Mother—

I am in good health—wound doing well. am happy as could be expected in place of this kind. 100 Officers in one room including 2 Generals. The 2d Lieut of my Co. is with me. very few are sick—We are waiting very anxiously to hear news of an exchange—Hope something will be done soon. I have rec'd no letters from you yet—Love to all

Very Affectionately Yours
Chas H Thayer
Capt 1st R.I. Cavalry

(Fig. 249)

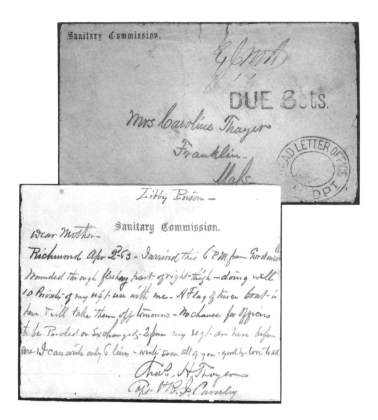

Fig. 249. Letters from Libby Prison written by Captain Thayer. Prisoner of War cover to Mrs. Caroline Thayer originating in Libby Prison on Sanitary Commission corner card. Marked "DUE 6 cts." with Dead Letter Office handstamp. SF5

The war which had ended on the military front on April 9, 1865, continued in the hearts and minds of veterans long after the war ceased. After the war one of the accusations against Jefferson Davis, President of the Confederacy, was that he and others in the Confederate prison system systematically planned the murder of all charges within their hands. Early in May, Captain Henry Wirz, commandant of Andersonville, was arrested for his part in the cruelty to prisoners. Along with General Winder who had died in February of 1865, and three others, Wirz was accused of conspiracy "to impair the health and destroy the lives of prisoners of war." A second charge leveled against him was murder "in violation of the laws and customs of war." Found guilty, Wirz was executed on November 10, 1865, the only person connected with Southern prisons executed for that reason. Except for the Lincoln conspirators, he was the only war criminal who was hung for activities during the Civil War.

Jefferson Davis said this on the subject of prisoners:

> When time shall have softened passion and prejudice, when Reason shall have stripped the mask from misrepresentation, then Justice, holding evenly her scales, will require much of past censure and praise to change places.

...on the monument at Andersonville appear these words of Davis on one side and on the other Grant's letter refusing to permit an exchange of prisoners.

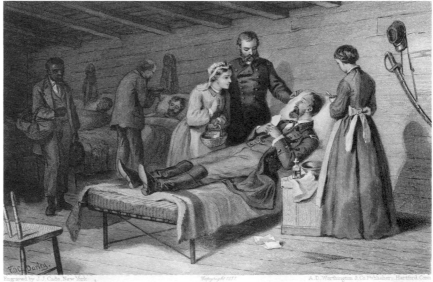

THE DYING SOLDIER.—THE LAST LETTER FROM HOME.

XVII

REFRESHMENT SALOONS AND SOLDIERS' RESTS

THE COOPER SHOP.

Union Volunteer Refreshment Saloon & Hospital
May 17, 1861 to August 28, 1865
Cooper Shop Refreshment Saloon & Hospital
May 27, 1861 to December 1, 1865
Citizens' Union Volunteer Hospital Association
September 5, 1862 —

Broadside of the Cooper Shop Refreshment Saloon

The "Cooper Shop", a two-storied brick building on Otsego Street in Philadelphia, opened on May 27, 1861. The building was originally used for the manufacture of barrel staves used by coopers (barrel makers) for the sugar cane industry, thus the name "Cooper Shop Refreshment Saloon". Troops passing through Philadelphia on the way to Washington and traveling north from Washington found the saloon a ready and handy refreshment stop along the way. The Union Volunteer Refreshment Saloon and adjacent Union Volunteer Hospital opened on May 17, 1861, ten days before the Cooper Shop. They were the two best known canteens in the North and could be compared with the United Service Organizations (USO) of World War II and yet were more. The Cooper Shop Hospital, next door to the Saloon, also assisted those in transit in need of medical help. The Cooper Shop Refreshment Saloon closed on December 1, 1865, and the Union Volunteer Refreshment Saloon on August 28, 1865.

By the time the Union Volunteer Refreshment Saloon closed after its four years of operation, over 600,000 meals had been served and over $85,000 raised in contributions. The Cooper Shop had served over 315,000 meals and close to $58,000 was raised during its years of furnishing aid and comfort to the Union forces passing through Philadelphia.

In both of these service canteens a soldier could write a letter, wash up, find something to eat and perhaps a bed on which to rest. The home-cooked meals were a welcome relief after the hardtack and worm-infested meat usually fried to a crisp in bacon grease.

Receipt for donation to the Cooper Shop

The army provided little in the way of extra medical care at the beginning of the war, a lack of services that was particularly felt by the troops in transit. The wounded were expected to care for themselves or in some way manage with the help of their families or friends. Later on, this system of caring for the wounded was improved so that those suffering injuries were cared for in government hospitals. Yet often their release was premature and those discharged from the service due to injuries were expected to manage as best they could and return to their homes. (Figs. 250, 251, 252, 253, 254)

Fig. 250. Cooper Shop, 1¢ blue (#63) paying circular rate, Philadelphia service carrier handstamp, also used as cancellation. Enclosed is a contribution receipt dated December 28, 1861. SF3

44. *The Tribute Book*, by Frank B. Goodrich, 1865.

The Union Volunteer Refreshment Saloon, organized under Bazilla S. Brown, had modest beginnings but as more troops passed through the area the citizens of Philadelphia were relied upon more and more to furnish the food, drink, laundry, and other necessities. The Eighth New York Regiment of 800 men was the first organization to be served by the Union Volunteer Refreshment Saloon, while the New York Seventh was the first served by the Cooper Shop.

Attached to the Union Volunteer Refreshment Saloon was the hospital cottage. "Here is a large table covered with writing-materials, where the soldier may write his letters. An attendant takes them, stamps them without charge, and dispatches them by the bushel basketful."[44]

The two Potter covers were secured at different times from different sources. The one to Washington, D.C. is a front only, while the other has a two-page letter dated February 10, 1862, from Waldo Potter to his brother, written from the Union Volunteer Hospital. Put-

Fig. 251. (Top) Cooper Shop, 2¢ circular rate, octagonal Philadelphia service carrier U.S.P.O. Dispatch handstamp. SF3

(Bottom) Two-cent (#73), postmarked Mar 10, '64. James Ruppell, cashier at Bank Penn Township, also received the previous letter with the two 1¢ stamps. Black overall Cooper Shop print on reverse. SF4

Fig. 252. Two-cent (#73), Philadelphia Post Office cancellation. Overall imprint of Cooper Shop on reverse. J. Spittall of Philadelphia was the engraver and printer. SF4

Wm. M. Cooper to Hon. A. Lincoln concerning Surgeon General Hammond. The Cooper family name may be an occupational name.

Fig. 253. (Top) Imprint of Cooper Shop on reverse of 3¢ (#65), canceled Philadelphia Apr 15, 1864. SF2

(Bottom) The 1¢ and 3¢ 1861 stamps (#63, 65). The one-cent paid the carrier fee. Reverse has saloon sketch. SF2

Fig. 254. The Aug 25, 1861 Philadelphia postmark is genuine but the stamp may have been added at a later date. Poignant letter to a wife written on Cooper Shop letterhead enclosed. SF1

ting these two letters together, one to a soldier relative of Company A in Washington, D.C. and the other to the brother in New York, brings life and zest to collecting Civil War patriotics. (Fig. 255, Plate 23) (Fig. 256)

Another design Volunteer Refreshment Saloon cover was forwarded by Congressman William D. Kelley. He was authorized to frank official mail but according to regulations, it had to be his own mail. His frank did not pay the carrier fee. Use of his frank to by-pass the payment of postage was illegal and one of the abuses that later led to the repeal of the franking privilege. (Fig. 257, Plate 24)

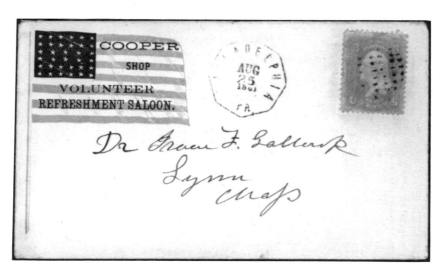

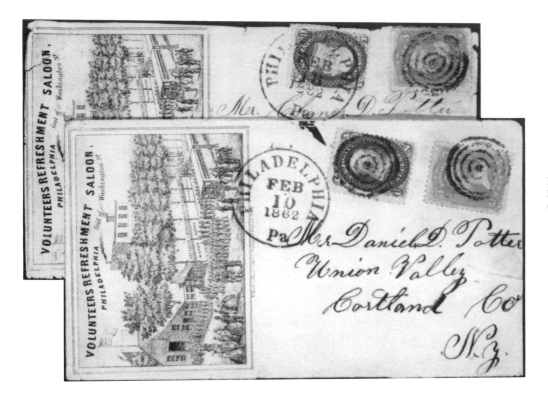

Fig. 255. Two Volunteer Refreshment Saloon covers, both postmarked Philadelphia. Carrier fee paid by 1¢ stamp. SF3

Fig. 256. (#U34) entire; 1¢ (#63) paid carrier fee. Philadelphia, Sep 15, 1861 postmark. On reverse, adhesive label of (Union) Volunteer Refreshment Saloon which had opened only four months earlier. SF2

Fig. 257. Corner card of Volunteer Refreshment Hospital bearing circular Philadelphia postmark and small circular FREE, franked by William D. Kelley, Member of Congress from Philadelphia. Postmarked Philadelphia, Jan 15, 1862, 1¢ stamp paid carrier fee. SF3

Covers from the Volunteer Refreshment Saloon and Hospital are known in various colors, in four designs, and with varying stamps. (Fig. 258) (Fig. 259, Plate 25) (Fig. 260)

With the end of the war the purposes of the saloons had changed but not the character. Arad Barrows, Chairman of the Union Volunteer Refreshment Saloon, was still very much interested in the welfare of those who passed through his establishment. On April 18, 1865, he wrote the following letter to Edward Stanton, Secretary of War:

Arad Barrow's letter to Edwin M. Stanton, Secretary of War

April 18th 1865

Hon Edward M. Stanton
Secretary of War
Washington—Dear Sir. We have two women each with one child at our Saloon, and one is about to be again confined. Their husbands deserted from the Rebel Army, and they came north in quest of them. By inquiry and advertisement we have not been able to find them. One of the women has a father and mother and the other friends in Richmond Va. [Richmond had been occupied by Federal troops only two weeks before on April 3, 1865.] Will you oblige us by sending passes and transportation for them to that point, their names are Emma W. Evans & child and Elisabeth Morris & child.

Very Respectfully
Your Obt Servant
Arad Barrows
Chairman

Out of the need for extended care there arose other benevolences associated with the War Between the States. As a result of this need, the Citizens' Union Volunteer Hospital Association was established in Philadelphia on September 5, 1862. Eventually this hospital grew to over 25,000 square feet and cared for over 30,000 troops the first year of its existence. (Fig. 261) (Fig. 262, Plate 26)

View of the Union Volunteer Refreshment Saloon

Other hospitals providing for long term care, privately financed, were established in Pittsburgh by the Pittsburgh Subsistence Committee and in Baltimore by the Union Relief Association of Baltimore. In Chicago the Soldiers' Home was supported mainly from the proceeds of the second Sanitary Fair.

Fig. 258. Union Volunteer Refreshment Saloon, Hornellsville, N.Y., Jul 24, 8 A.M., 1864 postmark. The design by Cobb is the scarcest of the refreshment saloon patriotics. SF3

Fig. 259. Three Union Volunteer Refreshment Saloon and Hospital covers illustrate different uses of these patriotics.

(Top) 1¢ drop letter blue design cover addressed to and mailed in Philadelphia with three strikes of the Philadelphia Penny Post. SF3

(Middle) Blue 2¢ cover is for circular rate that became effective July 1863. SF5

(Bottom) 3¢ rated cover printed in pale violet, Philadelphia to Roxbury, Mass. SF3

Broadside for a lecture, proceeds to be shared by the two major saloons in Philadelphia

Fig. 260. (Top) Postmarked Jan 31, '64, Washington, D.C., blue overall design. SF3

(Bottom) Postmarked Philadelphia, addressed to South Amherst, Mass. on a light brown printed cover. SF3

Crutch exchange where letters could also be written

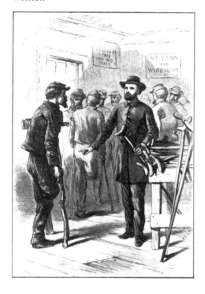

Fig. 261. Citizens' Volunteer Hospital. Soldier's letter certified by assistant surgeon, permitting it to move without the requisite postage. Postmarked Kingsessing (Philadelphia), Pa., Dec 1, "Due 3". SF2

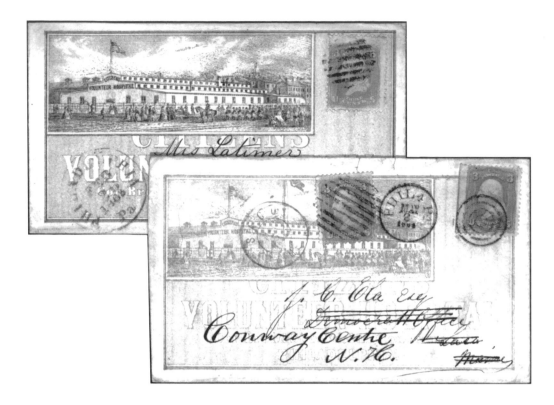

Fig. 262. (Top) Lilac design. Neither the Union Volunteer Hospital nor the Citizens' Volunteer Hospital were government establishments. They were primarily for convalescents and migratory soldiers or those mustered out of the service. SF3

(Bottom) Both Citizens' Volunteer Hospital covers are postmarked Philadelphia. The blue forwarded cover, upon reaching its destination in Maine, was sent to Conway Centre, N.H., and another 3¢ stamp applied for forwarding. SF3

XVIII

CONFEDERATE BENEVOLENCES AND HOSPITALS

Like the North, the Confederacy was ill-prepared for the large influx of sick and wounded that was soon to inundate the Confederate Medical Service. Medical supplies, medicines, surgeons, and ambulances and other conveyances were all in short supply. Most important and in the shortest supply was manpower. While the North had a relatively unlimited source in the heavy populated areas of the industrialized states that made up the Union, the South always had a manpower problem. Southern troops, while inherently of sterner stock and more conditioned to the out-of-doors, still succumbed equally to the effects of a well-placed bullet or shrapnel.

Similar to his northern brother-in-arms, Johnny Reb was continually plagued with camp diseases and maladies. By far the most debilitating was dysentery. Cures were nonexistent and the fatigue and drain of even the will to live was certainly a factor in the fighting elan of the troops. It has been said, but never confirmed, that General Robert E. Lee at Gettysburg suffered from a case of diarrhea and his lack of enthusiasm, in addition to disregarding General Longstreet's advice, contributed to the debacle at that battle. The cure was often worse than the affliction. Calomel, opium, and acetate of lead were considered common "cures" but others might include a pill made up of equal parts of red pepper and crude resin or administering "an infusion of raspberry leaves or whortleberry leaves."

The second most disabling disease was measles, particularly virulent among raw rural recruits who never developed a natural immunity to the disease. All in all, being a Confederate soldier was an unhappy lot. Besides dealing with being shot at, he was exposed to every major disease known at the time and some unknown, but in addition he lacked some of the basic amenities that the northern soldier was furnished through the United States Sanitary Commission and United States Christian Commission.

The profile of the average southern soldier was: age 26, 5'8¼" tall, weight 143½ pounds, black or brown hair (38%), blue eyes (45%), a farmer (48%), and American-born (75%). From the start of the conflict it was apparent that in order to field a sizable healthy force and to maintain their numbers, necessary steps had to be taken to assure that all men mustered into the Confederate Army be maintained at peak efficiency.

To begin with, medical education was pretty much the same in the North and South. After six to nine months as an apprentice to a doctor, the young aspirant to the practice of medicine would be furnished with a set of surgical instruments, a set of medical books, and a supply of medicine. From that point on, experience appeared to have been the best teacher. The northern doctor, however, through the efforts of the United States Sanitary Commission, was supplied with medical monographs, pamphlets, and books; this literature enhanced the understanding of medicine and surgical procedures. But the doctor in gray often had to rely on his intuition and experience gained from unsuccessful operations to further his medical knowledge and technique.

Soldiers' aid and hospital relief societies sprang up all over the South at the beginning of the conflict. In some states these relief societies could be found in every county. All operated independently and did not have the benefits of an umbrella organization such as the U.S. Sanitary Commission. It was not until late in 1862 that the Confederate government took over jurisdiction of all local hospitals, rest homes, and facilities that had made up the early medical and hospital network of the South.

Southern women have often been portrayed as male-dominated, helpless creatures, but this was not actually so. Like northern women, and even more so, they had to assume many of the physical labors previously performed by men because of the acute shortage of labor. Many traveled to see soldiers and relatives, and many aided the sick since there was no organization such as the U.S. Sanitary Commission or Christian Commission to aid the casualties. Even if there had been such a benevolent organization, the women would not have had time for it; they were confined to the farm doing men's work as the Confederate draft laws did not exempt fathers and/or farmers.

The only relief society formed on a Confederacy-wide basis was the Association for the Relief of Maimed Soldiers, although Mrs. Felicia Grundy Porter of Nashville, Tennessee had headed a body known as the Women's Relief Society of the Confederate States. Both became operational toward the end of the war with the former group concerned mainly with supplying artificial arms and legs for soldiers and sailors. There are no known covers from either of the two groups. In Atlanta there were three ladies' aid societies: The Ladies' Soldiers' Relief Society, The Ladies' Hospital Association, and the St. Phillips Hospital Aid Society.

Covers are known to exist with a manuscript notation "Forwarded by Louisiana Committee of Mobile" but the function of this committee was different from that of the Sanitary Commission or Christian Commission. The Louisiana Committee was primarily interested in the forwarding of mail in and out of New Orleans to Mobile while New Orleans was under the command of the repressive General Butler and then General Banks. There was no organized attempt by this group to marshal the spirits and energies of the South to alleviate and relieve the suffering of the Confederate soldier. Relief organizations were established on a state-by-state basis which not only was inefficient but tended to be unmanageable because they treated only casualties from their own states.

By the spring of 1862, while the hospitals were still very crowded, a study showed the sanitary conditions satisfactory and the food well prepared. It was not until the casualties of the battles of the Seven Pines (May 31 to June 1, 1862) and the Seven Days (June 25 to July 1, 1862) that it became more apparent that the system of localized hospitals such as the use of warehouses, churches, schools, hotels, private homes, and anything with a roof overhead had to be eliminated. Out of the chaos arose the construction of hospitals solely for treating the wounded and ill. The largest and most impressive were located in Richmond, which became the chief medical center of the South. The most famous of these hospitals was Chimborazo with a capacity of over 8,000 patients when it opened on October 11, 1861. It had five divisions and treated 76,000 during the war. Up to the time it was considered the largest hospital in the world. Other major hospitals in Richmond were Winder and Jackson. There were a total of 20 Confederate hospitals in Richmond.

The student of Confederate postal history might attempt to collect covers originating from or sent to the 153 Confederate military hospitals. But in over a quarter-century of our collecting Sanitary Fair stamps and related artifacts of southern hospitals and the medical establishment, the small number shown here is representative of that effort. While Confederate Medical Department covers are available, it was the hospitals that captured our interest. A list of those hospitals that are generally accepted as major Confederate Hospitals appears in Appendix III.

SOUTHERN MEDICAL COVERS (Figs. 263, 264, 265, 266, 267)

Fig. 263. Postmarked Gainesville, Ga., Sep 24. With "Paid" in the upper right. According to August Dietz, a cover lacking a value number is usually an indication of late usage—often in 1864. This ex-Kohn cover is addressed to Fair Ground Hospital No. 2 at Vineville, Ga., near Macon. SF2

Fig. 264. (Top) Dark blue, 10¢ (Confederate States #11), manuscript canceled and postmarked Columbus, Miss., Jan 5. At left appears notation "Please forward to Ripley" and "Forwarded 10". The "forwarded" is a "Due" marking and indicated that additional postage was charged and due for this extra service of forwarding the letter. One possible explanation of why a Christian Commission corner card should have had a Confederate stamp affixed might be that agents with both the Christian Commission and the Sanitary Commission were integral parts of a northern military division and these stores might have fallen into enemy hands along with other supplies. SF3

(Bottom) The 10¢ blue (#12), Marshall, Texas cancellation. Covers from Texas during the war are scarcer than from other southern states and a Christian Commission corner card from Texas is unusual. Earliest known cancellation on this stamp is May 1, 1863. It may be assumed that with the blockade troops in Texas would not have received a supply of this stamp until some time after that date. With the fall of Port Hudson, Louisiana on July 8, 1863 and Vicksburg four days earlier, all communication between Confederate states east and west of the Mississippi was cut. As a result Confederate mail west of the Mississippi was directed from the Trans-Mississippi sub-office at Marshall, Texas. Louisiana, Arkansas and Texas were given a semi-independent status with Marshall as the administrative center. As this cover to Liberty, Texas remained within the confines of Texas, Marshall as the sub-office postmarked this letter. There is no enclosure to indicate the actual point of origin of this letter. SF3

Chimborazo Hospital was constructed on Chimborazo Heights on the James River in Richmond. (Chimborazo was named after the tallest peak in the Ecuadorean Andes. An extinct volcano, it is referred to in legend as "Fire and Ice"—a somewhat prophetic name for a hospital.) It was well located near a fresh water supply, with good drainage. There was a nearby large farm for pasturage of cows and goats, and there even was a brewery with a capacity of 400 barrels of beer. Most importantly, there was a concerned citizenry to draw upon for hospital orderlies. The Confederate Secretary of War had designated Chimborazo and its grounds as an independent army post, with five surgeons in charge and 50 assistant surgeons. (Figs. 268, 268A, 269) (Fig. 270, Plate 27) (Fig. 271)

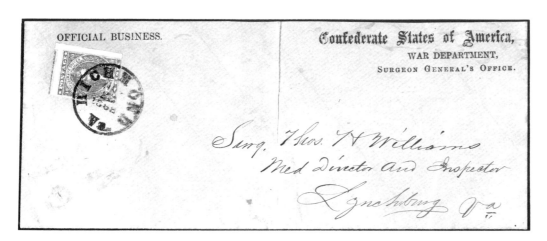

Fig. 265. Light blue 10¢ (#2) on light blue cover. Stamp shows portions of three other stamps. Richmond, Nov 22, 1862 postmark. Addressed to Surg. Thos. H. Williams, Medical Director and Inspector at Lynchburg, Va. who served directly under S.P. Moore, Surgeon General of the Confederate States Army. While the enclosed communication may have been of an official nature, all correspondence in all departments required the prepayment of postage except for the Post Office Department. SF3

Fig. 266. (Top) Manuscript town postmark dated Feb 6 endorsed by I.L. Harris, Jr. Assist. Surgeon. In the upper right is written "Phillips Legion", which was a part of the Georgia Volunteers. Directly below is a manuscript "Due 5". Addressed to Judge Iverson L. Harris at Milledgeville, Georgia, which was the state capital until occupied on November 22, 1864. SF2

(Bottom) Five cents pair (#6), light blue, postmarked Calhoun, Ga., addressed to Surgeon Lewis D. Ford at Augusta, Ga., site of the 3rd Georgia Hospital. "O.B." refers to official business. SF2

Fig. 267. (Top) Block of four (#6). Double rated. Addressed to the Institute Hospital in Richmond, Va. Postmarked Dec 16, Alexandria, La., which was occupied by Federal troops on March 16, 1864. sf4

(Middle) Adversity (homemade) cover. Vertical pair 5¢ blue (#7), red Aug 13, Alexandria, La. postmark. Stamps were printed by Archer & Daly of Richmond from plates made in London by De La Rue & Co. August 10, 1863 letter enclosed indicating that it originated at Taylor Hospital in Alexandria, La. sf3

(Bottom) The 2¢ orange brown (#8) with vignette of Andrew Jackson, circular Charleston, S.C., Apr 1 postmark. Addressed to Surgeon Robert Lebby, Medical Officer at the 1st Louisiana Hospital in Charleston. This issue to prepay drop letters and circulars, first known postmarked on April 21, 1863, compares with the 2¢ rate of the North, also with vignette of Andrew Jackson, which was issued in July 1863. sf5

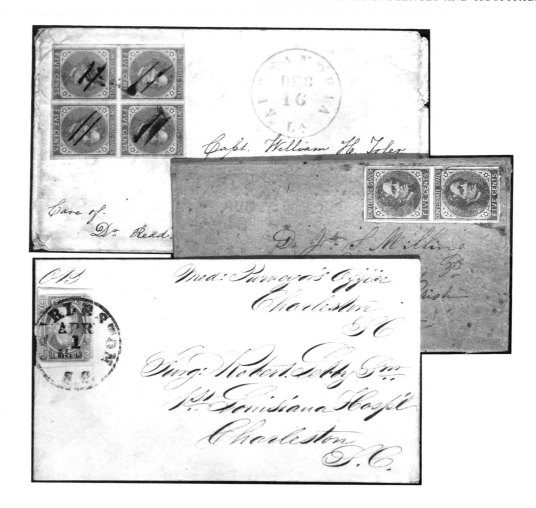

Fig. 268. The 10¢ (#11) milky blue, addressed to Chimborazo Hospital in Richmond. Palmyra, Va., July 12, 1864 postmark. sf3

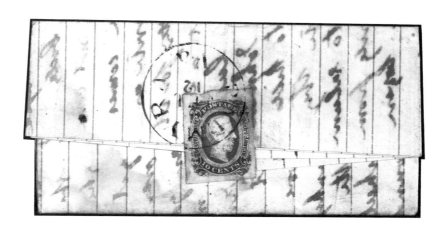

Fig. 268A. Reverse.

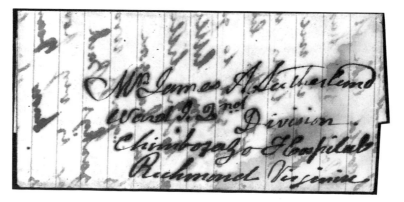

Fig. 269. (Top) The 10¢ greenish blue (#11), postmarked Feb 26, 1864, addressed to Catoosa Hospital in Griffin, Ga. Three days later on February 29 the cover was turned and used again. The stamp on the turned portion has been removed. SF3

(Middle) Milky blue 10¢ (#11), postmarked New Market, Va., May 29, to General Hospital No. 1 at Kettrell Springs, N.C. Lower left manuscript request "Please forward and oblige." SF3

(Bottom) Greenish blue (#11), Aiken, S.C., Sep 11 postmark. Docketed Sept 14, 1864. Turned cover addressed to the Asst. Surgeon in Macon, Ga. A total of 11 major Confederate hospitals were in or near Macon. SF3

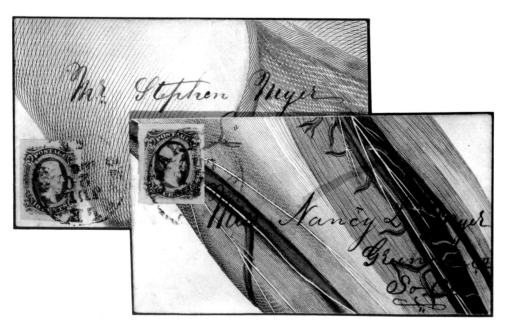

Fig. 270. (Top) Two colorful adversity covers made from a surgical text highlight that within the period of 26 days two different Confederate stamps were used from the same correspondent. Greenish blue (#11), to Mr. Stephen Myer in Greenville C.H., So. Ca., postmarked Charleston, S.C., July 20. SF4

(Bottom) Surgical cover to Miss Nancy L. Myer at Greenville C.H., So. Ca., postmarked Aug 15, Charleston, S.C., (#12) blue. As was #11, this stamp was first printed by Archer and Daly of Richmond and then in 1864 transferred to Keatinge and Ball of Columbia, S.C. Scott #12 is distinguishable from #11 by the additional line outside the ornaments at the four corners. SF4

Fig. 271. (Top) The 10¢ blue (#12), post-marked Atlanta; Medical Purveyor's Office, Atlanta, Ga. corner card. sf2

(Middle) From the Surgeon General's Office at the War Department of the Confederate States of America to George Sites, care of the Chief Medical Officer T.H. Fisher, Surgeon in Charge of General Hospital #3 at Lynchburg, Va. Greenish blue (#12), post-marked Richmond, Jul 10, 1863. sf2

(Bottom) Green 20¢ (#12), postmarked Hollow Square, Ala., on wallpaper cover addressed to an Alabama soldier in General C.A. Battle's Brigade of General Rodes' Division of the Army of Northern Va. The soldier had been transferred to Howard's Grove Hospital near Richmond and the letter was forwarded. sf3

The cover sent to Dr. Horace Taliaferro, the surgeon in charge at the General Hospital in Farmville, Virginia, has been forwarded to another doctor in Orange Court House, Virginia. The 20¢ Confederate stamp (Scott #13) has been canceled with a clear Richmond postmark dated March 19.

The earliest known use of the 20¢ green with a portrait of Washington is June 1, 1863. It was intended to be used either for the Trans-Mississippi rate of 20¢ or a double-rated 10¢. Its use, however, was limited, particularly with the closing of the Mississippi River after the surrender of Vicksburg on July 4, 1863. As a result there was a surplus of this stamp and a shortage of the more commonly used 10¢ stamp. This appears to be the case with this cover. Otherwise why the 20¢ fee—how was the addressor to know that his letter would need to be forwarded and would then require an additional 10¢ forwarding fee? There was no need for a 20¢ rate for a letter traveling such a short distance. (Fig. 272)

Mail was always important to those confined to a hospital and no less so to those at Chimborazo. According to H.H. Cunningham, writing in *Doctors in Gray*,

> An interesting petition from the Chimborazo occupants to Surgeon McCaw asked for the removal of the postmaster in that institution because he miscalled the names on more than half the letters, took too long to complete the call, and made unnecessary remarks about the writing on the back of the letters.

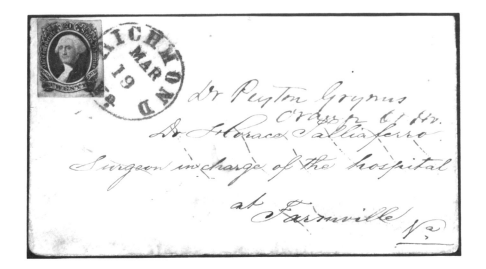

Fig. 272. Overpayment of 10¢ with the use of the 20¢ stamp (#13). SF4

WRITING HOME

(Rare Book Collection, UNC Library, Chapel Hill)

XIX

OTHER CIVIL WAR BENEVOLENCES

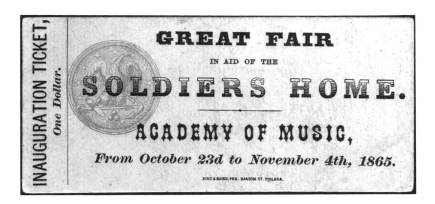

While the Sanitary Commission with its fairs and the Christian Commission with its spiritual emphasis have been the main concern of this study, there were other benevolences as well. All captured the interest of the civilian population and especially those who could see beyond the immediate day-to-day reporting of the war. Some of these people were sincerely interested in what was happening around them; others were promoters or carpetbaggers intent on taking advantage of the bereaved; and still others were businessmen, but each left his or her mark in postal history.

BUREAU OF REFUGEES, FREEDMEN AND ABANDONED LANDS

Gen. O. O. Howard, head of the Freedmen's Bureau

As early as 1863, Dr. Henry Bellows called on President Lincoln and Congress to create a Bureau of Emancipation "to superintend the transition of the freedmen (slaves) from a state of compulsory labor to a condition of self-supporting industry." Secretary of War Stanton also proposed a bureau in his report in 1864 stating, "…but not because these people are negroes, only because they are men who have been, for generations, despoiled of their rights." Finally, in March of 1865, both houses of Congress approved and President Lincoln quickly signed the bill creating the Bureau of Refugees, Freedmen and Abandoned Lands responsible for "supervision and management of all abandoned lands" and "control of all subjects relating to refugees and freedmen from rebel states."

Under the legislation the Secretary of War was authorized to provide food, clothing, and housing for the freed slaves. The bureau was authorized to lease and sell 40-acre plots of abandoned land to loyal refugees and freedmen. The officer chosen to head the bureau was Major General Oliver Otis Howard, former commander of the Army of the Tennessee, whose reputation for piety had won him the nickname "the Christian soldier". While benevolent in all that he did, Howard did not intend that the bureau be another charity, and on May 30, 1865, he issued an order that the relief establishments were to be discontinued as soon as possible and that only the "absolutely necessitous and destitute" were to be helped. The old, the infirm, the orphan, and the confused were aided where found, however. In practice, because of the large numbers of freed blacks, there was not enough land to furnish each one with the 40 acres he was promised. Some did receive the acreage; most did not. When the Sanitary Commission ceased operation on July 1, 1865, all leftover supplies and stores were turned over to General O. O. Howard. In 1872 Congress enacted legislation to end the Freedmen's Bureau. General Howard's name still lives in that distinguished institution of higher learning, Howard University. (Fig. 273)

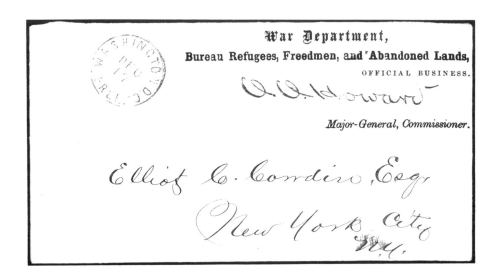

Fig. 273. Postmarked Dec 17 (1868 by enclosure), Washington D.C. Free, franked by Major-General Oliver Otis Howard, head of the Bureau of Refugees, Freedmen, and Abandoned Lands. Howard University is named after General Howard. SF3

AMERICAN UNION COMMISSION

The American Union Commission was founded in New York in October of 1864. Like the other commissions it attempted to muster forces across the country to aid the displaced former slaves. Unlike the Bureau of Refugees, Freedmen and Abandoned Lands, it was a private organization and depended on the munificence of a willing people. It was essentially religiously oriented and headed by the Reverend Joseph Parrish Thompson who said that the purpose in administering charities was to guard against creating a long state of dependence and thus holding the estimated 80,000 war refugees as paupers.

American Union Commission activities took the form of relocating displaced persons, white and black, to the extent of removing them to New York where their being unable to integrate made their plight a tragic one. While the Confederate government was aware of the displacements, it did nothing to alleviate the conditions of refugees who retreated with the southern troops as the war drew closer and closer to Richmond. One of the Commission's most highly-organized operations was the aid to the population of eastern Tennessee which had been devastated by the ebb and flow of each army through that area. (Tennessee was the site of 1,462 military actions of one degree or another, exceeded only by Virginia with 2,154.)

The period was a tragic one for both North and South. America, through the commissions, had learned that if the government would be of no help, then it was incumbent on the civilian population to step in and provide for the homeless refugees. (Figs. 274, 275)

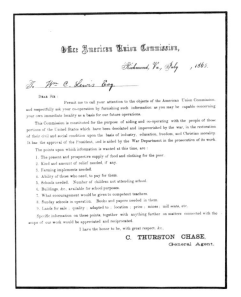

Broadside with announcement of needs of the American Union Commission

AMERICAN FREEDMEN'S UNION COMMISSION

The American Freedmen's Union Commission had its roots with the abolitionists under the direction of William Lloyd Garrison. It was an offshoot of the American Union Commission that tended to be less liberal. Its membership was made up primarily of Unitarians and Universalists, while the American Union Commission was made up mainly of Congrega-

Fig.274. (Top) Postmarked Feb 28, New York, American Union Commission. A private organization concerned with the plight of refugees, contraband (slaves), and displaced persons. It was nearly as well organized as the Sanitary Commission and Christian Commission. Founded in October 1864. SF2

(Bottom) American Union Commission, postmarked Richmond, Va., Aug 31 (1865), five months after the surrender of Richmond. With enclosure. SF2

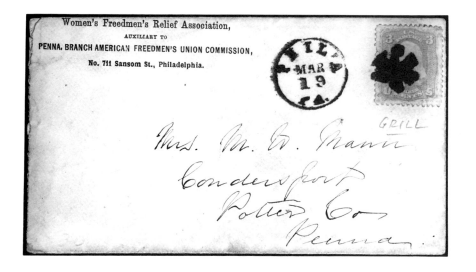

Fig. 275. The American Freedmen's Union Commission was dedicated to "establishing the corner stone of democracy...a public school system" in the South for both whites and blacks. Three-cent grilled stamp (#88) with killer cancel. SF2

tionalists. The purpose of the American Freedmen's Union Commission was to educate whites as well as blacks. The group did not regard the South as a proper field for missionary efforts. It went into the South not to convince a non-Christian or imperfectly Christian people but to aid a people impoverished by war in establishing the cornerstone of democracy—a public school system. It was disbanded in 1869, as its efforts were duplicated by the Bureau of Refugees, Freedmen and Abandoned Lands, a government agency.

TRACT SOCIETIES

Bible and Tract Societies had been a part of the American scene since the 1850s. Prior to the War Between the States, the American Tract Society was accused of condemning every sin except that of slavery. Funds for the publication of its religious pamphlets (tracts) were solicited from its members, churches, field agents, and also from wealthy gift-givers who often determined its policy toward the slavery issue. Additional income was received from the sale of religious tracts. When the war started, the American Tract Society had the advantage over other organizations of already being in operation. During the war members furnished pamphlets and religious booklets to soldiers and sailors.

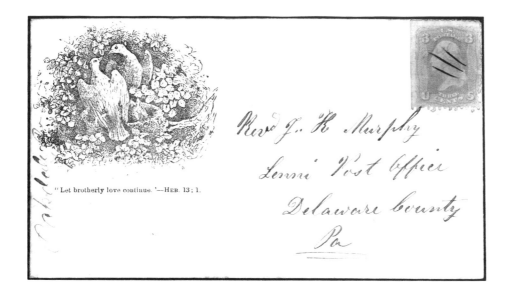

Fig. 276. Tract House on Chestnut Street in Philadelphia. Pen cancel, docketed Oakdale, Pa. On reverse, "Absent in body but present in spirit." SFI

"Old Abe", mascot of the 8th Wisconsin Volunteer Infantry

Following the war, while other relief agencies provided teachers, desks, and benches, the American Tract Society supplied primers, spelling books, and Scriptures for beginning readers at a nominal cost under the theory that if a student had to buy a book he would value it more. (Fig. 276)

OLD ABE AND THE ARMY OF THE AMERICAN EAGLE

The Army of the American Eagle was the brainchild of Alfred L. Sewell, who proclaimed himself the Commander of the Army of the American Eagle. Using the vehicle of children selling picture cards of "Old Abe", an eagle war "hero", he tied this promotion in with the Northwestern Sanitary Fair in Chicago in 1865. It was hoped that a child would buy a minimum of 10 picture cards of "Old Abe" for one dollar and he would then become a corporal in the Army of the American Eagle. By selling 4,000 of the pictures it was possible for the child to become a major general. One thing that Sewell insisted upon was cash with each order.

"Old Abe" was the name of the American Eagle captured in the region of the Flambeau and Eau Claire Rivers in Wisconsin who served as the mascot of the "Eagle" Regiment— the 8th Wisconsin Infantry Volunteers. The bird, affectionately named after President Lincoln, served four years on active service in 22 actions and 30 skirmishes. During the war he was derisively referred to as the "Yankee Buzzard", "Old Crow", "Wild Goose", or "Turkey Buzzard" by the Confederates. It was not uncommon for southern officers to offer bonuses or inducements to their troops for his capture.

Obverse

Reverse

Token of the Army of the American Eagle—
"Old Abe"

Officer's commission of the Army of the
American Eagle

The eagle was taken to the Second Sanitary Fair in Chicago, under the auspices of the state of Wisconsin, where he was proudly displayed along with relics and trophies. Everyone at the fair went to see this famous bird. When he shed his feathers from time to time, they were sold for five dollars each. P.T. Barnum offered $20,000 for the bird, but this, along with other offers to purchase, was refused.

"Old Abe" died on March 26, 1881, of suffocation from a fire in the capitol building in Madison where he was housed. The carcass was then stuffed and placed in the War Museum of the state capitol.

In the February 1970 (#65—Vol. 22, No. 1) issue of *The Chronicle of the U.S. Classic Postal Issues*, the late Henry Meyer showed a large envelope marked "Official Business" from the Headquarters of the American Eagle. He questioned why the envelope carried no stamp nor did it appear that any had dropped off. He drew attention to the fact that with 30 pictures it probably weighed more than the half-ounce basic letter rate and was subject to a double rate. Now comes another cover without postage that originated under an "Official Business" imprint and like the Meyer cover bears a Chicago postmark. This second cover, addressed to Quincy, Illinois, enclosed an officer's commission. There is no satisfactory explanation for this or the Meyer cover moving through the mail without prepayment of postage and with only the imprint "Official Business" on the envelope. The post office must have assumed that they were official business or else looked the other way. (Fig. 277)

The Army of the American Eagle enjoyed no special government privileges. The scheme had a purely profit motive except for the fact that while Sewell claimed that he received four to five hundred dollars a day, he directed some of these funds to the Northwestern Fair. Upon the opening of the second Sanitary Fair in Chicago in May of 1865, he tendered to the treasury $15,000. He was so successful with this project that he later launched another similar program and called it the "Little Corporal". In 1868, the same Alfred L. Sewell published *Our Branch and Its Tributaries: Being a History of the Work of the Northwestern Sanitary Commission and Its Auxiliaries.*

Fig. 277. Postmarked Chicago Ill., May 10, cover from Headquarters Army of the American Eagle bears no postage. Printed in upper left corner is bold "Official Business" which may have accounted for this non-prepayment. The Army of the American Eagle enjoyed no special official status. SF3

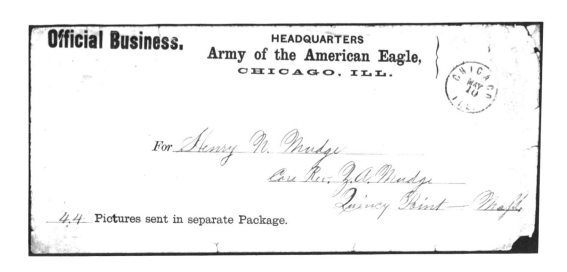

PENSIONS AND BOUNTIES

On July 16, 1862, Lincoln approved an act providing for the payment of pensions and bounties equally to regulars and volunteers wounded in the service or for the next of kin in the event of their death. The act became the basis for all subsequent legislation on pensions and bounties until 1890. For an enlisted man it provided that a widow be paid $8 a month and widows of officers whose rank was lieutenant colonel or higher were granted pensions of $30 a month. For grades in-between, the pensions varied accordingly. Before the end of the war Congress enacted further legislation providing for injuries from $25 a month for the loss of both hands or eyes down to $20 monthly for the loss of one hand and one foot. A bounty of $100, later raised to $300 for three years or $400 for five years, was to be paid over the term of service to Union soldiers. Independent agents solicited the business from widows, orphans, and the maimed in establishing claims.

Bounty jumping, that is, enlisting, deserting and re-enlisting, accounted for many of the estimated 200,000 to 268,000 desertions during the Civil War. Approximately 104,000 deserted from the Confederate Army. Some nefarious bounty agents in the North encouraged this activity with their fees. Bounties were never paid in the South. Over $300,000,000 in bounties was paid over the four years by the Federal Government and a like amount was paid by the states and localities. (Figs. 278, 279, 280, 280A)

Fig. 278. Patriotic cover from U.S. Pension and Bounty Land Office (not a government agency), 1¢ blue (#63), 35mm Auburn, N.Y., Mar 14 postmark, circular rate. SF3

When the war ended in April 1865, concern was then directed to the returned veteran. Those uninjured received an average of $250 for final pay, undrawn pay, unpaid bounties, and other claims that assisted their return to civilian life. Attention also went to the sick and wounded. A Soldiers' and Sailors' Home Fair was held in Philadelphia from October 23 to November 4, 1865. It was only later during the reconstruction era that separate soldiers' homes were provided in both the North and South for those who had served in the Civil War. (Fig. 281)

A total of $15,000 had been appropriated by Congress in July of 1862 for the purchase of prosthetic appliances for the Union soldiers. A Confederate veteran, destitute himself, returned to an impoverished homeland. Some northern states provided the limbless with artificial arms or legs, but many other disabled had to rely on the voluntary contributions of their neighbors. Private firms emerged to supply this need for these devices.

Fig. 279. (Top) Independent agents urged disabled soldiers, widows, and orphans to avail themselves of the services of a pension agent to secure benefits due a disabled soldier or next of kin. SF3

(Middle) Hurlbut, Williams & Co. of Hartford, Conn. published in 1866 a book of anecdotes and incidents of the rebellion and dedicated it to the Sanitary Commission. Part of the proceeds from this 705-page volume was donated to the Commission. SF1

(Bottom) Postmarked Fredericksburg, Va., Nov 30, printed frank of Leonard Myers, Member of Congress from Philadelphia. The Soldiers' and Sailors' Home held a fair in Philadelphia October 23 to November 4, 1865. Two large-size envelopes are also known. One was franked by Congressman Samuel J. Randall and was postmarked Phila Pa., Sep 23, and the other has a printed frank of Leonard Myers with Philadelphia station postmark. SF3

Fig. 280. Advertisement for artificial limbs, postmarked New York, Jun 4, killer cancel. SF3

Fig. 280A. Reverse.

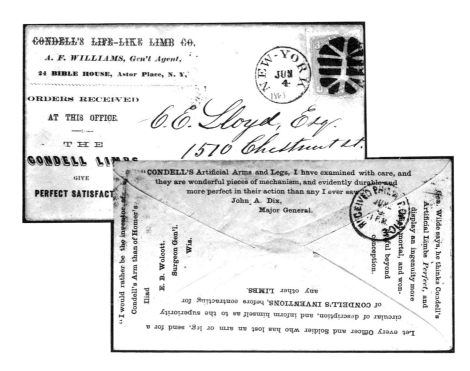

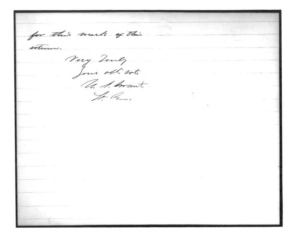

Fig. 281. From Washington at the "Head-quarters Armies of the United States". On December 18, 1865, Lt. General U.S. Grant, later President Grant, wrote to the chairman of the Soldiers' and Sailors' Fair in Philadelphia acknowledging receipt of the Frank B. Goodrich *Tribute Book*. The book is indispensable for the collector concerned with the benevolences of the Civil War period. SF5

OTHER BENEVOLENT INSTANCES

The Katharine Matthies collection, sold by Robert A. Siegel Auctions on May 21, 1969 in New York City, included a small section of patriotic envelopes used from foreign countries. One of those, pictured here, was described as a spectacular rarity and typifies the spirit of benevolence with the allegorical figures. It also brings into focus the fact that while America suffered the agony of a civil war there were many in Europe who also felt deep longings to help alleviate the hardships here. Europe at that time was in relative peace, with the Franco-Prussian War (1870–1871) still in the future. Curiously, it was in that war that all the innovations and benefits of the Sanitary Commission were once again put to the test, although by then the International Red Cross in Europe was a reality. (Fig. 282, Plate 28)

The theme of a compassionate woman ministering to a wounded soldier is repeated on these covers. Soldiers and their sweethearts or wives were a popular subject. (Fig. 283)

MAIL OF PROMINENT PERSONS ABOUT CIVIL WAR BENEVOLENCES

In April of 1863 Florence Nightingale, the nurse who introduced sanitary methods in the Crimean War some years earlier, wrote to Lord Nelson. The eight-page letter, all in her hand, tells of the appointment of nurses and the Nightingale Fund which had been established to train nurses. During the Crimean War (1854–1856) fought between Russia and England and her allies, the British Sanitary Commission revealed that deaths from sanitation-connected causes were so rampant that the British Army would have had to be replaced every nine months if her procedures had not been followed. It was largely as the result of her writing "Notes on Matters Affecting the Health, Efficiency and Hospital Administration of the British Army" that the British Sanitary Commission was formed. It was from this group that our own United States Sanitary Commission found direction. She died in 1910. Today the name Nightingale is synonymous with the nursing profession. (Fig. 284).

Fig. 282. (Top) France to the United States, strip of three and single of French 20 centimes stamp (Scott #15) tied by French diamond grid town marking #1872, Marckolsheim, France. Letter carried via British closed mail and paid through to Boston. Total charge was 15¢ or 80 centimes. Boston paid 15¢ was the current treaty rate first enacted April 1, 1857 between France and the United States. Rate continued until December 31, 1869. Of the 80 centimes the allocation was 21 centimes to the French, 11 centimes for transit through Great Britain, 32 centimes for sea postage, in this case British, and 16 centimes for inland U.S. rate. At the time the rate of exchange was 5.33 centimes to one cent U.S. SF5

(Bottom) Design similar to the French cover. To Nottingham, England with large N. York Br Pkt 5 postmark. On reverse, Nottingham, Jan. 12, '63 receiving mark. SF4

Fig. 283. (Top) Same design patriotic, postmarked Washington, Nov 29, 1862. Enclosed letter written by the brother of Lucy Wellman. SF2

(Middle) (#U59) entire, woman helping soldier. SF2

(Bottom) 3¢ rose (#65), postmarked Feb 10, Cherry Valley, Ill. SF2

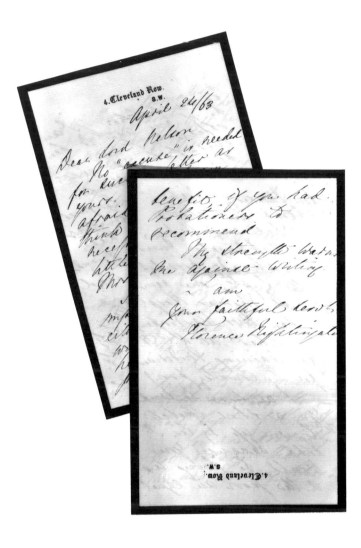

Fig. 284. Eight-page autograph letter signed of Florence Nightingale (1820–1910), April 24, 1863. Florence Nightingale promoted sanitary methods in military medicine during the Crimean War and was instrumental in establishing the British Sanitary Commission, the model for the United States Sanitary Commission. She is regarded as the founder of modern methods of nursing. SF5

Fig. 285. Franked by H(enry) Wilson, senator and later vice-president under Grant. Postmarked Washington, D.C. Free, Mar 20 (1866). Enclosure signed by a proxy for Clara Barton, founder of the American Red Cross. Abuses of the franking privilege typified by this cover resulted in the later withdrawal of the franking privilege altogether in the Grant administration and introduction of official stamps. SF2

In 1865, Clara Barton was appointed by President Lincoln to head the department searching for missing men from the Union Army. (It would be 16 years after the Civil War that Clara Barton saw her efforts to form the American Red Cross rewarded with its acceptance in this country.) In 1866, using the frank of Henry Wilson, then a senator from Massachusetts and later Vice-President of the United States, the "Office of Correspondence for Missing Men of the U.S. Army" sent out acknowledgments of requests for information on missing soldiers. The notice was signed by an aide to Clara Barton. (Fig. 285) There is no evidence that this office was ever able to completely fill the needs for information on missing soldiers. Yet responses to requests for information went to 22,000 families of soldiers. Methods of communication in 1866 were still inadequate; many soldiers were illiterate and unable to communicate with their families; many just disappeared, deserted, or were an unidentified battlefield casualty. For more on Clara Barton's work immediately following the war consult "Clara Barton and the Civil War Parole Camp at Annapolis", *The American Philatelist*, August 1960, Vol. 73, No. 11, p. 817.

Most authors and writers of the period and would-be authors and writers lent their talents to carrying on the war effort. Most, however, were content to lend what talent they had in the form of poetry or essays. Henry Wadsworth Longfellow, one of the most popular figures of the day, renewed his subscription to the Sanitary Commission and included his check for one hundred dollars. (Fig. 286)

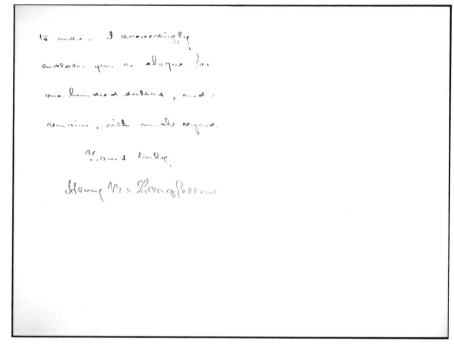

Fig. 286. Henry Wadsworth Longfellow renews his subscription to the U.S. Sanitary Commission. SF3

Jane Hoge, organizer of the Northwestern Sanitary Fair at Chicago

Despite the cares of the day Lincoln was called upon by Jane Hoge on January 23, 1864. She had written him twice before asking that her son, George B. Hoge, be appointed a Brigadier (General). Jane Hoge had been the person instrumental in the success of the first Chicago Sanitary Fair and after that had been active at the Chicago Branch of the U.S. Sanitary Commission. Now she was asking Lincoln again for the favor.

> Washington Jan 23rd 1864
>
> President Lincoln,
> Sir,
>   I leave Washington to night, & have only to beg you to remember my son's name, George B. Hoge, Col. of the 113th Ill. as one of those, whom you will request, to have appointed as Brigadier.
>
> Most respectfully,
> Mrs. A.H. Hoge
> Chicago Ill.

Five weeks later President Lincoln endorsed the reverse of Mrs. Hoge's letter:

> Submitted to the Sec.
> of War & Genl in Chief
>   A. Lincoln
> March 2, 1864

(Figs. 287, 288)

Earlier on November 25, 1862, replying to Mrs. Hoge from the Executive Mansion, Lincoln had written that it would be necessary for her son to receive a commission from the governor. Also, a General entitled to another staff officer would have to request her son

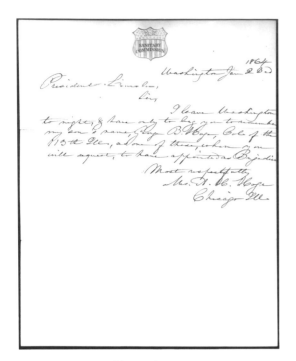

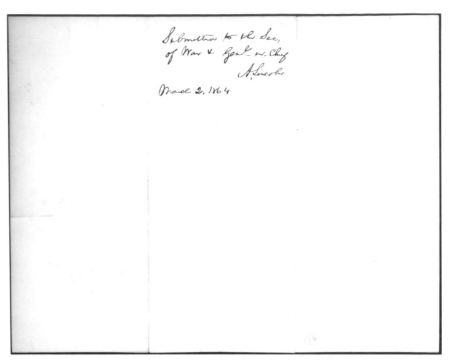

Fig. 287. Jane Hoge of the Northwestern
Sanitary Commission (Chicago) requests a
favor from President Lincoln. SF5

Fig. 288. (Reverse.)

Submitted to the Sec.
of War & Genl-in-Chief
A. Lincoln
March 2, 1864

before he could be appointed a Brigadier General. Apparently Mrs. Hoge did not follow these early instructions for securing the appointment but nonetheless wrote the President a second time. His reply of January 6, 1863 was more pointed and curt. He wrote that while she had secured a commission from the governor of Illinois for her son she did not find a Major General who needed a staff officer and would be willing to take her son on as a Brigadier. Lincoln wrote that it would be against the law for him to thrust her son on a Major General's staff; besides, it was "an indispensable courtesy" that the request come from the General. Her last effort, this letter of January 23, 1864, was influential in finally securing the appointment for her son, George Blaikie Hoge, as a Brevet Brigadier General, for on March 14, 1865, he received his commission. But he left the service on June 20, 1865.

From the Second Auditor's Office of the Treasury Department a Mr. Williamson telegraphed Mrs. Lincoln in Chicago in care of R.T. (Robert Todd) Lincoln: "Your Fair Contribution in plenty of time, & anxiously looked for. I'll write as requested."

The dating at the top of the telegram transcript of June 14, 1866 ties in with no major fair, and it is possible that Mrs. Lincoln made a contribution to one of the local fairs in aid of widows, orphans, or the disabled. It could also have been a late payment of a pledge made for the second Chicago Fair of 1865 that became a memorial to Lincoln. The shock of President Lincoln's assassination on April 14, 1865, over a year before, had left her mentally devastated. The postscript reads:

> Ask "P" to show this to Merrihew & get his approval. By common consent telegrms for Mrs. Lincoln have been franked & I do not think any telegraph Co. would deny the privilege, or object to its use.
>
> D.H.B.

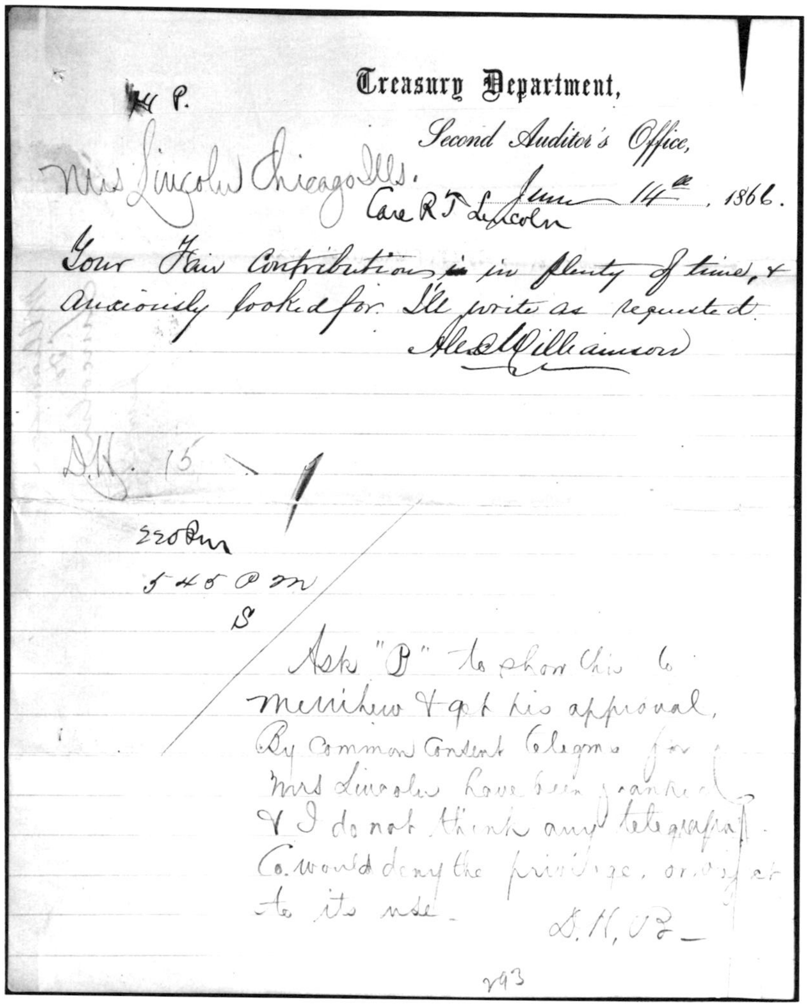

Fig. 289. Two references are made to the late President's wife. Addressed to Mrs. Lincoln, in care of her son, R.T. (Robert Todd) Lincoln, mention is made of a fair contribution and also the franking privilege of Mrs. Lincoln. SF4

On the back of the letter is a docket "Message for Mrs. A. Lincoln care of R.T. Lincoln Chicago Ills." (Fig. 289)

XX

MEDALS AND MUSIC

TOKENS AND MEDALS OF THE FAIRS

Most of the tokens and medals of the fairs are seldom seen and rarely can the collector locate them. However, that collector can be a philatelist as well as a numismatist, since the two hobbies have traditionally been intertwined and it is likely the philatelic specialist will want some background information on the allied numismatic items he might encounter. For purposes of definition, tokens have a value or an implied value while medals are more of a souvenir or of a commemorative nature. It has been estimated that between the years 1860 through 1864 more than 50,000,000 Civil War tokens were issued. These were mostly imitations of the one cent piece, and helped alleviate the severe coin shortage. George and Melvin Fuld, numismatic researchers, have identified nearly 10,000 die varieties.

Listings used by numismatists for these fair tokens and medals follow. We are deeply indebted to Rich Hartzog for his help on this section. Numbers used are Rulau/Fuld numbers.[45]

"R" represents scale of rarity with 10 the highest (one known). The rarity scale is subject to adjustment over time as new specimens are located. Actual mintages are not known for most pieces. The rarity scale is as follows:

R10 . . . . One known
R9 . . . . 2–4 known
R8 . . . . 5–10 known
R7 . . . . 10–20 known
R6 . . . . 20–75 known
R5 . . . . 75–200 known
R4 . . . . 200–500 known
R3 . . . . 500–2,000 known
R2 . . . . 2,000–5,000 known
R1 . . . . over 5,000 known

45. For further information on medals and tokens of the Civil War period consult: *Medallic Portraits of Washington* by Russell Rulau (based on Baker); *U.S. Civil War Store Cards* by George and Melvin Fuld; *Medals of the United States Mint* by R.W. Julian; *J.A. Bolen's Medals, Cards and Facsimiles* by Edwin L. Johnson; *Numismatics of Massachusetts* by Malcolm Storer, reprint 1981; *Civil War Sutler Tokens and Cardboard Scrip* by David E. Schenkman, 1983.

Token—Union Volunteer Refreshment Saloon—PA

Obverse: Union/Volunteer/Refreshment/Saloon/Instid./May 27, 1861.

Reverse: Second Annual/Fair/Held/June 15, 1863.

Copper 19mm (mentioned by Storer but not numbered)

Fuld PA 750W—1a Copper, plain edge R5

—1b Brass, plain edge R9

—1do Struck over U.S. copper-nickel cent, plain edge R10

—2a Similar, but different spacing of letters, plain edge;

rev. Fuld #1092 (Liberty head left surrounded by stars) . . . R9

—2b Same, brass, plain edge R9

—3a Same, rev. of PA 750W-1a copper, plain edge R3

	VF	Unc
W1a	$ 15.00	$ 30.00
1b	175.00	300.00
1do	—	750.00
W2a	150.00	250.00
2b	150.00	250.00
W3a	20.00	40.00

Sanitary Fair—New York Token

Obverse: BLESSED IS THE GIVER./GREAT FAIR/FOR THE/SANITARY/COMMISSION/
NEW YORK/MAY 1864. In seven irregular lines.

Reverse: GEORGE WASHINGTON PRESIDENT; head of Washington facing right, at each
side four stars.

(Fuld CWT die 1138)

Size 24mm (Storer 175, Baker 362)

Fuld NY 630BJ—1a Copper plain edge R4

—1b Brass plain edge R8

—1c Nickel plain edge R8

—1e White metal plain edge R8

—1fo Struck over French one franc silver R9

	VF	Unc
1a	$ 75.00	$150.00
1b	150.00	250.00
1c	175.00	300.00
1e	175.00	300.00
1fo	—	1,500.00

Commemorative Medal—Philadelphia

Obverse: Wounded soldier being ministered to by a doctor and nurse. Inscription around
edge: WE GIVE OUR WEALTH FOR THOSE WHO GIVE THEIR HEALTH,
FOR US.

In exergue: Pacquet F.

Reverse: IN COMMEMORATION/OF THE/GREAT CENTRAL FAIR/FOR THE/U.S.
SANITARY COMMISSION/HELD/PHILADELPHIA/JUNE 1864.

Copper 56mm, 901 struck, summer 1864. . . . . R3

VF	ExF
$125.00	$200.00

Silver 56mm (Storer 178) 4 struck, Aug. 1864, 2 known. R9

Unc

$2,500.00

Metropolitan Fair

Great Central Fair Token

Obverse: GREAT CENTRAL FAIR/PHILADELPHIA/JUNE 1864

Reverse: George Washington facing right

Fuld PA 750L-1a copper, 18mm, reeded edge (the most common of
fair tokens) R1

750L-1f Silver, 18mm R5

750L-1k Gilt-copper, 18mm R8

Also U.S. Mint Medal (Julian CM-43). There are 28 different die varieties (For
the M. and G. Fuld listing see *The Numismatist*, September 1952, p. 887.)

	VF	*Unc*
1a	$10.00	$ 25.00
1f	65.00	100.00
1k	75.00	125.00

Copper

Great Central Fair

Silver

Great Central Fair

These tokens were struck by a coining press located on the fair grounds. The copper pieces
were sold at 10 cents, the silver at 50 cents.

Copper   Silver

Great Central Fair

Sanitary Fair Nantucket Token

Obverse: GOD LOVETH A CHEERFUL GIVER/GREAT FAIR/IN AID OF THE/U.S./
SANITARY/COMMISSION,/NANTUCKET,/MASS. AUGUST, 1864. In nine lines,
the first three and last one are curved.

Reverse: Same as No. 362. (Fuld CWT die 1138)

Size 24mm (Storer 170, Baker 364)

Fuld 530 Ma — 1a Copper plain edge R5

— 1b Brass plain edge R7

— 1c Nickel plain edge R9

— 1e White metal plain edge R8

— 1f Silver plain edge R9

Great Fair at Nantucket

	VF	*Unc*
1a	$ 35.00	$ 75.00
1b	125.00	200.00
1c	175.00	300.00
1e	175.00	300.00
1f	500.00	750.00

It is to be noted that the Washington profile on Baker 364 is the same as that on Baker
362. (Dr. F.S. Edwards wrote from New York on July 23, 1864 that he had in his possession
the dies for a small medal that was prepared for the New York Metropolitan Fair but not
finished in time to be used. He stated that it could be fixed up for the Nantucket Fair and
sold for 25¢. Nine hundred were sent—one half to the fair and the other half to Dr.
Edwards.)

Northwestern Fair at Chicago

Soldiers' Fair Springfield Token

Obverse: SOLDIERS'/FAIR/DEC'1864./SPRINGFIELD, MASS./in five lines, all curved except the third, within an olive wreath.

Sanitary Fair at Wapakoneta, O.

Medals and tokens

Reverse

Union Volunteer Refreshment Saloon

Metropolitan Fair

Copper

Silver

Great Central Fair

Copper   Silver

Great Central Fair

Great Fair at Nantucket

Northwestern Fair at Chicago

Sanitary Fair at Wapakoneta, O.

Reverse: Bust in uniform, facing the left above: Washington, beneath the bust, J.A. Bolen.

Size 28mm tin, Baker 365 WM, 350 struck, about 20 known (Bolen 16, Schenkman B5, Rulau Ma-Sp65)................................ R6

	VF	*Unc*
	$25.00	$50.00

28mm copper, Baker 365A, 2 struck (Bolen 16) R9

	Unc
	$500.00

28mm copper, Baker 366. Second obverse, obverse of Baker 93. (uniformed bust left, BOLEN under bust) plain edge. R9

	Unc
	$250.00

Believed that A.R. McCoy restruck 366 using the Bolen dies.

There are other medallic remembrances of the Fair, using Bolen's reverse die. These occur with a Lincoln bust by Merriam and an Apollo bust by Merriam, all dating from the 1870s.

Commemorative Medal—Northwestern Sanitary Fair

Obverse: Bust of Lincoln facing right. Below truncation of bust: Pacquet F.

Inscription above: MEMORIA IN AETERNA. Below: ABRAHAM LINCOLN

Reverse: Standing figure of Columbia holding flag aloft. In background scene of ships on lake to right, and to left scene of encampment in front of which is "N.W. San. Com." (Northwestern Sanitary Commission). Inscription above: NORTH-WESTERN SANITARY FAIR. In exergue: CHICAGO, ILL./1865.

Copper: 57mm (King 501, Storer 169). Only 1,000 made in copper and dies destroyed. In Bangs & Co. sale of June 1878 the cataloguer, Edward Cogan, described this medal as very rare. Engraved by Anthony C. Pacquet, the engraver at the United States Mint.

	VF	*Unc*
	$200.00	$250.00

Similar to preceding—an electrotype copy, bronzed lead. Much thinner than the original. Very rare.

Wapakoneta, Ohio, Sanitary Fair Token

Obverse: MEMENTO/OF THE/SANITARY/FAIR/OF/WAPAKONETA, O.

Reverse: A trophy of flags and arms. An eagle upon a drum supported by crossed rifles, with bayonets. Above, rays. Upon each side, banners beneath four cannon balls.

Size 22mm

Fuld Ohio 905C—1a copper plain edge R8

—1b brass plain edge................................. R7

Not seen in tin/white metal in Fuld but

probably exists: Would be very rare R9

	VF	*Unc*
Brass	$125.00	$200.00
Copper	150.00	250.00
White metal	300.00	500.00

THE MUSIC AT THE FAIRS...

In 1861, a United States Sanitary Commission survey found that of 186 regiments, 143 had regimental bands and 43 had none. The Commission viewed bands as morale boosters that contributed to the esprit de corps of these troops.

In the event of a skirmish, it was usually the musicians who were unwillingly pressed into service as stretcher bearers and to tend the wounded. They were even expected to dig graves, usually in advance of an action, to provide for those killed in battle.

Music played an important part in the life of a soldier and no less for those left at home. General Robert E. Lee exclaimed that "it is impossible to have an army without music." William Mahar, professor of music at the State University of Pennsylvania, estimated in the September 1984 issue of *Civil War Times* that in the South over 750 songs were published by 40 firms before the end of the war. In the North almost 9,000 songs were published and of these at least one hundred of them sold more than 100,000 copies. Collectors of Civil War patriotic covers are familiar with many of the song sheets. (For a complete listing of these song sheets see *The Collectors Club Philatelist* Vol. XXXII, No. 1, January 1953— "Key to Patriotic Song Envelopes of the Civil War, Including a Check-List of Magnus Patriotic Song Lettersheets", by George N. Malpass.) Almost every subject was covered in these songs, and most were of a sentimental nature but many captured the spirit of the times as exemplified by the fairs. It was expected that each fair have its own march or polka, which added to the attraction of the fairs.

A grand march and two polkas were written for and dedicated to the Great Central Fair in Philadelphia. The polka is best described as a lively dance in two-four time characterized by three quick steps and a hop. Polkas had originated in Prague in 1831 in tribute to the Poles who had revolted unsuccessfully against Russia in 1830. First introduced in Paris about 1843, it became an extraordinary craze and by 1864 had crossed the Atlantic Ocean. President and Mrs. Lincoln enjoyed dancing the polka whenever they could.

Metropolitan Fair

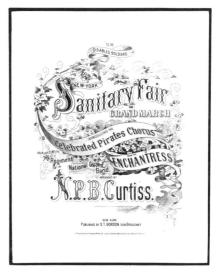

Metropolitan Fair

Brooklyn Sanitary Fair

Sheet music from the fairs

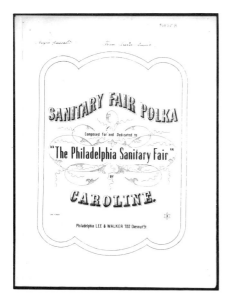

Great Central Fair

Great Central Fair

278

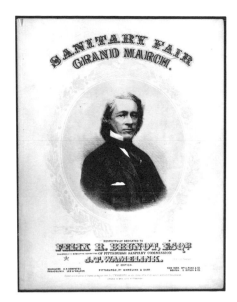

Pittsburgh Sanitary Fair

Mississippi Valley Sanitary Fair

Great Central Fair

XXI

CINDERELLAS AND EPHEMERA OF THE PERIOD

Other alleged stamps from fairs are considered to be labels as it is not certain whether they performed any postal service. Unlike Sanitary Fair stamps, none of the Cinderellas ever were used within the postal system. The older Cinderella fantasy stamps are rare and sought after by specialists in this fascinating phase of philately. These so-called fair stamps were prepared in between the period of the authentic, accepted Sanitary Fair stamps and the appearance of the first Christmas Seals in 1907. Some are as scarce as Sanitary Fair stamps themselves.

Most are the results of the efforts of S. Allan Taylor starting in 1864; his versatility, productivity, creativity, and merchandising talents have resulted in his representations appearing in most old-time collections. Briefly, S. (Samuel) Allan Taylor[46], 1838–1913, was known as the "Master Grafter" and this prince of forgers was one of the most colorful philatelic personalities of all time. His theory was that if collectors were fools enough to buy little bits of paper, then they were fair game for his make-believe stamps.

46. For more information on S. Allan Taylor refer to: "Sidelights on Literature", *The American Philatelist*, Vol. 49, No. 10, July 1936 and No. 11, August 1936 by Ralph A. Kimble and *Philatelic Literature Review*, Vol. 15, No. 2: 2nd Quarter 1966, by Jan Kindler.

Usually Taylor would prepare a composition "form" with a number of his subject designs. He would select a colored paper that was readily available. Then, using an assortment of woodcuts, engravings, electrotypes, and type blocks he would then proceed to print from the form on a small hand or foot press. He then cut apart the small, individual designs and while usually careful, he would sometimes overcut or undercut in the separation process so that one "stamp" might have a border or miscut from a neighboring different design. It is possible that one or more of these forms contained a Sanitary Fair stamp(s) since the paper Taylor used in creating his "stamps" is exactly that of the fair counterfeits. Sherwood Springer in the Fourth Edition (1966) of his ongoing work, *Springer's Handbook of North American Cinderella Stamps Including Taxpaid Revenues*, reported that he had never seen an unsevered pair of a Taylor-made.

Springer at first reconstructed a form by painstakingly putting together these miscuts and was partially successful. Then he came up with the idea that rather than trying to piece together many different colored stamps it might prove more logical to first separate the stamps by paper color and ink color and then proceed to put the jigsaw puzzle in place by once again matching the color and remnant of a nearby stamp.

Taylor's work includes among others the Springside Post Office, Tabernacle Fair Post Office, Warren Ave. Church Fair, and the Lincoln Subscription stamps. He advertised the Springside Post Office as a Pittsfield, Massachusetts issue. Note the similarity between the Warren Ave. Church Fair stamp and the Tabernacle Fair Post Office stamp.

The Union Home School Fair labels are both postmarked which would seem to indicate that they performed some postal function but search has revealed no other examples of their use. Sherwood Springer has speculated that they are authentic and not in the nature of a Cinderella. Both are on rough dull pink paper printed in black.

Little Wanderers Aid Society is no doubt another figment of Taylor's imagination. In Boston, where Taylor set up his printing business, there were orphans and abandoned children left on their own following the war. To shelter them a refuge home, "The Baldwin Place for Little Wanderers", was established. Once placed in this home, the children stayed for a short time before being sent out on trains to homesteads in the underpopulated areas of the East and Midwest. Their arrival was always scheduled for a Saturday in order for them to be cleaned up for introduction at church the next day. The children were presented and then placed with the first family that would treat them kindly and lovingly. Though many children were overworked and not well treated, many grew up to be upright and highly respected citizens.

In the 1860s the Little Wanderers' name was well known since there existed a home for Little Wanderers and this was probably known to Taylor also. Borrowing from the success of the sale of stamps at the Sanitary Fairs, he used the idea for promoting his own labels. In his publication *Stamp Collectors' Record* (Boston, February 1866) he noted:

> New Local. A stamp is to be used at a Bazaar shortly to be held in this city for the benefit of the Orphan's Aid Society and will do duty in the same manner as the stamp of the Sanitary Fair Bazaars. The design is the head of a child wearing a Glengarry cap and is evidently modelled after the scion of Guelph depicted on the 17¢ New Brunswick. The value expressed thereon is 10¢....

Volunteer aid societies did exist at that time but records reveal no bona fide organization known as the Little Wanderers Aid Society nor is there any record that Taylor used any of the proceeds for the welfare of orphans and abandoned children.

It has been suggested but never proven that the "Lincoln Subscription" labels were sold by supporters to raise money for his campaign of 1864. Some are known on cover along with stamps of the period. (Fig. 290)

The Orthodox Jewish Fair triangles were issued in the Jewish year 5639 which corresponds to 1878–1879. While these four issues do not fall within the Sanitary Fair period, they were issued within 15 years of the war's end and predated the popular Christmas Seals that came 28 years later. Each of the four values was printed in a different color. All are triangular shaped.

Little was known of these stamps until recently when Nathan Kaganoff, librarian at the American Jewish Historical Society of Waltham, Massachusetts, made a search of Jewish newspapers of the period. Mr. Kaganoff identified the central portrait as that of Sir Moses Montefiore (1784–1885), the Jewish philanthropist and important figure in the English and European community who was especially active in obtaining civil rights for his co-religionists.

In the December 6, 1878 *Jewish Messenger*, an orthodox Jewish newspaper published in New York, there appeared a notice that on Monday evening next (December 9th) "the fair in aid of the Norfolk Street Synagogue will be formally opened at Tammany Hall and will continue until December 22 (5639)...there will be a Floral Temple, Rebecca's Well, *Post Office*...". While this information does not definitely confirm that these stamps were issued in conjunction with the Norfolk Street Synagogue the date on the stamps does conform to the year date of the newspaper announcement. The fair, also known as the Shaare Rachim Fair, was important enough to be announced in *The American Israelite*, a reform Jewish newspaper published in Cincinnati, a city some distance away. Consideration as to the date must take into account that the Jewish New Year of 5639 began in the fall of 1878 which was the start of the Jewish New Year. This is the date that appears on the adhesive.

The Homoepathic Hospital Fair 10 cent stamp is blue in color. In 1869, the Ladies' Homoeopathic Hospital Fair Association held its fair in Philadelphia between November 17th and 30th for the purpose of raising funds toward the purchase of buildings and land to house the Homoeopathic[47] Medical College of Pennsylvania. The fair raised a total of $17,000. According to a writer at the time of the fair, "It was the handsomest [fair] held in this city since the great 'Sanitary'.[48] The returns from all the little schemes for raising money, such as the post office…were made through the tables with which they were connected." (Fig. 291)

47. "Homoepathic" as the name appears on the stamp is a contraction of the European spelling of "homoeopathic" and was the term used during the period. The present spelling is "homeopathic". The first homeopathic hospital in the United States was established in Allentown, Pennsylvania in 1832 by Dr. Constantine Hering.

48. Philadelphia had been the site of the Great Central Fair five years earlier and had been referred to in print and conversation as the "Sanitary".

Fig. 290. (First row) Warren Ave. Church Fair. Colors are: green on grayish, green on brown, green on yellow. Tabernacle Fair Post Office. Colors are: brownish vermilion on white, brownish vermilion on horizontal laid green. Size 20 x 24mm. SF1

(Second row) Springside Post Office. Colors are: black on bright green, black on rust-pink, black on gray, black on gold metallic surface colored paper, black on black, black on bluish gray, red on rose, red on white. Size 22 x 16mm. SF1

(Third row) Union Home School Fair, canceled, 29 x 30mm. SF1

(Fourth row) Little Wanderers Aid Society colors: 2¢ violet on white or yellow horizontal laid paper, red on white, brown on cream, black on violet surface colored paper; 5¢ green on white or yellow; 10¢ red on white pelure, black on violet, green or dark blue surface colored paper. Size 25 x 29mm. SF2

(Fifth row) Lincoln Subscription colors: 2¢ black on orange surface, 3¢ black on green, 4¢ black on pink, 5¢ blue on white, 10¢ black on yellow, 12¢ black on dark blue. Size 25 x 30mm. SF2

Fig. 291. (Top, middle) Orthodox Jewish Fair colors: 5¢ brownish vermilion, 10¢ blue, 25¢ violet, 50¢ green. Size 46 x 24mm. SF4

(Bottom) Homoepathic Hospital Fair, blue, 30 x 35mm. SF3

Two of its buildings were used as hospitals for the wounded by the army during the war. In 1885, the name was changed to Hahnemann Medical College. The college became Hahnemann University in 1981.

Cholera, dysentery, and measles which were prevalent during the war prompted the Medical Bureau to look into homeopathy as a possible answer to cures for these diseases and others. After an investigation, based primarily along the lines of conservative versus liberal medicine, the idea was completely rejected.

Samuel Hahnemann (1755–1843) founded homeopathy, a school of medicine which tries to cure diseases with small doses of a drug or remedy which in larger doses can produce in a healthy person symptoms of the disease. During the Civil War, with the exception of quinine, a drug widely used by all, homeopathy took the form of also using tested plants, herbs, and minerals. It was not until pharmaceuticals came into wider use that homeopathy expanded its treatment into compounded medicines.

XXII

EPILOGUE

While the Sanitary Commission began modestly, by the war's end its impact on the military and medical services was significant. It enrolled associate doctors and prepared medical monographs, with over 50,000 of these being distributed. The monographs contained information on the latest treatment of diseases and wounds. In all the four years of its operation during the war the Commission steadfastly refused to take on the duties and functions of government and always worked through government channels for any changes that it wanted. The Commission sought through public information to keep a populace informed about its activities so as to mold public opinion along lines that were believed to be most helpful toward minimizing pain and suffering. The Commission always stressed sanitary and preventative measures before relief measures, although the latter were not neglected either. By coaxing and urging change, the local sanitary inspectors prevailed upon medical practitioners to upgrade their techniques and sanitary concerns. In reforming the Medical Bureau, the U.S. Sanitary Commission hoped to put an end to incompetency and inefficiency.

The first open air pavilion type hospitals that it recommended were instrumental in preventing the spread of diseases. In its soldiers' homes the Commission protected the soldier and the public by caring for over 2,000 servicemen a day. It provided and planned the use of railroad cars and steamers to evacuate the wounded and thereby prevented local partiality in the treatment of the disabled. Hospital railroad cars were developed with elastic straps to act as shock absorbers in order to minimize the agony of the maimed and lame.

The Sanitary Commission supplied over one million nights of lodging for the soldiers in transit with no place to rest. It collected over $2,500,000 in back wages for soldiers. It furnished clothing where necessary, special food for those on restricted diets, wrote letters for patients, and then provided stamps for those letters.

Over 7,000 women's aid societies were united in a common cause by the Commission. By 1862 most women of the North had been brought into direct contact with the Commission. The Commission found women much superior to men in collecting stores and supplies because of their zeal and enthusiasm.

Charles J. Stillé, Corresponding Secretary of the Executive Committee of the Sanitary Commission, in his *History of the United States Sanitary Commission*, in 1866 reported that the total receipts for the Commission could not be stated with any precision. In addition to the supplies amounting to $15,000,000, the cash receipts to the Central Treasury to May 1, 1866 were $4,962,014.26. To this should be added an estimated $2,000,000 receipts from the branch treasuries which were never reported plus the free public services, i.e., free railroad transportation of supplies, telegrams, etc. Agents were reimbursed for their transportation but received no salaries. The total of all contributions in cash, stores, and public services came to approximately $25,000,000 for the four years.

The Commission was concerned with the lot of prisoners both from the North and South. At Camp Douglas much was accomplished to clean up "a disgusting hole" where Confederate prisoners were confined. The Commission never forgot that Confederate soldiers were Americans also.

The Commission thought that the American people would never forget its work in the war but twenty years after the war Charles Stillé sadly admitted that their work was all but forgotten. That the Red Cross had its genesis in the U.S. Sanitary Commission was forgotten as well. The Red Cross could promise more extensive operation through its international activities than an organization that was formed for "inquiry, advice and supply". The United States Sanitary Commission made the public aware of the benefits of hygiene and sanitation.

Dr. Bellows, its president, wrote Henri Dunant and he had this to say: "What chloroform is to surgery, humanity is to war. It does not stop bloodshed, but it spares needless suffering."

During the four years that the Sanitary Commission functioned during the War Between the States there were many accomplishments, the least of which were the stamps and covers that have been left to us. The war was a brutal and in some ways an unnecessary conflict yet philately has helped preserve this saga of American history. For the collector of patriotic covers there are the colorful corner cards of the era. For the collector of Confederate stamps and covers there are the activities of a fraternity of their own—the Confederate Stamp Alliance. For the collector of revenue stamps this period is one of the richest of all times. For the enthusiastic student of rates and routes, these four years yield a rich bounty. For the collectors of Official stamps, they find that their interests are a direct result of the abuses during the war. And for the collector of Sanitary Fair stamps this period in American history has provided a rich lore in stamps and covers that encompasses all the above disciplines. An attempt has been made to show a representation. It is now up to the future generations of philatelists to carry the study even further with new revelations and new delights as they occur.

Most appropriate today, as it was just about one hundred years ago, is the statement of J.W. Scott in *The American Philatelist*, Vol. 3, No. 3 of 1888: "…the series I have described [the Sanitary Fair stamps], which is composed of thirteen stamps [now fifteen], all told, and considering the small number, the interest attached to them and the great events they commemorate, is well worthy an honored place in the collections of American philatelists."

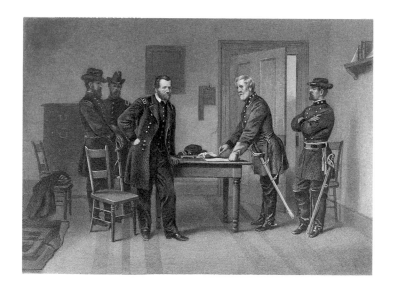

Lee's surrender to Grant at Appomattox

APPENDIX I

No. 3.

ORDER OF THE SECRETARY OF WAR, APPROVED BY THE PRESIDENT,
APPOINTING THE SANITARY COMMISSION.

WAR DEPARTMENT,
Washington, June 9, 1861.

The Secretary of War has learned, with great satisfaction, that at the instance and in pursuance of the suggestion of the Medical Bureau, in a communication to this office, dated May 22, 1861, Henry W. Bellows, D.D., Prof. A.D. Bache, LL.D., Prof. Jeffries Wyman, M.D., Prof. Wolcott Gibbs, M.D., W.H. VanBuren, M.D., Samuel G. Howe, M.D., R.C. Wood, Surgeon U.S.A., G.W. Cullum, U.S.A., Alexander E. Shiras, U.S.A., have mostly consented, in connection with such others as they may choose to associate with them, to act as "A Commission of Inquiry and Advice in respect of the Sanitary Interests of the United States Forces," and without remuneration from the Government. The Secretary has submitted their patriotic proposal to the consideration of the President, who directs the acceptance of the services thus generously offered.

The Commission, in connection with a Surgeon of the U.S.A., to be designated by the Secretary, will direct its inquiries to the principles and practices connected with the inspection of recruits and enlisted men; the sanitary condition of the volunteers; to the means of preserving and restoring the health, and of securing the general comfort and efficiency of troops; to the proper provision of cooks, nurses, and hospitals; and to other subjects of like nature.

The Commission will frame such rules and regulations, in respect of the objects and modes of its inquiry, as may seem best adapted to the purpose of its constitution, which, when approved by the Secretary, will be established as general guides of its investigations and action.

A room with necessary conveniences will be provided in the City of Washington for the use of the Commission, and the members will meet when and at such places as may be convenient to them for consultation, and for the determination of such questions as may come properly before the Commission.

In the progress of its inquiries, the Commission will correspond freely with the Department and with the Medical Bureau, and will communicate to each, from time to time, such observations and results as it may deem expedient and important.

The Commission will exist until the Secretary of War shall otherwise direct, unless sooner dissolved by its own action.

SIMON CAMERON,
Secretary of War.

I approve the above.

A. LINCOLN.

June 13, 1861.

APPENDIX II

NORTHERN GENERAL HOSPITALS AS OF DECEMBER 17, 1864

DEPARTMENT OF WASHINGTON

Name	Location	Beds
Armory Square	Washington, D.C.	1,000
Carver	Washington, D.C.	1,300
Campbell	Washington, D.C.	900
Columbian	Washington, D.C.	844
Douglas	Washington, D.C.	400
Emory	Washington, D.C.	900
Finley	Washington, D.C.	1,061
Freedman	Washington, D.C.	72
Harewood	Washington, D.C.	2,000
Judiciary Square	Washington, D.C.	510
Kalorama	Washington, D.C.	434
Lincoln	Washington, D.C.	2,575
Mount Pleasant	Washington, D.C.	1,618
Ricord	Washington, D.C.	120
Stanton	Washington, D.C.	420
Stone	Washington, D.C.	170
Seminary	Georgetown, D.C.	121
Augur	Near Alexandria, Va.	668
Claremont	Alexandria, Va.	164
L'Ouverture	Alexandria, Va.	717
1st Division	Annapolis, Md.	753
2nd Division	Alexandria, Va.	993
3rd Division	Alexandria, Va.	1,350
Fairfax Seminary	Virginia	936
U.S. General	Point Lookout, Md.	1,400

DEPARTMENT OF PENNSYLVANIA

Name	Location	Beds
Broad Street	Philadelphia	525
Citizens' Voluntary	Philadelphia	236
Convalescent	Philadelphia	766
Haddington	Philadelphia	1,329
Islington	Philadelphia	60
McClellan	Philadelphia	1,089
Mower	Philadelphia	3,100
Satterlee	Philadelphia	3,519
South Street	Philadelphia	288
Summit House	Philadelphia	1,204
Turner's Lane	Philadelphia	285
Officers'	Cammack Woods, Pa.	92

Chester	Chester, Pa.	878
Cuyler	Germantown, Pa.	646
U.S. General	Pittsburgh, Pa.	723
White Hall	White Hall, Pa.	1,369
York	York, Pa.	1,600
Beverly	Beverly, N.J.	1,000

DEPARTMENT OF THE OHIO

Name	Location	Beds
Brown	Louisville, Ky.	700
Clay	Louisville, Ky.	178
Crittenden	Louisville, Ky.	360
Eruptive	Louisville, Ky.	203
Foundry	Louisville, Ky.	200
Officers'	Louisville, Ky.	37
U.S. General	Ashland, Ky.	275
U.S. General	Bowling Green, Ky.	146
Main Street	Covington, Ky.	300
Seminary	Covington, Ky.	218
Joe Holt	Jeffersonville, Ky.	980
U.S. General	Lexington, Ky.	463
Nelson	Camp Nelson, Ky.	700
Jefferson	Jeffersonville, Ind.	2,399
No. 16	Jeffersonville, Ind.	144
U.S. General	Knoxville, Tenn.	1,190
Officers'	Knoxville, Tenn.	42

DEPARTMENT OF THE EAST

Name	Location	Beds
Ladies' Home	New York City, N.Y.	402
St. Joseph	New York City, N.Y.	325
Transit	New York City, N.Y.	62
David's Island	New York City, N.Y.	1,700
Ft. Columbus	New York City, N.Y.	100
Grant	Willet's Point, N.Y.	1,293
McDougall	Ft. Schuyler, N.Y.	1,184
Officers'	Bedloe's Island, N.Y.	103
Albany	Albany, N.Y.	482
Buffalo	Buffalo, N.Y.	150
Sisters of Charity	Buffalo, N.Y.	200
Elmira	Elmira, N.Y.	325
St. Mary's	Rochester, N.Y.	680
Troy	Troy, N.Y.	300
Ward	Newark, N.J.	927
Knight	New Haven, Conn.	607
Webster	Manchester, N.H.	475
Brattleboro	Brattleboro, Vt.	725

Baxter	Burlington, Vt.	500
Sloan	Montpelier, Vt.	469
Mason	Boston, Mass.	60
Readville	Readville, Mass.	1,000
Dale	Worcester, Mass.	480
Lovell	Portsmouth Grove, R.I.	1,464
Cony	Augusta, Me.	816

NORTHERN DEPARTMENT

Name	Location	Beds
Officers'	Cincinnati, Ohio	75
Marine	Cincinnati, Ohio	122
Washington Park	Cincinnati, Ohio	150
West End	Cincinnati, Ohio	120
Seminary	Columbus, Ohio	150
Dennison	Camp Dennison, Ohio	1,716
U.S. General	Camp Chase, Ohio	200
U.S. General	Cleveland, Ohio	330
U.S. General	Gallipolis, Ohio	350
U.S. General	Evansville, Ind.	702
U.S. General	Indianapolis, Ind.	256
U.S. General	New Albany, Ind.	860
Ohio	New Albany, Ind.	300
Corps d'Afrique	New Albany, Ind.	146
Madison	Madison, Ind.	2,430
Desmarres	Chicago, Ill.	150
Marine	Chicago, Ill.	110
U.S. General	Quincy, Ill.	950
U.S. General	Camp Butler, Ill.	525
U.S. General	Camp Douglas, Ill.	137
Simons	Mound City, Ill.	788
Harper	Detroit, Mich.	578
St. Mary's	Detroit, Mich.	276

Source: *Medical and Surgical History of the War of the Rebellion*, Medical Volume, Third Part, Surgeon General's Office. Prepared under the direction of Charles Smart, Major and Surgeon, United States Army, Washington, Government Printing Office, 1888, page 896.

PRINCIPAL HOSPITALS IN THE CONFEDERATE STATES

VIRGINIA

Name	Location
Chimborazo	Richmond
Camp Jackson	Richmond
Camp Winder	Richmond
Camp Lee	Richmond
Howard's Grove	Richmond
Stuart	Richmond
Louisiana	Richmond
General, No. 9	Richmond
General, No. 13	Richmond
General, No. 21	Richmond
General, No. 24	Richmond
General	Liberty
General	Huguenot Springs
General	Gordonsville
General, No. 1	Lynchburg
General, No. 2	Lynchburg
General, No. 3	Lynchburg
Ladies' Relief	Lynchburg
Pratt	Lynchburg
Way	Lynchburg
General	Farmville
General	Danville
General	Staunton
Confederate States	Petersburg
General	Petersburg
South Carolina	Petersburg
Poplar Lawn	Petersburg
Wayside	Petersburg
Small Pox	Petersburg
North Carolina	Petersburg
Virginia	Petersburg
General	Pearisburg
General	Charlottesville
General	Montgomery Springs
General	Emory
General	Harrisonburg
Washington	Abingdon
Wayside	Burkesville
Breckinridge	Marion

NORTH CAROLINA

Name	Location
Way, No. 5	Wilmington
General, No. 4	Wilmington
General, No. 5	Wilmington
Way, No. 7	Tarboro
Way, No. 1	Weldon
Way, No. 6	Charlotte
General, No. 11	Charlotte
Gen. Military No. 2	Wilson
Way	Goldsboro
General, No. 3	Goldsboro
General, No. 7	Raleigh
General, No. 8	Raleigh
Pittigrew	Raleigh
Sorrel	Asheville
General, No. 9	Salisbury
General, No. 10	Salisbury
Way, No. 3	Salisbury
General, No. 6	Fayetteville
General, No. 1	Kettrell Springs
General, No. 12	Greensboro
Way, No. 2	Greensboro

SOUTH CAROLINA

Name	Location
Ladies' General No. 3	Columbia
General, No. 1	Columbia
Second N. Carolina	Columbia
Way	Kingsville
Third N. Carolina	Charleston
First S. Carolina	Charleston
First Louisiana	Charleston
General	Georgetown
First Georgia	Charleston
Soldiers' Relief	Charleston
Way	Florence
Way	Greenville

GEORGIA

Name	Location
Erwin	Barnesville
Way	Fort Gaines
General, No. 1	Savannah
General, No. 2	Savannah

Name	Location
General	Columbus
Third Georgia	Augusta
Hardee	Forsyth
Clayton	Forsyth
General	Guyton
Lumpkin	Covington
Asylum	Madison
Kingston	Kingston
Polk	Atlanta
Bragg	Newnan
Foard	Newnan
Buckner	Newnan
Cannon	LaGrange
St. Mary's	LaGrange
Law	LaGrange
Oliver	LaGrange
Hood	Covington
Dawson	Greensboro
Gilmer	Marietta
Academy	Marietta
Foard	Marietta
Bell	Greensboro
Blackie	Madison
Prin	Griffin
Director	Griffin
Quintard	Griffin
Stout	Madison
Newsom	Thomaston
Fair Ground, No. 1	near Macon
Fair Ground, No. 2	near Macon
Empire	near Macon
Grant	near Macon
Institute	near Macon
Hill	Covington
Ocmulgee	Macon
City Hall	Macon
Blind School	Macon
Floyd House	Macon
Catoosa	Griffin
Medical College	near Macon
First Florida	Fort Gaines
Reid	West Point
Gamble	Newnan
Marshall	Columbus
Stout	Macon
Lee	Columbus

ALABAMA

Name	Location
Nott	Mobile
General	Mobile
General	Greenville
Way	Demopolis
General	Tuscaloosa
General	Selma
Way	Talladega
General	Spring Hill
General (Ross)	Mobile
Way	Selma
Ladies	Montgomery
Stonewall	Montgomery
Way	Eufaula
General	Mobile
General	Mobile
Madison House	Montgomery
Texas	Auburn
St. Mary's	Montgomery
General	Notasulga
Concert Hall	Montgomery
Watts	Montgomery
Officers'	Uniontown
General	Shelby Springs

MISSISSIPPI

Name	Location
General	Grenada
Way	Guntown
	Liberty

FLORIDA

Name	Location
General	Quincy
General	Tallahassee
General	Lake City
Way	Madison

TENNESSEE

Name	Location
General	Bristol
Hood	Bristol

Source: *Doctors in Gray–The Confederate Medical Service*, by H.H. Cunningham, published by the Louisiana State University Press, Baton Rouge, 1958.

GLOSSARY

ADHESIVE — A stamp intended to be affixed to a piece of mail by an adhesive substance as distinguished from one embossed or printed directly on an envelope.

ADVERTISED — A handstamp applied to an envelope indicating that the piece was undeliverable and had been advertised in a newspaper. Usually there was an additional fee charged by the post office for this service.

BACKSTAMP — A postal or other informational marking placed on the back of an envelope.

BLACK JACK — The U.S. two-cent black stamp of 1863 with an over-sized portrait of Andrew Jackson.

BLOCK — A multiple of unsevered stamps containing at least two parallel rows of stamps in any direction.

BOGUS — A term applied to stamp-like labels purporting to be authentic collectibles or to an authentic stamp which bears a sham addition.

CANCELLATION — A postal marking intended to make further use of a stamp impossible by obliterating or defacing the design.

> Manuscript Cancellation — A hand-written defacement of a stamp as contrasted with one made by a hand-stamp or mechanical device.

> Pen Cancellation — Usually refers to defacement by random pen strokes rather than by manuscript letters or words.

CARRIER STAMP — A supplementary special stamp used to pay the letter carrier's charge for local pick-up or delivery of mail. This system was abolished in 1863 when free delivery began.

CINDERELLA — A generic term applied to collectible stamp-like labels which are unlisted in general postage stamp catalogs as well as most specialized catalogs. Specific categories may vary with the customs of the country of issue. Cinderellas may be of postal, pseudo-postal, non-postal, or fiscal origin. They usually have the appearance of conventional postage stamps but are not valid for national or international mail services.

CIVIL WAR PATRIOTIC — Unofficial illustrated envelope displaying patriotic or nationalistic sentiments and used by both the North and the South during the Civil War.

CORNER CARD — The name and address of the sender or user of an envelope with or without illustration or decoration and usually in the upper left corner.

COUNTERFEIT — A fraudulent imitation of a genuine stamp made to defraud either a government authority or collectors.

COVER — A term denoting an entire envelope or folded letter used postally as the "cover of correspondence".

DEMONETIZED STAMP — Stamp declared invalid for postage and withdrawn from use, particularly during the early days of the Civil War.

DIE — An original piece of metal or other material on which a stamp's design is first engraved and from which multiples are made to form a printing base.

DROP LETTER — A letter delivered at the same post office at which it was mailed or held for collection there by the addressee.

ENTIRE — An envelope in its entire state as sold by the post office with an imprinted stamp.

ESSAY — A design which has been proposed for a stamp but not adopted. It may be in the form of an actual stamp or in any of several graphic arts media.

FACSIMILE — "An imitation of a genuine philatelic item produced and offered without any intention to deceive." (Kenneth Wood, *This Is Philately*)

FAKE — A genuine stamp altered in some way to falsely enhance its value to collectors; not synonymous with forgery or counterfeit.

FORGERY — Same as counterfeit; an imitation of an authentic specimen intended to deceive.

FORWARDING MARKING — A handstamped marking with the words "Forwarded by..." to indicate that the cover was forwarded from one point to another in order to reach the addressee.

FRAME — The border of a stamp that encloses the central feature.

FRANK — The mark or signature on a cover of a person permitted to send or receive mail free of postage.

HANDSTAMP — A hand-applied postal marking used to cancel a stamp or to designate rate, routing, postage due, etc., information.

IMITATION — Something derived or copied from an original. Occasionally used in philately to describe a non-genuine philatelic item whose origin is uncertain.

IMPERFORATE (abbrev. IMPERF.) — Refers to stamps printed in sheets without perforations or other means of separation.

IMPRINT — A marginal inscription on the selvage of a sheet of stamps identifying the printer or issuing authority.

INDIA PAPER — A thin, tough, absorbent paper used for taking proof impressions.

ISSUE — A term used to describe a related group of stamps placed on sale at a certain time.

LOCAL POSTS — Private postal systems serving mail routes in direct competition with or supplementing official services. Most were abolished by the Act of 1861.

MATCH AND MEDICINE STAMPS (Private Die Proprietary) — Special design tax or revenue stamps applied to matches, proprietary medicines, canned fruit, perfumes, and playing cards, largely during the Civil War.

MINT STAMP — A stamp in its original state of issue by a post office.

MOURNING COVER — A black-bordered envelope used to announce a death.

PAIR — Two unseparated stamps attached horizontally or vertically as originally issued.

PAPER

> Laid Paper — One of two main types of stamp paper texture showing a pattern of alternate parallel lines created by the wires on which it was formed.

> Wove Paper — The second basic type of stamp paper texture formed on a fine, closely interwoven mesh and showing no discernible pattern when held to the light.

PERFORATIONS (abbrev. PERF.) — The series of holes punched between stamps in a sheet to facilitate separation.

PHANTOM — "Stamps that are not what they seem" (F.J. Melville). Illusory or fictitious "stamps" intended to deceive collectors.

POSTMARK — A postal marking indicating office of origin of the cover or manner of postal conveyance; may be used to cancel or obliterate stamps also.

PROOFS — Special prints or impressions made during the preparation of a printing base, usually prior to the manufacture of stamps.

> Die Proof — A print made from the completed die for approval and record purposes.

> Plate Proof — Print made from an approved plate, cylinder, or stone, usually before printing begins but can be made thereafter (posthumous proofs) for special purposes other than checking.

> Progress Die Proof — Print made by an engraver from a die as he works on it to check the progress of his work.

> Trial Color Proofs — Prints, either from a die or a plate, in various colors not normal to the issued stamp and made to enable choice of the final color.

SE-TENANT — A term describing two or more adjoining, different, unseparated stamps.

STRIP — Three or more unsevered stamps in a single horizontal or vertical row.

BIBLIOGRAPHY

TARGET CANCELLATION—A type of cancellation consisting of concentric circles.

TÊTE-BÊCHE—A term describing a joined pair of stamps in which one is upside down in relation to the other.

TIED ON—A term indicating that the postal marking cancels the stamp and overlaps onto the envelope, thus assuring that the stamp was present when the envelope or cover was processed at the post office.

TURNED COVER—A letter sheet or envelope that was reversed to permit a second use in times of paper shortages; this practice was used primarily within the Confederacy and the resultant covers are much sought after by collectors.

WRAPPERS—Government postal stationery consisting of a blank sheet of paper gummed on one edge and bearing an embossed stamp design as used on concurrent envelopes; intended for mailing newspapers and similar matter.

PHILATELIC ARTICLES ON SANITARY FAIRS

Drayton, Evelyn S., "Civil War Sanitary Fair Stamps", *Stamps*, September 12, 1953, p. 374–376.

Hamilton, James H., "The Sanitary Fairs", *S.P.A. Journal*, Society of Philatelic Americans—Vol. 24 No. 3—November 1961, p. 131–133.

Mann, Percy, "Was the Plate of the 20 Cents 'Sanitary Fair' Stamps Used for the Experimental Work of the American Bank Note Co.?", *Philadelphia Stamp News*, Aug. 1914, p. 345–349.

Perry, Elliott, "The First Charity Stamps", *Pat Paragraphs #38*, July 1939, p. 1149–1164.

Severn, C.E., "The Sanitary Fairs and Their Issues", reprinted from *The Collector's Journal*, Chicago, (n.d.), 30 pages.

Wray, George Birch, "Sanitary Fairs—A Fascinating Study", *Covers*, Vol. XII No. 8, August 1952, p. 7–14.

—, "The Sanitary Fair Commission and Its Stamps", *Stamps*, October 24, 1953, p. 122–126.

PHILATELIC REFERENCES—GENERAL

The American Philatelist, The Journal of the American Philatelic Society—numerous.

Baker, Hugh J. and J. David, *Bakers' U.S. Classics*, from the columns in *Stamps*, 1962–1969, published by The U.S. Philatelic Classics Society, Inc., Columbus, Ohio, 1985, 343 pages.

Brazer, Clarence W., *Essays for United States Adhesive Postage Stamps*, 1941, 236 pages.

Cabeen, Richard McP., *Standard Handbook of Stamp Collecting*, published by Thomas Y. Crowell Company, New York, 1960, 628 pages.

Graham, Richard B., *The Chronicle of the U.S. Classic Postal Issues*, the U.S. Philatelic Classics Society, No. 47 (June 1964, p. 16–23), No. 50 (Jan. 1965, p. 110–113), and No. 58 (May 1968, p. 61–64).

The Collectors Club Philatelist, The Collectors Club, New York—numerous.

Dietz, August, *Dietz Confederate States Catalog and Handbook of the Postage Stamps and Envelopes of the Confederate States of America*, The Dietz Press, Inc., Richmond, Virginia, 1959.

The Essay-Proof Journal, Essay-Proof Society.

> #14, 1947, Vol. 4
> "Varieties of U.S. Essays & Proofs" by Clarence W. Brazer, p. 153–154.

> #68, Fall 1960, Vol. 17
> "Patent Papers Relating to the Improvement and Protection of United States Bank-Notes, Postage and Revenue Stamps" by Sol Altmann, p. 181.

> #132, Fall 1976, Vol. 33
> "Essays for U.S. Adhesive Postage Stamps" by Clarence W. Brazer—Revised by Falk Finkelburg, p. 199.

> #133, Winter 1976, Vol. 34
> "The 'Old Abe' Vignette What Was Its Use?" by Glenn E. Jackson, p. 10–15.

Gross, E. Tudor, "The First 'Window' Envelope", *The Collectors Club Philatelist*, Vol. XXI, No. 2, April 1942, p. 73–103; Vol. XXII, No. 1, Sec. 2, Jan. 1943, "Supplementary Notes", p. 1–28; Vol. XXII, No. 4, Sec. 1, Oct. 1943, "Supplementary Notes—Round Two", p. 263–270; Vol. XXIII, No. 2, April 1944, "Final Chapter", p. 53–55.

Konwiser, Harry M., *The American Stamp Collector's Dictionary*, published by Empire Stamp Galleries, New York, 1949, 309 pages.

Malpass, George N., "Check List of Publishers and Vendors of Civil War Patriotic Covers", *The American Philatelist*, Vol. 65, No. 4, January 1952, p. 282–293.

Patton, Donald Scott, *The Private Local Posts of the United States*, Vol. I, New York State, published by Robson Lowe Ltd., London 1967, 350 pages.

Scott 1992 Specialized Catalogue of United States Stamps, published by Scott Publishing Co., Sidney, Ohio.

Skinner, Hubert C., Gunter, Erin R., and Sanders, Warren H., *The New Dietz Confederate States Catalog and Handbook*, published by Bogg & Laurence Publishing Company, Inc., Miami, Florida, 1986, 270 pages.

Springer, Sherwood, *Springer's Handbook of North American Cinderella Stamps Including Taxpaid Revenues*, 1962, various editions.

U.S. Mail and Post Office Assistant 1860–1872, reprinted by the Collectors Club of Chicago, 1975.

FAIR HISTORIES

Goodrich, Frank B., *The Tribute Book*, published by Derby & Miller, New York, 1865—511 pages.

History of the Brooklyn and Long Island Fair, February 22, 1864, The Union Steam Presses, New York, 1864—189 pages.

History of the Great Western Sanitary Fair, C.F. Vent & Co., Publisher, Cincinnati, 1864—578 pages.

History of the North-Western Soldiers' Fair Held in Chicago, Dunlop, Sewell & Spalding, 1864—184 pages.

A Record of the Metropolitan Fair In Aid of the United States Sanitary Commission, Held in New York in April 1864, published by Hurd and Houghton, New York, 1867—261 pages.

Stillé, Charles J., *Memorial of the Great Central Fair for the U.S. Sanitary Commission*, United States Sanitary Commission, Philadelphia, 1864 — 211 pages.

A Tribute to the Fair (Metropolitan), Published in Aid of the Sanitary Commission, D. Appleton & Co., New York, 1864 — 253 pages.

FAIR NEWSPAPERS

The Boatswain's Whistle, National Sailors' Fair, Boston, Massachusetts, November 9 to November 19, 1864 — 10 issues.

The Canteen, Army Relief Bazaar, Albany, New York, February 22, 1864 to March 5, 1864 — 12 issues.

The Commissioner, The Bramhall Fair, Portland, Maine, October 28 & 29, 1863 — 1 issue and supplement.

The Daily Countersign, Mississippi Valley Sanitary Fair, St. Louis, Missouri, May 17, 1864 to June 4, 1864 — 13 issues.

The Daily Fair Journal, Wheeling Fair, Wheeling, West Virginia, June 28, 1864 to July 9, 1864 — 11 issues.

The Drum Beat, Brooklyn and Long Island Fair, Brooklyn, New York, December 22, 1864 (sic — February 22) to March 5, 1864 — 12 issues plus extra of March 11, 1864.

The Fair Record, Union Volunteer Refreshment Saloon, Philadelphia, June 15, 1863.

The Knapsack, Soldier's and Sailor's Fair, Philadelphia, October 24 to November 4, 1865 — 11 issues.

The Knapsack, Westfield Fair, Westfield, Massachusetts, December 28, 1864.

The Ladies' Knapsack, Great Western Sanitary Fair, Cincinnati, Ohio, December 21, 1863 to January 9, 1864.

The New Era, Baltimore, Maryland, April 18, 1864.

Our Daily Fare, Great Central Fair, Philadelphia, June 8, 1864 to June 21, 1864 — 12 issues plus #13 of Sept. 11, 1865.

Report of the Dutchess County and Poughkeepsie Sanitary Fair, Poughkeepsie, N.Y., March 15 to March 19, 1864.

Sanitary Fair Gazette, Northern Ohio Sanitary Fair, Cleveland, Ohio, February 22 to March 8, 1864.

Spirit of the Fair, Metropolitan Fair, New York, New York, April 5, 1864 to April 23, 1864 — 17 issues.

The Springfield Musket, Springfield Fair, Springfield, Massachusetts, December 20, 1864 to December 23, 1864 — 4 issues.

Voice of the Fair, Second Chicago Fair, Chicago, Illinois, May 30, 1865 to June 16, 1865.

The Volunteer, First Chicago Fair, Chicago, Illinois, October 27, 1863.

MISCELLANEOUS ARTICLES ON SANITARY FAIRS

Eglit, Nathan N., "U.S. Sanitary Fair Medals", *The Numismatist*, Publication of the American Numismatic Association, November 1962, Vol. 75 No. 11, p. 1487.

A History of the Delaware Department Held in Philadelphia, June 1864, by James B. Riggs, Printer, Wilmington.

Schnell, J. Christopher, "Mary Livermore and the Great Northwestern Fair", *Chicago History — The Magazine of the Chicago Historical Society*, Spring 1975, Vol. IV No. 1.

Thompson, William Y., "Sanitary Fairs of the Civil War", *Civil War History*, published by the State University of Iowa.

Wainswright, Nicholas B., *One Hundred and Fifty Years of Collecting by the Historical Society of Pennsylvania*, published by the Historical Society of Pennsylvania, Philadelphia, 1974.

MISCELLANEOUS FAIR INFORMATION OF INTEREST

The Book of Bubbles — A Contribution in Aid of the Sanitary Commission — New York Fair, Endicott & Co., New York, March 1864, 68 pages (one of the earliest limerick books).

The New Book of Nonsense — A Contribution to the Great Central Fair — June 1864, Ashmead & Evans, 1864, 53 pages.

Metropolitan Fair, in Aid of the United States Sanitary Commission, Charles O. Jones, Printer, New York, 1864, 16 pages.

Miscellaneous pamphlets and broadsides from various committees of the Great Central Fair in Philadelphia.

UNITED STATES SANITARY COMMISSION

Books

Flint, Austin (editor), *Contributions Relating to the Causation and Prevention of Disease and to Camp Disease*, published for the U.S. Sanitary Commission by Hurd & Houghton, New York, 1867 — 667 pages.

Gould, Benjamin A., *Investigations in the Military and Anthropological Statistics of American Soldiers*, published by the U.S. Sanitary Commission by Hurd & Houghton, Riverside Press, Cambridge, 1869 — 655 pages.

Hammond, William A., M.D., Surgeon-General U.S. Army, Etc. (editor), *Military, Medical and Surgical Essays*, prepared for the United States Sanitary Commission, published by J.B. Lippincott & Co., Philadelphia, 1864 — 552 pages.

Henshaw, Mrs. Sarah Edwards, *Our Branch and Its Tributaries: A History of the Work of the Northwestern Sanitary Commission*, published by Alfred L. Sewell, Chicago, 1863 — 432 pages.

Maxwell, William Quentin, *Lincoln's Fifth Wheel: The Political History of the United States Sanitary Commission*, published by Longmans, Green & Co., New York, 1956 — 372 pages.

Newberry, Dr. J.S., Secretary of the Western Department, *United States Sanitary Commission in the Valley of the Mississippi, Final Report* (Document 96), published by Fairbanks, Benedict & Co., Cleveland, 1871 — 543 pages.

Our Acre and Its Harvest: Historical Sketch of the Soldiers' Aid Society of Northern Ohio. Cleveland Branch of the United States Sanitary Commission. Published by Fairbanks, Benedict & Co., Cleveland, 1869 — 511 pages.

The Sanitary Commission of the United States Army: A Succinct Narrative of Its Works and Purposes., New York: Published for the Benefit of the United States Sanitary Commission, 1864 — 318 pages.

The Soldier's Friend, Published by the U.S. Sanitary Commission, printed by Perkinpine & Higgins, Philadelphia, 1865 — 128 pages.

Stillé, Charles J., *History of the United States Sanitary Commission*, published by J.B. Lippincott & Co., Philadelphia, 1866 — 553 pages.

The United States Sanitary Commission — A Sketch of Its Purposes and Its Work, Boston, 1863 — 299 pages.

UNITED STATES SANITARY COMMISSION

Pamphlets and Imprints
An Appeal to the People of Ohio, Indiana and Kentucky, Cincinnati Branch of the United States Sanitary Commission, Cincinnati, August 1862 — 4 pages.

Branch of the United States Sanitary Commission — Plan of Organization for Country Societies — 4 pages.

Brief Reports of the Operations of the Sanitary Commission in Tennessee, May 1862, by Dr. J. S. Newberry — 12 pages.

Circular to Associate Members, Washington, D.C., September 23, 1861 — 1 page.

Constitution and By Laws of the New-England Women's Auxiliary Association, Adopted January 1864, Prentiss & Deland, printers, Boston, 1864 — 7 pages.

Documents of the United States Sanitary Commission, May 18, 1861 to December 15, 1865 (First Printing) No. 1 to No. 95 (usually distinguished by being unbound, various sizes and last page blank, and identified "Sanitary Commission").

Documents of the United States Sanitary Commission, May 18, 1861 to December 15, 1865 (Second Printing in 1866), 3 Volumes (Vol I 1–60, Vol II 61–95), plus (Vol III 96 published in 1871).

The English Branch of the United States Sanitary Commission—The Motive of Its Establishment and the Result of Its Work by Edmund Crisp Fisher; William Ridgway, printer, London, 1865—31 pages.

European Branch of the United States Sanitary Commission—Report of Charles S.P. Bowles, Foreign Agent of the United States Sanitary Commission Upon the International Congress of Geneva For the Amelioration of the Condition of the Sick and Wounded Soldiers of Armies in the Field, R. Clay, Son & Taylor, London—67 pages.

Executive Organization of the United States Sanitary Commission Adopted October 8, 1863—7 pages.

Final Report of the Supply Department of the New-England Women's Auxiliary Association, Prentiss & Deland, printers, Boston, 1865—24 pages.

First Annual Report of the Soldiers' Aid Society of Northern Ohio, July 1, 1862, Fairbanks, Benedict & Co., Cleveland, Ohio, 1862—40 pages.

First Report of the Solicitor of the Protective War Claim and Pension Agency for the United States Sanitary Commission, January 1, 1865, King & Baird, printers, Philadelphia, 1865—24 pages.

How a Free People Conduct a Long War by Charles J. Stillé, printed by Anson D.F. Randolph, New York—16 pages.

How Can We Best Help Our Camps and Hospitals published by order of the Woman's Central Association of Relief, Wm. C. Bryant, printer, New York, 1863—39 pages.

List of Officers and Associates of the U.S. Sanitary Commission in Philadelphia and the Officers and Aids of the Women's Pennsylvania Branch of the U.S. Sanitary Commission, January 1, 1864, King & Baird, printers, Philadelphia, 1864—21 pages.

Minutes of the U.S. Sanitary Commission, June 12, 1861 to June 12, 1865, 22 sessions, 239 pages plus 23rd session Nov. 7, 1865, 9 pages plus 24th session Jan. 11, 1867, 11 pages, plus 25th session May 3, 1867, 3 pages.

Monographs:
A. Report on *Military Hygiene and Therapeutics.*—Report on Military Surgery to the Surgical Section of the New York Academy of Medicine, New York, June 21, 1861—27 pages.
B. *Directions to Army Surgeons on the Field of Battle* by J.G. Guthrie, Surgeon General to the British Forces during the Crimean War—8 pages.
C. *Rules for Preserving the Health of the Soldier.* July 12, 1861—10 pages.
D. *Report of a Committee Appointed by Resolution of the Sanitary Commission, to Prepare a Paper on the Use of Quinine as a Prophylactic Against Malarious Diseases.* McGill, Witherow & Co., Washington, 1862—16 pages.
E. *Report of a Committee Appointed by the Sanitary Commission to Prepare a Paper on the Value of Vaccination in Armies.* Collins, Printer, Philadelphia, 1861—32 pages.
F. *Report of a Committee of the Associate Medical Members of the Sanitary Commission on the Subject of Amputations.* David Clapp, Printer, Boston, 1861—10 pages.
G. *Report of a Committee of the Associate Medical Members of the Sanitary Commission, on the Subject of Amputations Through the Foot, and at the Ankle-Joint.* Bailliere Brothers, Publishers, New York, 1862—28 pages.
H. *Report of a Committee of the Associate Medical Members of the Sanitary Commission on the Subject of Venereal Diseases, with Special Reference to Practice in the Army and Navy.* John F. Trow, Printer, New York, 1862—17 pages.
I. —
J. *Report of a Committee of the Associate Medical Members of the Sanitary Commission on the Subject of Pneumonia.* Baker & Godwin, Printers, New York, 1862—24 pages.
K. *Report of a Committee of the Associated Medical Members of the Sanitary Commission, on the Subject of Continued Fevers.* Government Printing Office, Washington, 1862—27 pages.
L. *Report of a Committee of the Associate Medical Members of the Sanitary Commission on the Subject of Excision of Joints for Traumatic Cause.* Welch, Bigelow and Company, Printers, Cambridge, 1862—23 pages.
M. *Report of a Committee of the Associate Members of the Sanitary Commission on Dysentery.* Collins, Printer, Philadelphia, 1862—40 pages.
N. *Report of a Committee of the Associate Members of the Sanitary Commission on the Subject of Scurvy.* Government Printing Office, Washington, 1862—29 pages.
O. *Report of a Committee of the Associate Medical Members of the Sanitary Commission on the Subject of the Treatment of Fractures in Military Surgery.* J.B. Lippincott & Co., Philadelphia, 1862—15 pages.
P. *Report of a Committee of the Associate Members of the Sanitary Commission on the Subject of the Nature and Treatment of Miasmatic Fevers.* Bailliere Brothers, Publishers, New York, 1862—23 pages.
Q. *Report of a Committee of the Associate Members of the Sanitary Commission on the Subject of the Nature and Treatment of Yellow Fever.* Wm. C. Bryant & Co., Printers, New York, 1862—25 pages.
R. —
S. *Hints for the Control and Prevention of Infectious Diseases, in Camps, Transports, and Hospitals.* Wm. C. Bryant & Co., Printers, New York, 1863—36 pages.
T. *Report of the Ladies Sanitary Committee of St. Thomas' Colored Episcopal Church, Auxiliary to The United States Sanitary Commission.* Crissy & Markley, Printers, Goldsmiths Hall, Library Street, Philadelphia, 1864—4 pages.

Monthly Bulletins of the Operations of the Cincinnati Branch of the United States Sanitary Commission, February 1863 to November 1864.

Northwestern Sanitary Commission, Branch of the United States Sanitary Commission, Chicago, October 17, 1861 to December 31, 1864—8 pages.

Operations of the United States Sanitary Commission at Beaufort and Morris Island, New York, September 17, 1863—8 pages.

Origin, Struggles and Principles of the United States Sanitary Commission (Extracted from the January 1864 number of the North American Review)—42 pages.

Outline of Plan for Classifying the Archives and Preparing the History of the United States Sanitary Commission—14 pages.

Philadelphia Associates of the United States Sanitary Commission—An Appeal to the People of Pennsylvania for the Sick and Wounded Soldiers, Philadelphia, October 20, 1861—40 pages.

Preamble and Resolutions of the Associates in Philadelphia in Relation to the Reorganization of the Army Medical Department, Philadelphia, January 22, 1862—7 pages.

Relief Services Among Disabled and Needy Soldiers and Their Families in the City of New York from November 1865 to November 1, 1866, New York, November 3, 1866—1 page.

Report Concerning Special Relief Service of the U.S. Sanitary Commission, Boston, Mass. No. 1. Year Ending March 31, 1864, Prentiss & Deland, printers, Boston, 1864—28 pages plus June 10, 1864 3-page insert.

Report of the Cincinnati Branch U.S. Sanitary Commission from December 1, 1861, to December 1, 1864, Three Years. Printed by order of Cincinnati Branch U.S. Sanitary Commission, 1865—15 pages.

Report of Delegates from the General Aid Society for the Army at Buffalo, N.Y. to Visit the Government Hospitals and the Agencies of the United States Sanitary Commission. by Rev. George W. Hosmer, D.D., Buffalo, 1862—16 pages.

Report of the General Superintendent of the Philadelphia Branch of the U.S. Sanitary Commission to the Executive Committee, February 1, 1864, King & Baird, printers, Philadelphia, 1864—28 pages.

Report of the General Superintendent of the Philadelphia Branch of the U.S. Sanitary Commission to the Executive Committee, January 1, 1865, King & Baird, printers, Philadelphia, 1865 — 51 pages.

Report of the General Superintendent of the Philadelphia Branch of the U.S. Sanitary Commission to the Executive Committee, January 1, 1866, King & Baird, printers, Philadelphia, 1866 — 82 pages.

Report of the Iowa Sanitary Commission from the Organization (To its close) Ballou & Winall, printers, Dubuque, 1866 — 71 pages.

Report of the Secretary with Regard to the Probable Origin of the Recent Demoralization of the Volunteer Army at Washington and the Duty of the Sanitary Commission, McGill & Witherow, printers, Washington, 1861 — 46 pages.

Rules for Preserving the Health of the Soldier, 4th edition, Government Printing Office 1861 — 16 pages.

Rules for Preserving the Health of the Soldier, Sanitary Commission (no date) — 14 pages.

The Sanitary Commission Bulletin, November 1, 1863 to August 1, 1865, 40 issues — 1280 pages.

The Sanitary Commission of the United States Army — Its Organization, Purposes, and Work., by an Englishman, London, 1865 — 24 pages.

Second Annual Report of the New England Women's Auxiliary Association, Prentiss & Deland, printers, Boston, 1864 — 19 pages.

Second Annual Report of the Woman's Central Association of Relief, May 1, 1863, Wm. S. Door, printer, 1863 — 35 pages.

Second Report of the Solicitor of the Protective War Claim and Pension Agency of the U.S. Sanitary Commission, January 1, 1866, King & Baird, printers, Philadelphia, 1866 — 13 pages.

Second Report of the Woman's Relief Association of the City of Brooklyn, Auxiliary to the United States Sanitary Commission, Brooklyn, April 30, 1864 — 20 pages.

Second Semi-Annual Report of the Woman's Central Association of Relief, November 1862, Baker & Godwin, Printers, New York, 1862 — 19 pages.

Semi-Annual Report of the Soldiers' Aid Society of Northern Ohio, Cleveland Branch of the Sanitary Commission from July 1, 1864 to January 1, 1865, printed by the Soldiers' Aid Society of Northern Ohio, 1865 — 7 pages.

Statement of the Receipts and Disbursements of the United States Sanitary Commission from June 27, 1861 to May 14, 1878 — 5 pages.

Third Annual Report of the General Aid Society... Buffalo, N.Y. January 1, 1864, to January 1, 1865. Franklin Printing House, Buffalo, 1865 — 16 pages.

Third Annual Report of the New England Women's Auxiliary Association, Prentiss & Deland, printers, Boston, 1865 — 28 pages.

Third Annual Report of the Soldiers' Aid Society of Toledo, Ohio, October 1864, Pelton & Waggoner, printers, Toledo, 1864 — 15 pages.

Third Annual Report of the Woman's Central Association of Relief, May 1, 1864, Sanford, Harroun, printers, 1864 — 35 pages.

Third Semi-Annual Report of the Woman's Central Association of Relief, November 1863, Baker & Godwin, printers, New York, 1863 — 23 pages.

To Dr. J. S. Newberry, Sanitary Commission, New York, November 5, 1862 by Dr. Henry Bellows — 10 pages.

To the Women of Ohio, Indiana and Kentucky, Cincinnati Depot Branch of the United States Sanitary Commission, Cincinnati, December 13, 1861 — 8 pages.

The United States Sanitary Commission, by Henry W. Bellows, D.D., reprinted from Johnson's Universal Encyclopedia, G.D. Putnam's Sons, New York (no date) — 51 pages.

United States Sanitary Commission Century Club Meeting, January 9, 1862 — To Meet the Commission and Associate Members — 12 pages.

United States Sanitary Commission Historical Bureau, New York, December 25, 1865 by Jno S. Blatchford, General Secretary — 1 page.

The United States Sanitary Commission — The Board as the Embodiment of the Inner Life of the Commission — 7 pages.

United States Sanitary Commission to Dr. Quackenbush — Surgeon General State of New York, March 11, 1863 — 8 pages.

United States Sanitary Commission to Mrs. Moore, Corresponding Secretary of the Women's Pennsylvania Branch, New York, March 3, 1863, signed by Henry W. Bellows — 3 pages.

The Working of the United States Sanitary Commission with Regard to Armies in the Field, by E. C. Fisher, 1865 — 25 pages.

NEWSPAPER

The Sanitary Reporter, published by the U.S. Sanitary Commission, Western Department, Louisville, Ky., Vol. I No. I, May 15, 1863 to Vol. II No. 22, April 1, 1865.

WESTERN SANITARY COMMISSION

Book

The Western Sanitary Commission: A Sketch, Published for the Mississippi Valley Sanitary Fair, printed by R. P. Studley & Co., St. Louis, 1864 — 144 pages.

Pamphlet

Report of the Western Sanitary Commission for the Year Ending June 1, 1863, St. Louis, Mo., Western Sanitary Commission, 1863 — 32 pages.

UNITED STATES CHRISTIAN COMMISSION

Book

Smith, Rev. Edward P., *Incidents of the United States Christian Commission*, published by Lippincott & Co., Philadelphia, 1869 — 512 pages.

Pamphlets

First Annual Report of the United States Christian Commission, February 1863 — 128 pages.

Second Annual Report of the United States Christian Commission, April 1864 — 284 pages.

Third Annual Report of the United States Christian Commission, January 1, 1865 — 160 pages.

Fourth Annual Report of the United States Christian Commission, January 1, 1866 — 222 pages.

Information for Army Meetings, James B. Rodgers, Printer, Philadelphia, August, 1864 — 36 pages; November, 1864 — 37 pages.

Article

Cannon, M. Hamlin, "The United States Christian Commission", *Mississippi Valley Historical Review*, Vol. 38, June 1951, p. 61–80.

GENERAL CIVIL WAR REFERENCES

Amann, William Frayne (editor), *Personnel of the Civil War*, published by Thomas Joseloff, New York, 1961 — 2 volumes.

Boatner, Mark Mayo, III, *The Civil War Dictionary*, published by David McKay Co., Inc., New York, 1959 — 974 pages.

Bowman, John S., Executive Editor, *The Civil War Almanac*, published by World Almanac Publications, New York, New York, 1983 — 400 pages.

Duncan, Captain Louis C., *The Medical Department of the United States Army in the Civil War*, reprinted by Olde Soldier Books, Inc., Gaithersburg, Md., 1987 — 407 pages.

Livermore, Thomas L., *Numbers and Losses in the Civil War*, published by the Civil War Centennial Series, Indiana University Press, Bloomington, Indiana, 1957 — 150 pages.

Long, E.B., *The Civil War Day by Day — An Almanac 1861–1865*, published by Doubleday & Co., Garden City, New York, 1971 — 1135 pages.

Lossing, Benson J., *Pictorial History of the Civil War in the United States of America*, Thomas Belknap, Publisher, Hartford, 1874 — Vol. II.

Medical and Surgical History of the War of the Rebellion — Surgeon General's Office — Government Printing Office, Washington, 1875 – 1888 — 6 volumes.

Nicolay, John G. and Hay, John (editors), *Abraham Lincoln — Complete Works — Comprising his Speeches, Letters, State Papers, and Miscellaneous Writings*, The Century Co., N.Y., 1902 — 2 volumes — 770 pages.

OTHER SOURCES

Appleton's Cyclopedia of American Biography, D. Appleton & Co., New York, 1888, 6 volumes with index.

Barrett, Joseph O., *History of 'Old Abe' — The Live War Eagle*, published by Alfred L. Sewell, Chicago, 1865 — 71 pages.

Bellows, Anna K., *Recollections of Henry Whitney Bellows*, Geo. Ellis, Printers, Boston, 1897 — 29 pages.

Billings, John D., *Hardtack and Coffee — The Unwritten Story of Army Life*, edited by Richard Harwell, The Lakeside Press — R.R. Donnelley & Sons Company, Chicago, 1960 — 483 pages.

Biographical Dictionary of the American Congress 1774 – 1927, United States Government Printing Office, 1928, House Document #783, 1740 pages.

Carse, Robert, *Department of the South — Hilton Head Island in the Civil War*, published by the State Printing Company, Columbia, S.C., 1961 — 156 pages.

Censer, Jane Turner (editor), *The Papers of Frederick Law Olmsted — Defending the Union — The Civil War and the U.S. Sanitary Commission, 1861 – 1863*, Vol. IV, The Johns Hopkins University Press, Baltimore and London, 1986 — 757 pages.

Civil War Navy Chronology, compiled by the Naval History Department, Washington, 1931.

The Civil War Sketch Book of Charles Ellery Stedman, Surgeon United States Navy, Presidio Press, San Rafael, Calif., 1976 — 218 pages.

Commager, Henry Steele (editor), *The Blue and the Gray*, Fairfax Press, New York, 1982 — 1201 pages.

Concise Dictionary of American Biography, published by Charles Scribner's Sons, New York, 1964 — 1273 pages.

Concise Dictionary of American History, published by Charles Scribner's Sons, New York, 1962 — 1156 pages.

Davis, William C. (editor), *Fighting for Time*, National Historical Society, printed by Doubleday & Co., Garden City, N.Y., 1983 — 464 pages.

Nevins, Allan (editor), *Diary of the Civil War — George Templeton Strong*, The Macmillan Co. printers, New York, 1962, Vol. III — 664 pages.

The Eagle Regiment — A Sketch of Its Marches, Battles and Campaigns from 1861 – 1865, Recorder Print, Belleville, Wisc., 1890 — 166 pages.

Frank Leslie's Scenes & Portraits of the Civil War, with an introduction by Joseph B. Carr; Mrs. Frank Leslie, Publisher, N.Y., 1894 — 512 pages.

Gardner, Alexander, *Gardner's Photographic Sketch Book of the Civil War*, Dover Publications reprint, New York, 1959 — 100 plates.

Harper's Pictorial History of the Civil War, published by the Puritan Press Co., Chicago, 1894 edition — 2 volumes.

Kaplan, Justin, *Walt Whitman — A Life*, Simon and Schuster, New York, 1980 — 429 pages.

Kirkland, Frazar, *The Book of Anecdotes of the War of the Rebellion*, Hartford Publishing Co., Hartford, 1866 — 705 pages.

Leekley, John (editor), *Reflections on the Civil War — Bruce Catton*, Berkley Books, New York, 1981 — 246 pages.

Lord, Francis A., *Civil War Sutlers and Their Wares*, published by Thomas Yoseloff, New York, 1969 — 162 pages.

Lytle, William M. and Holdcamper, Forrest R., *Merchant Steam Vessels of the United States 1790 – 1868*, edited by C. Bradford Mitchell, published by The Steamship Historical Society of America, Inc., Staten Island, New York, 1975 — 322 pages.

McPherson, James M., *The Negro's Civil War*, published by Vintage Books, 1965 — 358 pages.

Miller, Francis Trevelyan (editor), *The Photographic History of the Civil War*, New York, 1911 – 1912, 10 volumes.

Moore, James, M.D., *History of the Cooper Shop Volunteer Refreshment Saloon*, published by James B. Rodgers, Philadelphia, 1866 — 212 pages.

Post, Lydia Minturn (editor), *Soldiers' Letters, Published in Aid of the U.S. Sanitary Commission*, published by Bunce & Huntington, New York, 1865 — 472 pages.

Roper, Laura Wood, *FLO — A Biography of Frederick Law Olmsted*, Johns Hopkins University Press, Baltimore & London, 1973 — 555 pages.

Stinson, Byron, "Drug Addiction: 'The Army Disease'", *American History Illustrated*, Vol. VI No. 8, p. 10–17, December 1971, published by The National Historical Society, Gettysburg, Pa.

Walton, Clyde C. (editor), *Private Smith's Journal — Recollections of the Late War*, The Lakeside Press — R.R. Donnelley & Sons Company, Chicago, 1963 — 253 pages.

HOSPITALS, DOCTORS AND PRISONS

Adams, George Worthington, *Doctors in Blue*, published by Henry Schuman, New York, 1952 — 253 pages.

Antrim, Earl, *Civil War Prisons and Their Covers*, Collectors Club, N.Y., Handbook Number 12, 1961 — 215 pages.

Bradford, Thomas Lindsley, M.D., *History of the Homoeopathic Medical College of Pennsylvania; The Hahnemann Medical College and Hospital of Philadelphia.*, published by Boericke & Tafel, Philadelphia, 1898.

Brooks, Stewart, *Civil War Medicine*, published by Charles C. Thomas, Springfield, Illinois, 1966 — 148 pages.

Chidlaw, Rev. B.W., *Story of My Life*, published by Robert Clarke & Co., Cincinnati, 1890 – 382 pages.

Civil War Medicine article in April 1961 issue of *M.D.*

Cunningham, H. H., *Doctors in Gray — The Confederate Medical Service*, published by the Louisiana State University Press, Baton Rouge, 1958 — 339 pages.

Daniel, Dr. F. E., *Recollections of a Rebel Surgeon*, published by Von Boeckmann, Schultze & Co., Austin, Texas, 1899 — 264 pages.

Hesseltine, William B., *Civil War Prisons — A Study in War Psychology*, published by Ungar Publishing Co., New York, 1978, 4th printing — 290 pages.

Hoge, Mrs. A., *The Boys in Blue; or Heroes of the 'Rank and File.' — Incidents…from Camp, Battle-field, and Hospital…*, published by E.B. Treat & Co., New York, 1867 — 477 pages.

Hospital Transports, A Memoir of the Embarkation of the Sick and Wounded from the Peninsula of Virginia in the Summer of 1862, published by the United States Sanitary Commission, printed by Ticknor and Fields, Boston, 1863 — 167 pages.

Johnson, Charles Benevlyn, *Muskets and Medicine*, published by F.A. Davis Co., Philadelphia, 1917 — 276 pages.

Munroe, James Phinney, *Adventures of an Army Nurse in Two Wars*, published by Little, Brown & Co., Boston, 1903 — 355 pages.

Narrative of Privations and Sufferings of United States Officers & Soldiers While Prisoners of War in the Hands of the Rebel Authorities., a report of the United States Sanitary Commission, published at the Office of "Littell's Living Age", Boston, December 1864 — 86 pages.

Narrative of Privations and Sufferings of United States Officers and Soldiers While Prisoners of War in the Hands of the Rebel Authorities., printed for the United States

Sanitary Commission by King & Baird, Philadelphia, 1864 — 283 pages.

Perry, Dr. Martha Derby, *Letters from a Surgeon of the Civil War*, published by Little, Brown & Co., Boston, 1906 — 225 pages.

Reed, William Howell, *Hospital Life in the Army of the Potomac*, published by William V. Spencer, Boston, 1866 — 199 pages.

Steiner, Paul E., *Physician-Generals in the Civil War*, published by Charles C. Thomas, Springfield, Illinois, 1966 — 194 pages.

Welch, Spencer Glasgow, *A Confederate Surgeon's Letters to His Wife*, published by Continental Book Co., Marietta, Ga., 1954 — 127 pages.

Wheelock, Julia A., *The Boys in White; The Experience of a Hospital Agent In and Around Washington*, published by Lange & Hillman, New York, 1870 — 268 pages.

Whitman, Walt, *Memoranda During the War — Written on the Spot*, Author's Publication, Camden, N.J., 1875–76, 68 pages.

—, *The Wound Dresser*, published by Small, Maynard & Co., Boston, 1898 — 201 pages.

PHILANTHROPIES — RED CROSS AND CIVILIAN

Brenner, Robert H., *The Public Good: Philanthropy and Welfare in the Civil War Era*, Alfred A. Knopf, New York, 1980 — 234 pages.

American Association for the Relief of the Misery of Battle Fields, published by Gibson Brothers, Printers, Washington, D.C., 1866 — 18 pages.

Clara Barton, produced by the Division of Publications, National Park Service — U.S. Dept. of the Interior, Washington, 1981 — 79 pages.

Evans, Thomas W., M.D., *Ambulance and Sanitary Materiel — A Report of Class XI, Group II, Paris Exposition, 1867*, published by E. Briere, Paris, 1867 — 31 pages.

Gumpert, Martin, *Dunant — The Story of the Red Cross*, published by Blue Ribbon Books, Garden City, New York, 1942 — 323 pages.

History of the Red Cross, the Treaty of Geneva and Its Adoption by the United States, Government Printing Office, Washington, 1883 — 227 pages.

The Philanthropic Results of the War in America, dedicated by permission to the United States Sanitary Commission, published by Sheldon & Co., New York, 1864 — 160 pages.

(Red Cross) *L'Oeuvre D'Un Grand Peuple* (in French) — Deuxieme edition, Paris, 1864 — 66 pages.

Work of Humanity in War, Plan and Results of the Geneva Congress and International Treaty, prepared under the direction of the American Branch of the International Association for Relief of Misery of Battlefields, published by Anson D.F. Randolph & Co., New York, 1870 — 35 pages.

WORK OF WOMEN DURING THE CIVIL WAR

Andrews, Mathew Page, *The Women of the South in War Times*, published by The Norman, Remington & Co., Baltimore, 1920 — 466 pages.

Brockett, L.P., *Woman's Work in the Civil War — A Record of Heroism, Patriotism and Patience*, published by Ziegler, McCurdy & Co., 1867 — 799 pages.

Brumgardt, John R. (editor), *Civil War Nurse — The Diary and Letters of Hannah Ropes*, University of Tennessee Press, Knoxville, Tenn., 1980 — 149 pages.

Cumming, Kate, *A Journal of Hospital Life in the Confederate Army of Tennessee from the Battle of Shiloh to the End of the War*, published by John P. Morton & Co., Louisville, Ky., 1866 — 200 pages.

Dannett, Sylvia, *Noble Women of the North*, published by Thomas Yoseloff, 1959 — 419 pages.

Edmonds, S. Emma E., *Nurse and Spy in the Union Army*, published by W.S. Williams & Co., Hartford, Conn., J.A. Stoddard & Co., Chicago, Ill., 1865 — 384 pages.

Gillespie, Mrs. E.D., *A Book of Remembrance*, published by J.B. Lippincott Company, Philadelphia, 1901 — 393 pages.

Greenbie, Marjorie Barstow, *Lincoln's Daughters of Mercy*, published by Putnam's Sons, New York, 1944 — 211 pages.

Hurn, Ethel Alice, *Wisconsin Women in the War Between the States*, published by the Wisconsin Historical Commission, May 1911 — 190 pages.

Livermore, Mary, *My Story of the War — A Woman's Narrative of Four Years Personal Experience*, published by A.D. Worthington, Hartford, Conn., 1888 — 700 pages.

Michigan Women in the Civil War, published by the Michigan Civil War Centennial Observance Commission, Lansing, 1963 — 144 pages.

Moore, Frank, *Women of the War*, published by S.S. Scranton & Co., Cincinnati, 1867 — 596 pages.

Schwartz, Gerald (editor), *A Woman Doctor's Civil War — Esther Hill Hawks' Diary*, University of South Carolina Press, 1984 — 301 pages.

Simkins, Francis Butler and Patton, James Welch, *The Women of the Confederacy*, published by Garrett and Massie, Inc., Richmond and New York, 1936 — 306 pages.

Smith, Adelaide W., *Reminiscences of an Army Nurse During the Civil War*, pub-

lisher Greaves Publishing Company, New York, 1911 — 263 pages.

Wormeley, Katharine Prescott, *The Other Side of War with the Army of the Potomac, Letters from the Headquarters of the United States Sanitary Commission*, published by Ticknor & Co., Boston, 1889 — 210 pages.

Young, Agatha, *The Women and the Crises — Women of the North in the Civil War*, published by McDowell, Obolensky, New York, 1959 — 389 pages.

LOCAL AND STATE SOURCES ON BENEVOLENT ENDEAVORS

The Annual Reports of the Soldiers' Aid Society of Waltham, Mass., for the Years Ending July 1, 1863–64, Free Press Office, Waltham, 1864 — First Annual Report, 1863, 17 pages; Second Annual Report, 1864 — 14 pages.

The Bible in the Army — A Statement of the Distribution of the Scriptures Among the Military and Naval Forces of the Union, by the New York Bible Society, New York, 1862 — 31 pages.

Clark, Rufus W., *The Heroes of Albany — A Memorial of the Patriot-Martyrs of the City and County of Albany*, published by S.R. Gray, Albany, 1866 — 870 pages.

Coatsworth, Stella S., *The Loyal People of the Northwest* (Chicago), published by Church, Goodman & Donnelley, Chicago, 1869 — 402 pages.

The Connecticut War Record, Sept. 1863 to April 1865 (New Haven).

Constitution, By-Laws, and Officers of the Discharged Soldiers' Home. West Springfield Street, February 1, 1863., Press of Geo. C. Rand & Avery, Boston, 1863 — 21 pages.

Final Report of the New York Medical Association for the Supply of Lint, Bandages, etc. to the United States Army — Presented July 25, 1861, printed by Baker & Godwin, New York, 1861 — 32 pages.

First Annual Report of the Discharged Soldier's Home, with Constitution, By-Laws, List of Officers . . ., printed by Bazin & Chandler, Boston, 1863 — 32 pages.

Green, Mason A., *Springfield 1636–1886 History of Town and City*, C. A. Nichols & Co., Publishers, 1888 — 645 pages.

Hammond, William A., *A Statement of the Causes Which Led to the Dismissal of Surgeon-General William A. Hammond from the Army: with a Review of the Evidence Adduced Before the Court*, New York, Sept. 1864 — 73 pages.

Illinois State Sanitary Bureau — Report of Transactions from September 12, 1863 to January 1, 1864, printed by Baker & Phillips — 98 pages.

McCloskey, Henry, *Manual of the Common Council* (Brooklyn), published by Brown & Co., New York, 1864 — 403 pages plus supplements.

INDEX

Niven, John, *Connecticut for the Union—
The Role of the State in the Civil War*,
Yale University Press, New Haven, 1965—
491 pages.

*Report of a Meeting of the Massachusetts
Soldiers' Relief Association, Held in Washington, D.C., December 8th, 1862*, M'Gill
& Witherow, Printers, Washington, 1863—
16 pages.

*Report of the Michigan Soldiers' Relief
Association for the Years 1865 and 1866*,
Joseph L. Pearson, Printer, Washington,
1866—15 pages.

Rose, William Ganson, *Cleveland—The
Making of a City*, World Publishing Co.,
Cleveland and New York, 1950—
1272 pages.

Taylor, Frank H., *Philadelphia in the Civil
War 1861–1865*, published by the City,
1913—360 pages.

Terrell, W.H.H., *Indiana in the War of the
Rebellion—Report of the Adjutant General*,
A reprint of Vol. I of the 8 vol. report published originally in 1869, reprint by the Indiana Historical Society, 1960—603 pages.

*Third Annual Report of the Michigan Sol-
diers' Relief Association for 1864—Report
of the Executive Committee*, Washington,
December 12, 1864—28 pages.

ABOUT THE AUTHORS

A short personal history might be of interest. It may be obvious that the writers are not professional writers. We are stamp collectors interested in not only these issues but also in United States stamps, presidential free franks, philatelic literature, and all things connected thereto. When the book was started in 1977 Bob was 56 years of age and Margie a few years less than that.

Bob graduated from the University of Wisconsin in 1942 and then went into the service for over three years, mostly in the Southwest Pacific, during World War II. He was in the automatic merchandising business and was the founding president of the National Bulk Vendors Association. Margie graduated from Northwestern University where she was in the School of Commerce. She is also an advanced philatelist and a housewife. We are the parents of two grown daughters and seven grandchildren. We make our home in Glencoe, Illinois and Bellevue, Washington.

Headquarters Armies of the United States,
Washington D.C. Dec. 18th 1865

Mr. Wm D. Lewis
Ch. Soldiers & Sailors Fair

Dear Sir:

I have the
pleasure of acknowledging
the receipt this day of
"The Tribute Book" which I
have been honored with
by the Executive Commit-
tee of the Fair of which
you are Chairman.

Please return my
thanks to the Committee

for this mark of their
esteem.

Very Truly
Your obt. sert.
U. S. Grant
Lt. Gen.

Buffalo, June 7. 1864

My Dear Miss Edsall,

In compliance
with your request I send you
some autographs, and you have
my best wishes for the success
of your fair.

Our brave soldiers
will need all the relief that
it is possible to give, and the
sympathetic heart of woman
must be their last hope

Respectfully yours
Millard Fillmore

Head-Quarters Armies of the United States,
Washington June 15.

Hubert P. Main Esq
Sir,
Your note enc—
$5.00 in aid of the N.W. Sanitary —
was duly received and the amount —
handed to the Treasurer as requested
Sanitary Resp'y
Your Obt. Servt.
U. S. Grant
Lt. Gen.

OFFICE OF THE GREAT CENTRAL FAIR
FOR THE SANITARY COMMISSION
Philadelphia, 1307 Chestnut St

March 30th 1864

Liberal patronage for the benefit
of the sick and wounded soldiers is
respectfully solicited.

U. S. Grant
Lt. Gen. U.S.A.

Washington
A. T. Goodman
Dear
of the 12th ins
The Speech
at the opening
Fair at Clevel
Entirely extem
I had not e
o hence can
no manus
. Very Truly
J.

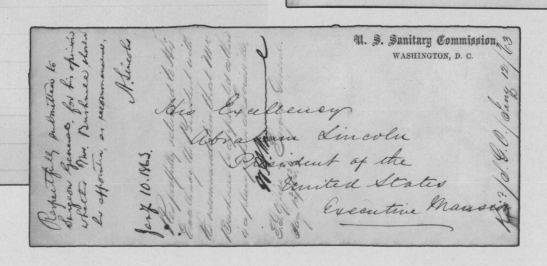

U. S. Sanitary Commission,
WASHINGTON, D. C.

His Excellency
Abraham Lincoln
President of the
United States
Executive Mansion

Respectfully submitted to
Surgeon General, for his opinion
whether Mrs. Barlow's plan
be adopted, as recommended.
A. Lincoln
Jan. 10. 1863.